CLASS IN CONTEMPORARY CHINA

China Today series
Greg Austin, *Cyber Policy in China*
David S. G. Goodman, *Class in Contemporary China*
Stuart Harris, *China's Foreign Policy*
Michael Keane, *Creative Industries in China*
Pitman B. Potter, *China's Legal System*
Xuefei Ren, *Urban China*
Judith Shapiro, *China's Environmental Challenges*
LiAnne Yu, *Consumption in China*

CLASS IN CONTEMPORARY CHINA

David S. G. Goodman

polity

First published in 2014 by Polity Press

Polity Press
65 Bridge Street
Cambridge CB2 1UR, UK

Polity Press
350 Main Street
Malden, MA 02148, USA

ISBN-13: 978-0-7456-5336-5
ISBN-13: 978-0-7456-5337-2(pb)

A catalogue record for this book is available from the British Library.

Typeset in 11.5 on 15 pt Adobe Jenson Pro
by Toppan Best-set Premedia Limited
Printed and bound in Great Britain by Clays Ltd, St Ives PLC

The publisher has used its best endeavours to ensure that the URLs for external websites referred to in this book are correct and active at the time of going to press. However, the publisher has no responsibility for the websites and can make no guarantee that a site will remain live or that the content is or will remain appropriate.

Every effort has been made to trace all copyright holders, but if any have been inadvertently overlooked the publisher will be pleased to include any necessary credits in any subsequent reprint or edition.

For further information on Polity, visit our website: www.politybooks.com

Contents

Tables

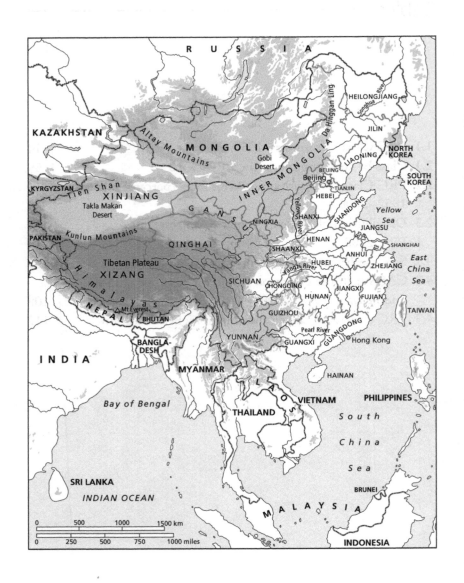

Chronology

1894–95	Sino-Japanese War
1911	Fall of the Qing dynasty
1912	Republic of China established under Sun Yat-sen
1927	Split between Nationalists (KMT) and Communists (CCP); civil war begins
1934–1935	CCP under Mao Zedong evades KMT in Long March
December 1937	Nanjing Massacre
1937–45	War of Resistance to Japan
1946–9	Civil war between KMT and CCP resumes
October 1949	KMT retreats to Taiwan; Mao founds People's Republic of China (PRC)
1950–3	Korean War
1953–7	First Five-Year Plan; PRC adopts Soviet-style economic planning
1954	First Constitution of the PRC and first meeting of the National People's Congress
1956–7	Hundred Flowers Movement, a brief period of open political debate
1957	Anti-rightist Movement
1958–60	Great Leap Forward, an effort to transform China through rapid industrialization and collectivization
March 1959	Tibetan Uprising in Lhasa; Dalai Lama flees to India

1959–61	Three Hard Years, widespread famine with tens of millions of deaths
1960	Sino-Soviet split
1962	Sino-Indian War
October 1964	First PRC atomic bomb detonation
1966–76	Great Proletarian Cultural Revolution; Mao reasserts power
February 1972	President Richard Nixon visits China; 'Shanghai Communiqué' pledges to normalize US–China relations
September 1976	Death of Mao Zedong
October 1976	Ultra-leftist Gang of Four arrested
December 1978	Deng Xiaoping assumes power; launches Four Modernizations and economic reforms
1978	One-child family planning policy introduced
1979	US and China establish formal diplomatic ties; Deng Xiaoping visits Washington
1979	PRC invades Vietnam
1981	Gang of Four sentenced
1982	Census reports PRC population at more than 1 billion
December 1984	Margaret Thatcher co-signs Sino-British Joint Declaration agreeing to return Hong Kong to China in 1997
1989	Tiananmen Square protests culminate in 4 June military crackdown
1992	Deng Xiaoping's Southern Inspection Tour re-energizes economic reforms
1993–2002	Jiang Zemin, General-Secretary of CCP (1989–2002) and President of PRC (1993–2003) continues economic growth agenda
November 2001	WTO accepts China as member

2002–12	Hu Jintao, General-Secretary CCP (and President PRC from 2003)
2002–3	SARS outbreak concentrated in PRC and Hong Kong
August 2008	Summer Olympic Games in Beijing
2010	Shanghai World Exposition
2012	Xi Jinping appointed General-Secretary of the CCP (and President of PRC from 2013)

Preface ──

In the late 1960s, at the time I started studying China, there seemed to be little academic challenge in attempting to understand class in research on that country. It was the era of China's Cultural Revolution. Class was either apparently clearly defined, or a function of elite politics, operating within a tight ideological framework. The only interpretation beyond that was the occasional attempt to apply Djilas-type 'new class' analysis to the development of the People's Republic of China.

Class in China became more intellectually interesting with 'reform and openness' after 1978. Economic growth led to greater social differentiation, the emergence of entrepreneurial classes, the growth of the middle classes, the disempowerment of the state socialist working class and dramatic changes in rural China, including the massive expansion in numbers of migrant workers. It also became possible to undertake fieldwork in China, to interview people and carry out social surveys, rather than base research on state-controlled documentary sources. One result was that research in China led to questions about the applicability and suitability of class analyses that had been derived from the experience of other countries. Starting with research in Hangzhou in 1991, my attempt to understand the social consequences of economic change in China led to a series of related projects.

The Australian Research Council has been a frequent supporter of this research through a series of research grants since 1991, and their contribution is gratefully acknowledged. The inquiry into class and social stratification in China has been greatly assisted by the project to examine The New Rich in Asia, which was the key project of the Asia Research Centre at Murdoch University, Western Australia, during the 1990s. Later, at the University of Technology, Sydney, the China Research Centre's project to examine The New Rich in China followed up on the earlier work in considerably greater detail, both conceptually and with the more specific geographical focus. More recently still, during 2009–11, the Seminar on Class at the University of Sydney, which culminated in the China Studies Centre's 2011 workshop on Class and Class Consciousness in China, was a significant learning experience.

Many people have contributed either knowingly or unwittingly to my understanding of class and social stratification in China. My greatest intellectual debt has been to Dorothy Solinger, who has been an academic model throughout my career for her thoroughness and her humanity. At Murdoch University, Richard Robison, Gary Rodan and Kevin Hewison stimulated my renewed interest in the topic. Also at Murdoch University, Sally Sargeson and Rachel Murphy were students from whom I learnt more on this topic than I suspect they learnt from me. I have benefited greatly from working with Yingjie Guo and Wanning Sun, both now at the University of Technology, Sydney: scholars of excellence on social and political change in China. Similarly, I owe a considerable debt to Xiaowei Zang, now at City University Hong Kong, not only for his prolific output and research, but also for his friendship and professional cooperation. At Nanjing University, my colleagues Zhou Xiaohong and Zhou Peiqin have been courageous analysts of social change in China, as well as helpful and informative discussants. At both the University of Technology, Sydney (2002–8) and the University of Sydney (since 2008), my work on class and social stratification could not have been so successfully undertaken on a number of projects without my co-researchers Beatriz Carrillo and Minglu Chen. At the University of Sydney, Jeffrey Riegel has been a more than useful sounding board for all things Chinese. In the last five years Kirsty Mattinson, now at Xi'an Jiaotong-Liverpool University in Suzhou, has been an invaluable companion and guide to class and social change on the ground in China. In addition, I would like to thank two anonymous reviewers and Jonathan Skerrett at Polity for their helpful advice on the draft manuscript. None of these people are to be held responsible for the words that follow, though I hope not only that they do not find too much that is disagreeable but also that they recognize their influence.

David S. G. Goodman
University of Sydney and Nanjing University
February 2014

Abbreviations, Measures and Note on Chinese Names and Transliteration

Abbreviations

ACFTU	All China Federation of Trade Unions
BCG	Boston Consulting Group
CASS	Chinese Academy of Social Sciences
CCP	Chinese Communist Party
CHFS	China Household Finance Survey (Texas A&M University and The People's Bank of China)
CHIP	Chinese Households Income Project (CASS Institute of Economics)
FBIS	Foreign Broadcast Information Service (USA)
GDP	Gross Domestic Product
NBS	National Bureau of Statistics
NCNA	New China News Agency
NPC	National People's Congress
PPCC	People's Political Consultative Conference
PPP	Purchasing Power Parity
PRC	People's Republic of China
PLA	People's Liberation Army
RMB	Renminbi (The People's Currency)
RMRB	Renmin Ribao (*The People's Daily*)
SASAC	State-Owned Assets Supervision and Administration Commission
SE2	Special Economic Zone

SOE   State-Owned Enterprise
TVE   Town and Village Enterprise
WTO   World Trade Organization

Measures
mu 亩   land area equivalent to 667 sq metres or 0.17 of an acre
yuan 元   dollar RMB: 1 GBP equals approximately 10 Chinese
          dollars; 1 US$ equals approximately 6 Chinese dollars.

Note on Chinese Names and Transliteration
Names in Chinese are usually presented as family name followed by a
personal name. That practice is followed here, with two exceptions. The
first is where Chinese people have a non-Chinese personal name, in
which case the personal name is presented before the family name. The
second is where a person with a Chinese name has indicated, usually
through publication, that they wish to be known by their personal
name followed by their family name.

In most cases, the *pinyin* (拼音) system of transliteration is used
throughout this book for representing Chinese words (and sounds) in
English. The exceptions are works that have already been published in
an alternative transliteration system, or where words (usually people's
names) are only or more usually known in an alternative transliteration
system.

1 Introduction
Understanding Class in China

Class has been and remains central to the understanding of social and political change in the People's Republic of China (PRC). Founded in 1921, the Chinese Communist Party (CCP) made revolution explicitly through mobilizing and acting on behalf of China's workers and peasants. When it came to power in 1949, and established the PRC, it did so in the name of the Chinese working classes. It implemented class-based prescriptions for the new regime's development, and every citizen was officially categorized and provided with a specific class identification to enable this to happen. During the Mao Zedong-dominated period of the PRC's politics from the mid-1950s to the late 1970s, which culminated in the Cultural Revolution, these formal class identities became particularly important in determining individual life chances not only for those classified in the early 1950s, but also their children and (eventually) their grandchildren. In late 1978 the CCP determined to adopt a more market-oriented development strategy. As part of that change, those earlier class identities have increasingly come to play a less formal role in determining access to public goods, employment and lifestyle. Nonetheless, throughout the reform era, the social structures that were put in place during the 1950s and 1960s have continued to shape social mobility and individual life chances for successive generations.

The PRC remains an explicitly class-based political system, informed by the CCP's Marxist–Leninist ideology. Its legitimacy rests to a large extent on the leadership of the CCP and the latter's role as 'the vanguard both of the Chinese working class and of the Chinese people and the Chinese nation' (Constitution of the Communist Party of China, 14 November 2012). According to the Preamble to the state Constitution, the PRC is a 'people's democratic dictatorship led by the working class and based on the alliance of workers and peasants, which is in essence the dictatorship of the proletariat' and while 'the exploiting classes as such have been abolished in our country . . . class struggle will continue to exist within certain bounds for a long time to come' (Constitution of the PRC, 14 March 2004).

These class-based perspectives may seem somewhat outdated given the dramatic socio-economic change the PRC has experienced since 1978. Nonetheless, they still not only inform the development of the government's social policy, but also infuse the whole of the educational system and the language of politics and social interaction. Children are socialized from an early age into the language of class through schooling and education. Undoubtedly, in the post-Mao era the social impact of a continued state-sponsored class analysis may sometimes be less than positive and conforming, but even resistance and reaction to the CCP's direction on this topic serves to underline the continued importance of ideas of class as determinants of change.

Certainly there have been significant socio-economic changes with reform, which have had a major impact on China's class structure. To start with, there has been dramatically increased urbanization and income inequality. In the 1970s, the PRC had approximately 80 per cent of its population living as peasants on or off the land, but by 2013 roughly half the total population lived in towns and cities across the country. In the early 1980s, China could be characterized by a high degree of income equality. Inequality was necessarily hidden in many ways but the standard measure of income inequality, the Gini coefficient (where 0 represents total equality and 1 total inequality) was about 0.20 in 1981. In 2013 (when the population was 1,354 million) it stood, by various domestic PRC accounts, at anywhere between 0.47 and 0.61.

During the 1970s Chinese society was described by the CCP, strictly using the conventions of Marxism–Leninism, in terms of two classes and a stratum: workers, peasants and intellectuals. Even outside the PRC and the CCP's ideological framework, the description could not be much broader. There were officials of the Party-state, workers, peasants and a relatively small middle class (though not identified as such within the PRC) of managers, administrators and teachers. The subsequent years resulted in considerably greater social differentiation as part and parcel of spectacular economic growth. The highest-profile new social category to emerge is that of entrepreneurs, though not all are the fabulously wealthy of popular imagination. At the same time, socio-economic change has resulted in the development of the professional middle classes and the expansion of the managerial classes; in size, certainly, but also in kind as some professions (lawyers, psychologists, sociologists, communication specialists, for example) have re-emerged. As industry – and particularly the state sector, which had been developed in the 1950s as the mainstay of the PRC's state socialism – has been restructured, the former public-sector working class has been dramatically affected: reduced in size and politically downgraded. Now there is an additional, new category of industrial worker: the peasant migrant worker who leaves the countryside for short and longer periods of employment. The changes in the workforce and the market have necessarily impacted on the peasantry as well as leading to the emergence of a new urban underclass.

Given the extent and scale of the changes wrought by reform, it is little surprise that Chinese people's sense of class identity often seems to be at odds with the CCP's ideological prescriptions. There has been a tendency not only for people to shy away from the CCP's categories of class analysis, but also to deliberately describe themselves as being of a lower class than a more objective assessment of their wealth, status and position might indicate (Chen 2013; Gao 2013). Then there is the question of the emerging middle class. Until 2002, consistent with Marxist–Leninist ideology the Party-state did not acknowledge any social, economic or political role for a middle class at all. Even though since that year there has been an emerging state-sponsored discourse encouraging the development of the middle class, it often rests uneasily with the CCP's ideological formulations. Yet, according to a national survey undertaken during 2013, 7.2 per cent of China's population saw themselves as upper class, 59.2 per cent as middle class and 33.6 per cent as lower class (Boehler 2013). Though the percentages have varied over time, this survey confirmed a constant trend since the mid-1990s, where a majority of Chinese have indeed reported themselves as middle class (Bian and Lu 1996; Wang and Davis 2010).

One deceptively obvious reason for these differences is linguistic. Ideas about class and classes are rendered in a number of different ways in Chinese, of which two are most commonly used. One is 阶级 (*jieji*), which refers usually to class in the particular construction which comes from the CCP's Marxist–Leninist ideology rather than more generally. Thus, workers, peasants and capitalists are all described as classes in this way. The other is 阶层 (*jieceng*), which linguistically denotes stratum or strata. Thus, the (emergent) middle class is most usually now described as 中产阶层 (*zhongchan jieceng*) – literarily, the middle propertied stratum. When used in these ways, though, the distinction between class and stratum is merely a convenient fiction. Lu Xueyi, the prime architect of the current structure of class that dominates academic enquiry and government policymaking, made it clear that *jieceng* was adopted after 2002 to refer to class as it might be understood elsewhere in the world in order to make a distinction between the contemporary situation, on the one hand, and on the other, class as interpreted by both Marx and Mao Zedong, and specifically as applied in China's revolutionary era before 1949, and under state socialism before 1978 (Lu Xueyi 2005: 419).

As Li Chunling, one of China's leading sociologists (from the Institute of Sociology at the Chinese Academy of Social Sciences (CASS)) has pointed out, the understanding of class in China varies with the observer (Li Chunling 2010), and this too is a marker of the social and political change that has emerged with reform since 1978. The various different perspectives on class of the public, consumers, Party-state ideologists, government policymakers and academic sociologists have commonalities, overlap and are necessarily related. All the same they are not identical and the result is considerable complexity within the PRC in the understanding and function of class that reflects the social processes involved. Class as socio-economic structure, class as performance (the rehearsal of identity), and class as ideological formulation are all involved in the development of China's political economy.

UNDERSTANDING CHINA AND CLASS

The PRC is clearly undergoing substantial social change, yet the precise nature of these changes, let alone the consequences for the political economy, are far from clear. There are commentators ready to describe the emergence of capitalism in the PRC and the consequent challenge to the regime from the activities of the newly emergent (since the 1980s) class of capitalists (Nee and Opper 2012). There are others who, while acknowledging the emergence of capitalist practices in economic development, still highlight the role of cadres and former officials, and their social capital and political connections as the basis of a system of bureaucratic capitalism in which officials are embourgeoised, and entrepreneurs are bureaucratized (Huang 2013; So 2013). Still others emphasize the extent to which the structures of state socialism remain in place despite the marketization of the economy. While the PRC may no longer be state socialist, these authors highlight not only the roles of bureaucrats and technocrats as the key economic decision-makers, through a redistributive rather than a market-based economy, but also the ways in which they and their families (rather than the entrepreneurial classes) are the primary beneficiaries of the PRC's development (Szelényi 2008).

The extent to which the social basis of the Chinese political system has changed, and the likely consequences of those changes, depends on an examination of possible trends within and among various classes and not just changes in the ruling class. In particular, this includes not only the impact of change on the old urban working class, but also the extent to which the migrant workers – on whom much of the economic power of the PRC since the early 1980s has been based – are forming a new working class. And while the precise definition of the middle class in the Chinese context is for the moment a matter of some conjecture, it would seem possible from the analysis of expanding middle classes elsewhere that they too might be agents of political change, if not necessarily for the advocacy of liberal democracy (Robison and Goodman 1992).

The aim of the analysis presented here is not simply to aid the understanding of social and political change in China, but also to contribute to the wider understanding of class and its role in social change. Any account of class must necessarily highlight the discontinuities apparently represented by both 1949, when the PRC was established, and 1978, when the decision was taken (if tentatively at first) to move away from the earlier policies of state socialism and towards a socialist market economy. At the same time, it is also clear that there are continuities in Chinese society through both 1949 and 1978. Although the establishment of the People's Republic came justifiably clothed in the rhetoric of revolution, in practice 1949 also institutionalized not only the rule of the new revolutionary elite but also to some extent the continuation of the social structure as it existed immediately before 1949. While the changes of late 1978 started a process that liberated those regarded as remnant class enemies from the old (pre-1949) society, economic growth and social change has in the longer term privileged still further many of those who became privileged in elite and essentially middle-class positions during the PRC's first thirty years. Indeed, one key determinant of class profiles would seem to be a high degree of path dependence, to which education, wealth, political power and social status all contribute.

Class in China is best understood in terms of the intergenerational transfer of compound inequalities of wealth, status and power, rather than solely in terms of ideas of class and stratification drawn from the experience of socio-economic development elsewhere. This is not to argue for a Chinese exceptionalism, but rather to highlight the ways in which class and the conceptualization of class in and applied to China since the early twentieth century have met some of the intellectual and political challenges that are a necessary part of class analysis, particularly for and when applied to active revolutionaries and ruling Communist Parties. From its very beginnings, the CCP has discussed (and experimented with) how to identify and how to manage the relationship between socio-economic structure and identity, class and class consciousness. In addition, China's experience raises questions about (before 1949) the role of the peasantry in revolution, especially in less economically developed countries; and (after 1949 and the establishment of the PRC) the question of whether ownership of the means of production is as important as control and management as a defining relationship to the means of production (for the ruling class). More recently, the increasing socio-economic complexity that has resulted from economic development raises questions about class structure, and especially the role of the middle classes.

Class everywhere highlights difference and inequality, and is probably more important as a mobilizing concept than a precise or reliable analytical tool. This mobilizatory aspect of the concept of class is clearly apparent in practical politics, especially for parties that are part of, or draw on, the Marxist tradition. It is also apparent in the business world where class differences not only assist producers and marketeers in their search for target audiences, but form an essential part of advertising to consumers (Silverstein et al. 2012). For social scientists, class also draws attention to the fundamental inequalities that constitute society: of power, wealth, social standing, lifestyle, culture and opportunity (Crompton 2006: 658). But it does more than that. It also draws attention to the relationships and interactions between different kinds of inequality, especially in terms of the development and influence of sources of power and authority in society (Savage 1995: 25). This is the meaning and crucial significance of compound inequality: where different kinds of inequality reinforce privilege or disadvantage.

The CCP's understanding of class, and the history of its development, is then the obvious place to start the examination of class in contemporary China, not least because it provides a guide to the language and practice of class in China. It also demonstrates the ways in which the CCP's experience interacted with the development of class analysis more generally in the twentieth century. It is a history dominated by Mao Zedong, who first provided the CCP with a method of class analysis that facilitated successful revolution, and then pushed his analysis to such a level of near self-destruction that after his death (in 1976) and the decision to change the PRC's development strategy (in 1978) there was an official concern to ensure such politics never recurred. It is also a history probably best understood in terms of the changes in the CCP's ideological formulation of the relationship between socio-economic conditions and political consciousness in the shaping of class identity. In Marx's class analysis an individual's socio-economic position is seen as determining their political behaviour, and a class as a social group is expected to behave in line with its economic interest. But class action is not guaranteed. The capitalist class may well act to protect its interests. The working class (of whom much is expected, for it is their 'historical mission' to overthrow the capitalists) on the other hand will need to acquire a high degree of class consciousness in order to act. For the CCP before 1957, the emphasis was on socio-economic conditions leading to political consciousness. During 1957–76, class essentially came to be seen almost entirely in terms of political correctness, struggle and the transformative power of consciousness, sidelining for much of the time considerations of socio-economic conditions. Since 1976, the CCP has essentially come to approach 'class as socio-economic conditions' and 'class as political consciousness' as two separate matters.

REVOLUTIONARY CLASS ANALYSIS

The CCP had been established in 1921 by Chinese intellectuals seeking to create an agenda of radical change and impressed by the Russian Revolution. A key problem, though, was the relative absence of industrialization and its associated proletariat, or indeed any significant social base that could be mobilized as such. The CCP had, in Jerome Chen's words, 'accepted the historical mission, the revolutionary character, and the internationalism of the proletariat as defined by Marx' (Jerome Chen 1973: 84), but socio-economic conditions in China essentially left them wondering how to proceed.

The debate on class inevitably preoccupied the CCP for much of its early life as it sought to develop an adequate strategy for the Chinese revolution. There was intense elite conflict within the leadership of the CCP, which was as much about personality as about the identification of the proletariat, the relationship with the Nationalist Party (also supported and developed with the help of the Soviet Union) and different approaches to revolution. For the most part, until the mid-1930s, the leadership of the CCP was made up of individuals who had either returned from or who worked closely with the Soviet Union, and their interpretation of class was bound up with that experience. Their main focus was to work with the small Chinese working class, mainly in Shanghai and the areas of and surrounding colonial concessions, and they rejected the view that the proletariat was only a metaphor for the progressive forces in a Marxist view of history, as others did. While recognizing that the peasantry was the majority of the working population, they were for the most part unable to see much revolutionary potential in them.

There were, however, others in the CCP who thought differently. One of these was Mao Zedong who had been involved in successful peasant mobilizations in the mid-1920s in his native Hunan Province. He too embraced the commitment to the proletariat throughout his life. Officially published collections of his articles and speeches even after the foundation of the PRC still began with the admonition: 'Workers of all countries, unite!' At the same time, from 1926 onwards, he came to argue that the 'principal aspect of the principal contradiction' in Chinese society – the social polarization that would lead to revolutionary change – was between peasants and landowners.

There is unfortunately little reliable information available about land distribution during the Republican Era (1911–49). Research from extant contemporary surveys suggests a dramatic economic inequality. Of the rural households, 4 per cent were landlords who owned 39 per cent of the land. Another 6 per cent of households were rich peasants who hired labour to help them farm the 17 per cent of the land that they owned, while 22 per cent of rural households were owner-farmer middle peasants who owned 30 per cent of the land. Additionally, 36 per cent of rural households were poor peasants who owned 14 per cent of the land; and 24 per cent of rural households were tenant farmers, with 8 per cent of rural households being agricultural labourers. These figures provide only the most approximate of guides and there were, in any case, intense local variations. Tenancy was greater in the south than in the north of the country, and there were areas of the north where there were few, if any, landlords; and, where there were landlords, they were often absentee landlords (Esherick 1981).

In Mao's view, the peasantry had the majority and the potential to make the revolution, but it would still be led by the proletariat – not only because the proletariat too were oppressed by capitalism, but also because they were politically organized through the CCP, and represented the most advanced and productive force politically, combined with the fact that many of those now in the proletariat were displaced peasants. This last notion was part of the key to the second radically different element in Mao's approach to class analysis. From the 1920s on, he argued that an individual's objective socio-economic class nature could be modified through changed consciousness arising from a learning experience, usually ideological education and training or participation in revolutionary struggle (Schram 1981: 409). Mao was not so much arguing that peasants could become workers (though this type of thinking about class transformation did at times also become manifest), but rather that the peasantry could assume the political attitudes, and potential for revolution, of the proletariat.

Mao's interpretation of class, then, from an early stage in the development of the Chinese Communist Revolution, combined both objective socio-economic conditions and the possibility of these being restructured through conscious actions. At the same time it was anything but a simple analysis based on a straightforward polarization. Mao always detailed the complexities of the social structure, not least in order to provide policy prescriptions and political direction. Class was always first and foremost a political tool, and not just a description of a perceived economic reality. In addition to poor peasants and rich landlords, there was a large range of other classes. He recognized that in urban areas there was a small but growing working class, as well as a class of local native entrepreneurs (as opposed to foreign entrepreneurs, who were also numerous) who might be regarded as a 'national bourgeoisie' in terms of their political support for change, at least in a nationalistic direction. In the rural areas, Mao saw that in between the landed local elite and the poor peasantry there were several categories of relative wealth, landowning or landlessness, power and influence, all of which could, under the appropriate circumstances, be mobilized to revolutionary goals. In addition, a wide range of other social categories existed, each of which also had to be taken into account as the CCP developed its strategy in the field, and some of which might conceivably prove to have considerable revolutionary potential. These included artisans, street sellers, bureaucrats, monks, bandits, vagabonds and compradors in the service of foreign capital.

In crude terms, Mao's method was to target the rich and the powerful through the mobilization, and with the support of the poor and powerless, but without alienating the slightly less rich and powerful whose support was also necessary to sustain economic development. This was an iterative process so that the targets of particular campaigns were not only always changing but were also sometimes those who had benefited in earlier campaigns. To achieve success under these circumstances required a fine appreciation of both socio-economic and political distinctions, as well as a high degree of organization and a well-trained cadre force.

By 1934 the CCP was facing annihilation. Various attempts to foment urban revolution had failed. Those who had championed rural mobilization had established rural soviet areas, of which the most famous was the Jiangxi Soviet (in Southeast China) where Mao Zedong (and others) were based. But by 1934 it was under threat from the forces of Chiang Kai-shek and the Nationalist Party Government. It was abandoned and the CCP set out on what became the Long March, heading first to West China and then eventually managing to re-establish itself in Yan'an in North China. Along the way, in January 1935, the CCP turned to Mao Zedong, his analysis of the Chinese revolution and a strategy for change based on peasant mobilization.

Japan's invasion in 1937 provided the opportunity for Mao's approach to class and class mobilization to be put into operation on a far larger scale than had previously been the case, as CCP areas of resistance and influence expanded. In the process it enabled the CCP to increase its extractive capacity – money and food from the rich, soldiers from the peasantry. Policies and programmes were developed in the effective CCP capital of Yan'an and then disseminated to other CCP-governed areas, especially those in North China. By 1945 and Japan's defeat, the CCP was in control of a substantial portion of North China and well placed to challenge the Nationalist Party for control of China, which was subsequently resolved in their favour through the 1946–9 Civil War.

This ultimate success meant that Mao and his ideas achieved a considerable and almost unassailable authority within the CCP. It also meant that the CCP's descriptors of class not only became extremely refined but were ready to be fully implemented when the PRC was established in 1949. On the eve of the declaration of the PRC (June 1949) Mao Zedong had, in general terms, described the new Chinese state that was about to come into existence as 'a people's democratic dictatorship' led by four classes: the workers, the peasants, the urban petty bourgeoisie and the national bourgeoisie. Political leadership would go to the workers, with the support of the peasants. The petty bourgeoisie were a kind of service class; while the national bourgeoisie (local native entrepreneurs as opposed to foreign entrepreneurs) were allowed to be part of 'the people' but were warned that, because they remained exploiters, they could, if their behaviour warranted it, find themselves redefined as enemies of the state (Mao 1949).

Starting in 1950 and over a period of essentially three years, every citizen was assigned a class descriptor that appeared on their household registration documents. These descriptors were from a fairly detailed schedule (Oksenberg 1974; White 1976: 2), which Mao Zedong had played a leading role in preparing (Schram 1984: 52). Some of the sixty-two class descriptors are detailed in table 1.1 (Kraus 1981: 185). Regulations assigned two class labels to each individual: class origin (*jieji chengfen* 阶级成分) and class background (*jiating chushen* 家庭出身). Class origin was determined by a person's activities during 1946–9; class background by the father's activities when the individual in question was born. As is readily observable, these class descriptors exemplified the dual perspectives that had driven Mao's understanding of class for many years: socio-economic position and political attitudes as implied by behaviour.

The original intention was that class origin and class background should be kept quite separate but in the event differences started to blur, especially as individuals began to realize the implications of

Table 1.1 PRC Class Descriptors, 1950

A. Non-economic class designations	Revolutionary cadre
	Revolutionary soldier
	Dependent of revolutionary martyr
	Military officer for an illegitimate authority
B. Urban class designations	Worker
	Enterprise worker
	Transport worker
	Handicraft worker
	Sailor
	Pedicab worker
	Idler
	Petty bourgeois
	✦ Urban pauper
	✦ Peddler
	✦ Small shop-owner
	✦ Small factory-owner
	✦ Office employee
	✦ Liberal professional
	Capitalist
	✦ Commercial capitalist
	✦ Industrial capitalist
	✦ Comprador capitalist

Table 1.1 *(Continued)*

C. Rural class designations	Hired agricultural labourer
	Poor peasant
	Middle peasant
	✦ Old middle peasant
	✦ New middle peasant
	✦ well-to-do middle peasant
	Rich peasant
	Small land lessor
	Landlord
	✦ Enlightened landlord
	✦ Overseas Chinese landlord
	✦ Landlord who is concurrently an industrialist or a merchant
	✦ Sub-landlord
	✦ Hidden landlord
	✦ Bankrupt landlord
	✦ Despotic landlord

registering under one class or another. The CCP apparently also originally intended that once the new classifications had been used to establish social control and socialize property relations, they might die away and certainly not be inherited. In the event, it rapidly became clear that class background as identified at this time was to become the main determinant of every aspect of an individual's and their family's life chances. Access to education, careers and marriage partners was determined to a large extent by these class descriptors. In particular, those from the 'red' class backgrounds, people who had fought or died on the CCP side in the revolution, or who were from worker or poor peasant backgrounds, were highly favoured, while those from the 'black' class backgrounds associated with the rich or resistance to the CCP were discriminated against, and often scapegoated in later political campaigns (Kraus 1981). Without a doubt, the application of class descriptors in the early 1950s provided every Chinese citizen with a new and coherent understanding of politics that lasted for decades (Unger 1984: 130). Although 'bad' class labels were removed from personal records early in the reform era (January 1979) and all class descriptors increasingly slipped from use, they were still required on applications to enter higher education, public service or the CCP. In 1984, a new national standard system for identifying class background based on these same class descriptors – Regulation GB 4765-84 – was developed and remained operational until 2004.

In the short term, classification was an essential part of the process by which the CCP established social order with the establishment of the new regime. It was followed remarkably quickly by the socialization of the means of production. In rural China, land reform was followed by campaigns to bring the peasantry first into lower-stage cooperatives, and then higher-stage collectives, a process completed by the end of 1956. In urban areas, also by the end of 1956, most enterprises had been brought under state control.

Land reform was designed less to redistribute wealth than to eradicate the power and influence of the local ruling class and to establish the new regime's structures of social control. Certainly there was land redistribution. Landlordism and landlessness were both abolished. The poorest 20 per cent of the rural population doubled their Republican-era income, and two thirds of the peasantry became middle peasants (Selden 1988: 9). At the same time, politics dominated these acts. More land was redistributed (700 million *mu* 亩) than had been owned by landlords (Esherick 1981); and land reform was itself a political performance. Work teams organized villagers to attend struggle meetings to denounce the local landlord or landlords. Landlords had to be found by the Party-state even where the pattern of landholding might be otherwise, with cadres often being allocated quotas to identify local 'landlords' (Huang 1995: 105).

The urban environment was politically and organizationally complex in 1949, not least because much of the economy in the coastal provinces had been dominated by foreign investment and involvement. The Party-state developed its reach into enterprises in a two-pronged offensive, empowering workers under CCP leadership at factory level, and bringing factory owners and entrepreneurs under closer control through national political campaigns, in which it appealed to the patriotism of the capitalist class on the one hand and was prepared to use more force on the other (Andreas 2012: 108). At first, the Party-state worked in cooperation with private owners to establish economic stability but, starting in 1952, the urban equivalent of land reform known as the 'Five Anti' Campaign (against bribery, tax evasion, fraud, theft of government property and the stealing of state secrets) led to struggle sessions, confessions of economic crimes and ultimately the collectivization of businesses. By the end of 1956, almost the entire urban population was assigned to a state-regulated work-unit (*danwei* 单位) so that housing, welfare (including education for children) and security were provided at the point of employment. By this stage, almost all economic activities were either under direct or indirect state control as (respectively) state-owned enterprises or collectives, and from 1955 on there was a wage system for state staff and workers with twenty-six grades of officials, seventeen grades of technician and eight grades of workers (Korzec and Whyte 1981).

THE BOURGEOISIE WITHIN THE PARTY

Success in implementing the socialization of both industry and agriculture left the CCP willing to accept by the end of 1956 that class conflict might have been largely resolved in China. Since there no longer was private property, it was reasonable to assume that the principal contradiction (between the bourgeoisie and the proletariat) had been resolved and that class conflict would be no more. In a report to the Eighth CCP Congress in September 1956, Deng Xiaoping (then General-Secretary of the CCP) hailed the homogenization of a single working class that united everyone. (Deng 1956: 213–14).

The optimism expressed by the CCP's leaders, including Mao Zedong, especially over the end of social contradictions and class conflict, was to prove short-lived. Mao's appeal to the professional middle classes – scientists, technicians and intellectuals – who would be necessary to the next stages of the PRC's development to (constructively) criticize the work of the government and the Party, now that the future of socialism in China had been ensured, backfired dramatically. Although he first suggested that it would be possible to 'Let a hundred schools of thought contend, a hundred flowers bloom,' reactions from other CCP leaders, critics of the CCP and the Party-state, and Mao's subsequent reaction to the critics, radicalized Mao and his interpretation of class under socialism. After the professional middle classes expressed their (to him, hyper) critical views of the Communist Party-state, he announced that 'Class struggle is by no means over . . . The proletariat seeks to transform the world according to its own world outlook, and so does the bourgeoisie. In this respect, the question of which will win out, socialism or capitalism, is not really settled' (Mao 1957a: 385).

The rediscovery of the bourgeoisie under socialism was to become a major concern of China's politics during the next two decades. From the middle of 1957 until his death, Mao increasingly saw opposition, not only within society, but even within the CCP. There was a need in his view for constant struggle, both to ensure the revolutionary nature of those better disposed towards socialism, and to eradicate the remnant enemy. As early as 1957, he had identified Rightist supporters within the CCP, who represented the main danger 'because their ideas are a reflection of bourgeois ideology inside the Party, and because they yearn for bourgeois liberalism, negate everything and are tied in in a hundred and one ways to bourgeois intellectuals outside the Party' (Mao 1957b: 440).

The immediate aftermath of the so-called Hundred Flowers Movement (where criticisms of the CCP and the PRC were voiced) was an Anti-Rightist Campaign of political censure, exclusion and often imprisonment, which fell heavily on those who had spoken up. In this campaign the class labels from the earlier classification were added to a person's work record for the first time, and this became standard practice for the next two decades. In particular, designation as one of the 'five bad elements' – landlords, rich peasants, counter-revolutionaries, bad elements and rightists – became commonplace for the targets of this and later political campaigns. These labels were not intended as class designations but rapidly came to be seen as such, to the extent that the 'five bad elements' were balanced by the 'five red categories'– workers, peasants, cadres, descendants of revolutionary martyrs and revolutionary intellectuals – the privileged beneficiaries of political campaigns and socio-economic development.

Mao Zedong's ideas on class and particularly the bourgeoisie were often inconsistent and inchoate after 1957. During the Great Leap Forward (1958–61), when Mao encouraged a fast speed of economic development based on mass mobilization, he expressed his ideas about the PRC's new class structure on a number of different occasions. He identified four 'big classes'. Two of these were 'exploiting classes' and two were 'labouring classes'. The labouring classes were the vast majority of the population, the workers and peasants. Though Mao often talked about the four 'big classes' politically, it was usually only 'the enemy and us' (Schram 1984: 36).

In the first exploiting class were 'imperialism, feudalism, bureaucratic capitalism, the remnants of the Nationalist Party [from the pre-1949 civil war] the 300,000 Rightists [the targets of the 1957 campaign, though in fact there had been 550,000] and their agents'. Mao described this exploiting class as 'the enemy' and estimated that they were 5 per cent of the population 'or about 30 million'. Although Mao described this exploiting class as a 'hostile class', he still argued that they could have their 'bad' class labels removed if they were genuinely reformed and in the process changed their class nature.

The second exploiting class was the bourgeoisie. On the whole, when Mao Zedong talked of the bourgeoisie, as he did increasingly with the onset of the Cultural Revolution, he was identifying those within the CCP who, by virtue of their position of privilege in the Party-state, had developed 'bourgeois' ideas. Theoretically, these ideas were expressed as antithetical to the cause of the proletarian revolution and the CCP, and as having come from bureaucratism and deficiencies in the work-style of cadres, which had resulted in the changed class character of both the CCP and its cadres (Schram 1983: 61). This definition of the bourgeoisie followed on from the idea of 'bourgeois elements' first expressed in May 1957. Over time, as this method of analysis was accepted by the CCP, the main question then became how to identify the bourgeoisie within the CCP, and who they actually were. By 1966 and the launch of the Cultural Revolution, it became clear not only that Liu Shaoqi, the President of the PRC, was the 'Number One Person in Authority Taking the Capitalist Road' and that Deng Xiaoping, a close associate of Mao Zedong's from the early 1930s on, was the second ranked 'Capitalist Roader', but also that most of the leading cadres in the Party-state were in this category.

There were also two other meanings provided for the term 'bourgeoisie'. The first of these was to indicate the remnant bourgeoisie from the old pre-1949 society, or the 'national bourgeoisie' of the pre-1957 period. These had been owners of capital and entrepreneurs who could be worked with but who had to be watched because their political reliability was uncertain. In the post-1957 era the term was used, despite the socialization of industry, to warn of the influence that these people and their ideas still exercised. The second was used to explain the power of the new PRC bourgeoisie not in terms of their position of privilege within the Party-state, but through the material benefit they extracted, and the greater share of distribution they received.

This description of what came to be known as 'bourgeois right' started in 1958 with an argument by Zhang Chunqiao (later to become a CCP leader during the Cultural Revolution of 1966–76) that criticized the use of material incentives in encouraging production. Zhang's argument was that in an era of full supply under socialism, there should be unrestricted distribution of goods and therefore the only people advocating restrictions would be those seeking to preserve their privileges (Zhang Chunqiao 1958). In the early 1960s, as measures were taken to improve production in the wake of the dislocations of the Great Leap Forward and famine, Mao himself became concerned at the exercise of bureaucratic power and the use of material incentives to encourage production in rural areas (Schram 1983: 51). Much later still, in 1975, this argument became the basis of a full-grown critique of the bourgeoisie within the CCP, articulated by both Zhang Chunqiao (Zhang Chunqiao 1975) and Yao Wenyuan (another CCP Cultural Revolution leader). Yao presented the case somewhat apocalyptically, saying that unless material incentives were restricted a fully capitalist system would ensue (Yao 1975: 7–8).

Struggle was central to Mao's world view after early 1957 both because he saw it as an effective method of social transformation and because of the inter-elite conflict that he engineered, largely to get his own way. He was determined to push his ideas on class, struggle and transformation, and when others resisted, he characterized them as class enemies. The abandonment of the Great Leap in 1961 was followed the next year by Mao's call to 'Never Forget Class Struggle' where he once again warned of the dangers of not recognizing the potential power of 'new elements of the bourgeoisie' (Kraus 1981: 79). It was a move that then led directly, albeit in an extended and somewhat convoluted process, to Mao's launch of the Cultural Revolution against the cadres and organization of the CCP in 1966. Mao's call to 'Seize Power

from those in Authority Taking the Capitalist Road!' closed universities, colleges and schools as young people responded to the call to join
in a large mass rectification movement aimed at the CCP, state administration, intellectuals, their teachers and authority figures. Although
some pre-Cultural Revolution leaders of the Party-state managed to
survive as Mao Zedong supporters, most of those occupying such
positions were dismissed from office, often quite brutally. It was a
humiliating experience that was to have repercussions after Mao
Zedong's death.

With the identification and removal of the bourgeoisie within the
Party-state in the late 1960s, the CCP's lens of class analysis turned to
focus on the working classes. In the first half of the 1970s, the use of
class labels really came into its own. There was considerable positive
discrimination in favour of the 'five red categories' in general, but particularly for the 'workers, peasants and soldiers' who were hailed as the
most revolutionary of classes. In higher education, for example, once
colleges and universities started to be re-opened, admission was less
on the basis of intellectual than political merit, with preference going
to those designated as 'worker, peasant and soldier' students. It was
essentially class as performance, with individuals required to meet, and
seeking to meet, revolutionary credentials through participation in
activities and individual behaviour: a system described by one noted
commentator as a virtuocracy (Shirk 1984: 58).

CLASS BY IDEOLOGY; CLASS BY OCCUPATION

Mao's death in September 1976 sparked dramatic change in the leadership of the CCP and in the direction of the PRC's development strategy. The 'Gang of Four' – Jiang Qing (Mao's wife), Zhang Chunqiao,
Yao Wenyuan and Wang Hongwen – who had become leading CCP
advocates of Mao's position on class and struggle were arrested in early
October 1976, and gradually over the next two years many of those

leaders of the Party-state who had been removed in the Cultural Revolution returned to office. The PRC's development strategy started to change at the end of 1978 when the decision was taken to promote reforms that would reduce the role of government in economic management, introduce marketization to the domestic economy and open the domestic economy to global interactions. In terms of class analysis, the CCP attempted to return decisively to 1956–7 in its formulations. One of the first public acts of the new reform era was the removal in November 1978 of black 'class labels' from individuals and their families who had been criticized and discriminated against as Anti-Rightists since the late 1950s. This was followed on 29 January 1979 by the announcement of the decision to remove the negatively discriminating class label from the families of the former exploiting classes, where they had proven in the interim to be law-abiding and not to have run into further problems.

Many of the ideas about economic development adopted at the start of the reform era had their origins in the discussions that had occurred during 1956–7 (Solinger 1981). Certainly, the emphasis in politics was on a return to the formulas of that time, though CCP leaders were also not averse to pointing out the lessons of the intervening years. As Ye Jianying, the CCP's senior military figure, stressed in 1979, elite differences should not be regarded as class conflict between the bourgeoisie and the proletariat (Ye Jianying 1979: 44–5). The CCP's formal 1981 judgement on Mao and the Cultural Revolution was more of the same: workers and intellectuals were of the same class, and there was overall class unity within a heterogeneous working class. There could be no violent class conflict under socialism; nor could a bourgeoisie emerge from within the CCP (Lin and Shen 1981: 12).

The strength of reaction to Mao's politics of Cultural Revolution at the end of the 1970s and beginning of the 1980s was entirely understandable. At the same time, it left the CCP with a considerably oversimplified and static understanding of class. Now there were only two classes: everyone who was not a peasant was a worker. Moreover, in reaction to – and rejection of – the emphasis on transformative class consciousness at the height of the Mao-dominated era of China's politics, consciousness was completely discounted as another variable in the CCP's understanding of class (Guo 2012: 727). For a while, it seemed as if that ideological formulation was adequate, but by the mid-1990s three problems had already become apparent.

Chronologically, the first stimulus for further change appeared in the form of a critique from within the Party-state that focused on the wealth and privilege that seemed to be generated by members of the Party-state and their families. Even if Mao's idea that the bourgeoisie could emerge from within the CCP had been abandoned, nonetheless there were concerns about the ways in which cadres were attracted by improving their private lifestyles. The CCP's theoretical journal *Red Flag* was particularly critical of cadres' children, who it said could too easily 'regard themselves as a special people separated by dress, eating habits, work place and education' from ordinary people (Wang Renzhong 1982).

The second major problem facing the CCP's description of Chinese society was not just that there were obvious rising inequalities, but that these inequalities had been seen as unjust and were seen to have angered a majority of Chinese citizens. There was concern that if action was not taken to counter growing inequality, then discontent would threaten social and political stability (Kelly 2013: 44).

There was a further real issue in that social change was running ahead of the CCP. The CCP's description of Chinese society was in a sense delegitimizing what was happening, and was certainly not encouraging individuals to become self-starting economic actors who would use their initiative in return for material incentives – an important objective towards the overall goal of economic development (Guo 2012: 726). Entrepreneurship was hindered by entrepreneurs' concerns that they might be politically punished, and so for a long time private businesses were largely confined to the small-scale, and the retail and service sectors (Gold 1990: 157). Despite often having a high social profile, the social status of entrepreneurs has remained fairly low, with a significant culture of 'wealth hatred' (Zang 2008: 70).

The CCP's response came slowly and in stages as it moved towards identifying and privileging the middle class and encouraging the development of a middle-class society. This practical change was delivered without abandoning the legitimacy afforded by its historical mission and commitment to the working class. In large part the ideological niceties could be observed because of both imprecision about the meaning of the concept of 'middle class' and the breadth of definition now afforded to the idea of the 'working class'. Even people who were exceptionally wealthy by global standards, and responsible for decisions that impacted the lives and livelihoods of many others, were regarded as 'workers . . . because they were originally members of the working class and now work under a political system opposed to exploitation' (Jiang Zemin 2001: 169; Fang Yu 2001).

The first stage was the redefinition of socialism away from public ownership, and towards the 'three advantages' – 'advantageous to the development of productive forces, to increasing the comprehensive strength of a socialist nation, and to raising people's standards of living'. The CCP itself then becomes the representative of 'advanced productive forces, the whole nation, and advanced culture'. For their part, class relations then became less important than economic activity (Guo 2008: 41).

The second stage was the CCP's rediscovery of class consciousness and its utility. The CCP had debated during the 1980s and into the 1990s if, whether and how class consciousness was related to socioeconomic position. In the 1980s the CCP had been mechanistic in its interpretation of this relationship. Workers had working-class consciousness. Greater social complexity challenged that assumption. The CCP's response was to describe political consciousness as entirely separate from and not related to socio-economic position. This separation thus draws attention to occupational hierarchies at the same time as it provides for class identification to operate as an incentive structure determined solely by political consciousness (Guo 2012: 730). The significance of an emphasis on occupational hierarchies is that it highlights functional interdependence and integration in the social and economic division of labour of an increasingly complex society.

As part of encouraging economic activity, the third stage was for the CCP to embrace business people and entrepreneurs more fully than previously. Business people had not been permitted to join the CCP from the mid-1950s until the start of the reform era. In the 1980s some business people became CCP members, and some who were already Party members became business people, but the political status of business people was always somewhat suspect. Following the suppression of demonstrations in Tiananmen Square during June 1989, in which some entrepreneurs and business organizations were implicated, business people were once again banned (in theory) from Party membership (Dickson 2008: 36). From 2000 on, however, Jiang Zemin, then President of the PRC and General-Secretary of the CCP, announced that business people were welcome to apply for CCP membership, though it would still be necessary for the CCP to ensure they were 'educated and guided' (Jiang 2001: 169). The re-entry of business people into the CCP was justified by Jiang Zemin in terms of his Three Represents Theory, seen as his major contribution to CCP ideology. The CCP should now 'represent' China's 'advanced social and productive forces, advanced culture, and the interests of the overwhelming majority' (Jiang 2002).

On the other side of the equation, Jiang Zemin also focused on the management of inequality as a social issue (Lewis and Xue 2003). At the 16th Congress of the CCP in 2002 he announced that the goal was to 'control the growth of the upper stratum of society, expand the middle, and reduce the bottom' (Jiang 2002). Jiang Zemin described the centrality of developing the middle-propertied stratum, and from this beginning the CCP developed a state-sponsored discourse of the harmonious middle class. The goal now was to be an olive-shaped middle-class society, which would be both *xiaokang* (小康) and harmonious (Guo 2008: 50). *Xiaokang* is a difficult term to translate, lying partway between 'comfortably well-off' and affluent, though it also implies social health. In the words of an exponent, *xiaokang* implies 'a competitive society, in which all members and their families own their private resources and live a life based on law and governed by elites' (Lu Hanlong 2010: 111). The CCP committed itself to ensuring the majority of the Chinese population would eventually become middle class in those terms.

A certain fetishization of the middle class has been apparent in the various official statements made about its development (Guo 2009), not least since as many commentators have indicated there has been a notable lack of sociological certainty in its identification (Rocca 2010: 57). Middle-class society is an aspiration rather than a carefully thought-out idea. Nonetheless, the identification of the middle class as a potential driver of change is clear. Individuals are being encouraged to pursue new 'social norms of middle-class identity often defined around consumer practices'. The new model citizen is someone with high cultural capital, and the economic capacity to consume. This message is intended not only to justify the existence and the behaviour of the wealthy, but also to encourage such active economic behaviour, even amongst migrant workers and the poorest sections of society (Anagnost 2008: 498–9). As will be seen in chapter 4, where its conceptualization and practice is discussed further, the idea of a new Chinese middle class has not gone without criticism in China.

Though Jiang Zemin's 2002 statement offered the prospect of a less antagonistic interpretation of social change, both because it concentrated on strata and highlighted the growth of the middle as the most dynamic element, a comprehensive overview of class was still missing. This came with the support of a group at the CASS Institute of Sociology, led by Lu Xueyi, which, alongside the orthodoxy of class by ideology, developed a typology of class by occupation (Lu Xueyi 2002). CASS is the leading research activity and think tank under the PRC State Council. While the exact relationship between the CCP's definition of class by ideology and Lu Xueyi's description of class by occupation was, and even to some extent remains, ambiguous, in practical terms there is widespread acceptance of both. Certainly the CASS approach informs government policy development and dominates the more academic discussion of class in the PRC.

Lu and his colleagues first developed their strata as class (*jieceng*) scheme in a 2002 report, and it has been the basis for a series of reports since that date. It is discussed in detail in chapter 2. The classification was informed by the work of sociologists outside China, notably Anthony Giddens and John Goldthorpe, who emphasized the importance of occupational class (Giddens 1973; Goldthorpe 1980); and Erik Olin Wright, who from a Marxist perspective stressed social class and authority relationships (Wright 1997). Ten strata were identified, derived in practical terms from surveys of the working population around the country, determined by 'occupation . . . the possession of organizational authority, economic and cultural resource' (Lu Xueyi 2002: 9).

ANALYSING CLASS IN CONTEMPORARY CHINA

The combination of Weberian (occupational class) and Marxist (social class) perspectives in the work of the CASS sociologists mirrors developments elsewhere in the sociology of class. Remarkably, despite earlier disagreements, sociologists appear to have generally achieved a degree of agreement on a basic three-class division in industrial society, which can be reached if the Marxist view of history and the historic mission of the proletariat is (at least temporarily and for academic purposes) put aside (Wright 1997: 29). There are three main sources of class power: property, qualifications and labour (Giddens 1973). These have led to the identification of 'a dominant class based on the ownership of capital, an intermediate class based on the acquisition of educational and/or organizational assets, and a subordinate class based on the possession of physical labour' (Edgell 1993: 81). In addition, there may also be constituent classes or subclasses within each of these three main classes, as well as one or more underclasses completely outside consideration of class position.

This tripartite framework provides a useful way to approach a society's class structure in general terms, and with a few slight adaptations it can be employed in examining the PRC beyond the perspectives of the CCP. The extent to which the three main classes so described have more than a categorical existence necessarily depends on the interaction between their economic configuration, political behaviour, social mobility and symbolic construction, all of which are matters for further consideration. There is the added advantage in taking this approach to understanding the PRC that it facilitates comparisons with other industrial societies. It is clear, for example, right from the start that while the PRC has much in common with other industrial societies, it is also differentiated as a Communist Party-state. One crucial result, as was previously the case in other earlier state socialist systems, is that position in the state system is more important than property ownership as a source of economic power (Bourdieu 1998: 14–18; Szelényi 1978). The PRC has a socialist market economy: a mixed economic system in which a growing market sector interacts and hybridizes with, but largely remains subordinated to, a more established state sector. While some economic capital may indeed be owned by individuals or even corporations, control of economic capital or ownership of the product of capital, as well as the exercise of political capital, are equally if not more significant.

The next chapter (chapter 2) details the changing structure of social and economic inequality that have occurred in the PRC since the start of the reform era in 1978, and how the resultant patterns of stratification have been conceptualized by commentators both outside and inside China. It provides a basic overview of the social trends and practices that shape class formation. In particular, it highlights the importance of the rural–urban divide, institutionalized through the household registration system that still more widely acts as a significant brake on social mobility by ensuring that most Chinese must live where they are born. It also highlights the significance of China's scale and intense regional variation; and of the still privileged position of the public sector – including not only state-owned and collective economic enterprises, but also the military and civil security, and all government agencies and state hospital, education and welfare systems – in the political economy. The chapter then reviews various attempts to construct a class narrative around these trends, including the now dominant account of class provided by the CASS sociology group. While the latter is comprehensive in its ambition, the application of its principles is found unconvincing, not least because of its teleology designed to discover a growing middle class.

Against this background of social change, each in turn of the following three chapters considers the development of the dominant class, the middle or intermediate classes, and the subordinate classes. In each case, the broad class in question and its component parts is examined in terms of socio-economic configuration, status, identity, behaviour and cohesion.

The dominant class (chapter 3) consists of those who wield economic power through control and management, as well as through ownership of the means of production. Its membership comes largely from the political leadership, though there are clearly also some large-scale entrepreneurs with significant status and influence. However, this is still a political economy where the public sector dominates politically despite the increasing size of the non-public marketized sector. The public sector of the economy remains substantial, especially in strategic industries. Moreover, a large part of the explanation of its continued dominance is that the marketized sector of the economy has both structural and associational links with the public sector. Many economic enterprises are hybrid public-private, or public-marketized sector activities, and where entrepreneurs have not emerged from within government and the public sector they have been brought into political activities and accommodation with and by the Party-state.

Chapter 4 begins by considering the state-sponsored discourse that has encouraged the desirability of having and growing a middle class since 2002. It suggests that the development of the middle class is more aspirational than structural. Despite a substantial body of different entrepreneurial, professional and managerial middle classes whose class position comes from the possession of skills, knowledge and experience, and their organizational abilities, they are more limited in numbers than the state's rhetoric and encouragement suggests. Paradoxically, they are to be found more in the public sector than elsewhere, which indicates that the growth of the middle class is likely to be somewhat limited. These observations about the middle class in terms of socio-economic structure aside, there still can be no gainsaying the power of a middle-class identity, especially in the marketplace.

The subordinate classes are clearly even more diverse than the middle classes, and considerably more divided, particularly along the lines of rural–urban household registration. Chapter 5 examines those whose position in the political economy is derived from their manual labour: the urban working class, the peasant migrant workers, and the peasantry. It details the previous strong identity and class consciousness of the urban working class and how this has been effected by the restructuring of the public sector, which has been and will continue to be a key feature of reform in the PRC. It also details the extent and the ways in which a new industrial workforce of peasant migrant workers has come into existence. The impact of reform on rural life has been significant, not least because most rural households have members who are migrant workers, though not all gravitate to large urban areas. The discussion of the peasantry highlights the inherent variability of the rural political economy, particularly in terms of both regionalism and proximity to urban centres and communication channels.

Having detailed the development of the dominant class, the middle classes and the subordinate classes in the contemporary era, chapter 6 returns to examine the likely consequences of change for China's political economy. The prospects for regime change, and specifically for the establishment of capitalism and liberal democracy, are the most common frameworks applied in the literature by those attempting to understand China's political economy of change. Here it is argued that neither is a likely short- to medium-term outcome, not least because socio-economic change, while substantial and continuing, remains limited. For the moment at least, China remains an example of market socialism, dominated by its cadres and public sector. These conclusions are borne out by consideration of more specific questions, all of which are much debated in the secondary literature: the impact of the market on the composition and operation of the dominant class; the potential role of the entrepreneurial and middle classes as agents of political change; the possible emergence of a new working-class consciousness; the dimensions of peasant activism; and the impact of economic inequality on regime legitimacy.

In conclusion, chapter 7 revisits the argument about inequality and class formation. Not only are there severe and possibly growing inequalities, but almost all the most acute are historically reproduced and institutionalized. Contemporary China is a society characterized by its low social mobility and high intergenerational transfer of privilege and disadvantage. This is a meaning of class well understood by most Chinese, who when faced by the ambiguities that are a consequence of the CCP's simultaneous description of class by ideology and class by occupation, have come to socialize their understanding in their own experience.

2   Social Stratification under Reform _____

It is always an over-simplification to identify turning points in the development of a society: there are inevitably continuities across such specific moments as well as discontinuities. Nonetheless, December 1978 has to count as a major marker of change in the development of the PRC. The Third Plenum of the 11th Central Committee of the CCP which met at that time is usually held to be the beginning of the period of 'reform and opening' because of its decisions and their consequences. The plenum decided to turn its back on the politics of the Mao-dominated era once and for all, to formally review (and learn the lessons of) the CCP's more recent history and, most importantly, to adopt a new development strategy that would introduce market forces into the state socialist economic system, decentralize administration, separate the functions of government and party more clearly, lessen the government's role in economic management, and open the domestic economy to global interactions (Goodman 1985; Naughton 1995).

The social impact of these changes has been both dramatic and considerable (Bian 2002; Zhou and Qin 2010). Social scientists both inside and outside the PRC, and the CCP itself, have all agreed that the development of the socialist market economy has resulted in considerable inequality and increased stratification (World Bank 2012: 8; Sun and Guo 2013). There is still uncertainty and debate about the extent and consequences of those inequalities (Li, Sato and Sicular 2013), the dynamics of change, and the resultant stratification and class formation. The view of the class structure prepared by the CASS Institute of Sociology has been embraced by the Party-state and dominates discussion. Nonetheless, this remains an issue of considerable debate within China and generally amongst social scientists.

MARKERS OF CHANGE

After the mid-1950s, China's social structure was dominated by the then prevalent CCP ideology of class, as well as the distinction between state and collective sectors of the economy and the household registration system. Theoretically, the economy was divided into three ownership sectors: the state, the collective (where ownership was socialized by the people living or working in a unit) and the private sectors. Almost 80 per cent of the urban workforce was in the state sector and they not only had their employment guaranteed for life – the so-called 'iron rice bowl' – but received substantial benefits, including housing, education for their children and health care. These terms of employment and benefits were not shared by workers in the collective sector, which included all agricultural activity and the rest of the urban workforce (Davis 1985; Walder 1986: 45). The private sector was negligible after 1956, reserved largely for welfare recipients.

The introduction of the household registration system (hukou 户口 colloquially or huji 户籍), first in 1955 but more assiduously and draconically after 1960, tied almost every individual to their mother's place of birth for life, and severely limited the opportunities for moving somewhere else (Cheng and Selden 1994). Each household and all its individual members were classified according to whether they lived in an urban or rural area; and whether they had a right to buy from the public supply of grain (non-agricultural household registration) or were expected to feed themselves under all circumstances (agricultural household registration). After 1960, the development of the household registration system effectively brought a strict rural–urban dichotomy, which was particularly pernicious for peasants unable to either move to urban areas or to access the benefits of urban life (Chan, Madsen and Unger 2009). At the same time it also restricted the movement of the urban workforce and often effectively tied the individual to their work-unit (Davis 1992; Walder 1992: 526). Migration restrictions were very strict and hierarchical. While downward movement to a lower-order city or rural area was possible, upward reassignation was much harder. In the mid-1950s and early 1960s, large numbers of urban residents were required to resettle elsewhere and, starting in the late 1960s, there was a decade in which several million 'educated youth' were sent to the countryside from the cities (Bernstein 1977). In such cases the migrants were provided with a new household registration that prevented any return to their place of departure. On the other hand, in total only 329,000 rural residents were ever permitted to change to a hierarchically superior household registration before 1979 (Wang Chunguang 2012: 269).

By the late 1970s, the PRC had become remarkably equal and des-tratified (Whyte 1975; Parish 1984): an equality of poverty, especially for the 80 per cent of the population who lived on and off the land (Parish and Whyte 1978: 44). Destratification is perhaps more usually a term applied to pre-industrial societies where social and political life is dominated by the family and by a small state administration with no division of labour and no room for the secular, and seems particu-larly apposite as a description of China's case during the 1960s and 1970s (Stockman 2000: 203). In China's case, the Party-state had even made inroads into family life, through its policies of rural collectiviza-tion (Lu Xueyi 2012: 22) and the domination of urban life by the work-unit system (Bray 2005).

Since 1978 change has happened gradually and without a blueprint. On the contrary, the CCP's strategy has been experimental and often based on trial and error. Nor for that matter has the state economic sector, or the state's role in economic management, been abandoned (Naughton 2010; NBS 2013). There have been a number of milestones related to employment, business structures, housing, education and patterns of consumption, all of which are key markers of stratification. One of the first acts of the new development strategy was the introduction of the 'One-child Policy' of population control which applied to urban married couples, with few exceptions. Only rural couples, ethnic minorities and couples who themselves were only children were permitted additional children. Announced in 1978, it was implemented from the start of 1979. By 2007, it was claimed that 35.9 per cent of the population were subject to the one-child restriction (Guan 2007). Family size declined from 4.41 members in 1982 to 3.1 in 2012 (Lu Xueyi 2012: 11). An unintended consequence has been a dramatic shift in the sex ratio of live registered births: as of 2010, there were 118 males for every 100 females.

Socio-economic change started in the countryside at the end of the 1970s with the introduction of the household responsibility system, which essentially decollectivized agriculture and led rapidly to the development of town and village enterprises (TVEs) and to the phenomenon of migrant workers: rural residents who moved out of agricultural work and in some cases moved to urban areas and cities to look for work (Kam Wing Chan 2012). Because the household registration remained (and remains) in place, these migrant workers, their families and dependents are not treated as urban residents. By 2013, the National Bureau of Statistics (NBS) calculated that the number of migrant workers had grown to 262.61 million (*Xinhua* 18 January 2013), roughly half of whom were working in urban areas. By that time too there were already second-generation 'migrant workers' who had largely grown up in urban areas. About half of all rural migrant workers in urban areas, together with their families and dependents (altogether a migrant population of about 125 million people), are estimated to stay in urban areas for six months or more at any one time (Li, Luo and Sicular 2012).

In 1984, market reforms were extended to urban China, although initially development was slow, with some reluctance to take initiatives on the part of potential private business people, and some hesitation from the Party-state. Marx had argued in *Das Kapital* that employing more than eight people led to exploitation. Accordingly, the CCP decided to permit the development of small-scale individual household businesses (*getihu*, 个体户) of up to eight employees. Later, in 1988, somewhat larger private businesses (*siying qiye*, 私营企业) were recognized but these were seen as adjuncts to the state sector, stepping in where the latter was less able to act. Most private business remained small throughout the 1980s (Dickson 2010: 295). Foreign investment and involvement in China started at this time, though it was heavily regulated except in the then newly established Special Economic Zones – Shenzhen, Zhuhai, Shantou and Xiamen, and later (in 1988) Hainan Province – and in open cities and export-processing zones that followed the successful development of the SEZs.

The potential for further socio-economic change was signalled in the wake of the Party-state's decision to emphasize the development of the marketized sector of the economy in 1992, and particularly with the restructuring of state and urban collective sector enterprises in and after 1995, which by 1999 reduced the urban workforce in the public sector by 29 per cent (Khan 2005). The housing reform that started in 1998 removed a large amount of urban housing from the ownership of work-units and in many cases provided former residents with significant subsidized private housing. From the mid-1980s to 2000, urban owner-occupied housing grew from 10 to 75 per cent (Davis 2003), and by 2013 was estimated to be about 85 per cent (Li Gan 2013). In 1999, the decision was taken to dramatically expand the number of students in higher education. By 2005, 7 per cent of the national population and 17 per cent of the urban population of eighteen-year-olds were higher education graduates, compared to less than 1 per cent and 11 per cent during the 1980s (Li Chunling 2010: 139). By 2010, 27 per cent of the urban population of eighteen-year-olds was in higher education (*RMRB* 11 March 2011).

Immediately after the Tiananmen Incident of 1989, and the challenge that the CCP felt to its leadership, entrepreneurs of all sizes had been banned from joining the Party itself. This was a strange move since in urban areas some of the earliest non-state business people were already Party members. It came to be seen as an even stranger decision in and after 1992, when the CCP encouraged the development of the marketized sector of the economy; and again, in the middle of the 1990s, when both cadres and state-sector managers were encouraged to leave their 'iron rice bowls' behind and 'go into the sea' (*xia hai* 下海) of the new economy. By the late 1990s, it was clear that entrepreneurs, far from being banned by the CCP, were beginning to be feted, and with Jiang Zemin's formulation of the 'Three Represents' in 2002 were actually being welcomed into the CCP.

The household registration system remains in place, despite considerable lobbying within the PRC and speculation that it might be abolished, though accompanied by minor reforms in both principle and practice as well as considerable complexity in its continued operation (Chan and Buckingham 2008). Lobbying for other legislative and regulatory changes that have potential to impact socio-economic change has been more successful. In 2003, the number of state-owned enterprises (SOE) was reduced in number, and 117 of those at the national level (known as Central State-owned Enterprises) as opposed to those that report to provincial or even sub-provincial authorities were brought under the direction of the State-owned Assets Supervision and Administration Commission (SASAC) of the State Council. In 2004, some assistance was provided to alleviate rural poverty through the abolition of rural taxes and fees. In 2006, legislation was passed into law that approved the recognition of private property and private property rights. In 2007, a new PRC Bankruptcy Law came into play that brought the 1986 (and only SOE-focused) legislation up to date with regulation that was also applied to the private sector, though the forty-six SOEs deemed to be strategically important were still protected from the possibility.

In addition to wealth creation, the Party-state's attention has also focused on inequality and poverty as matters of concern for public policy, especially since 2002. Poverty alleviation measures were put in place in urban China during the mid-1990s, as the state-sector work-force was reduced, in the form of a 'Minimum Livelihood Guarantee' (*zuidi shenghuo baozheng*, 最低生活保证 usually shortened to *dibao* 低保), but the number of those supported was low and the support less than recognized as necessary (Solinger 2006). At the 17th National CCP Congress in 2007, Hu Jintao announced his 'New Vision of Scientific Development', designed to alleviate the rural–urban differ-ence, reduce regional disparities, narrow income inequality and estab-lish a social security network. Research based on the large-scale China Household Income Project, with samples from the National Bureau of Statistics during the last decade, shows that while poverty continues to be reduced, economic inequalities not only remain, but in some cases – such as the rural–urban divide – have increased and (as of 2012) were still increasing (Li, Luo and Sicular 2012). According to the NBS, in 1978 income inequality between rural and urban China had been 1:2.6 – 134 *yuan* compared to 343 *yuan* GDP per capita per annum. By 2012, the ratio had increased to 1:3.1 – 7,917 *yuan* to 24,565 *yuan* (Xinhua 18 January 2013).

RURAL–URBAN RELATIONS

The fundamental importance of the rural–urban relationship to an understanding of inequality and stratification in China goes far beyond the significance of the size and proportion of the rural and agricultural population (still about half the overall total in 2013). It is not just, as Whyte has recently suggested, that the policies of the Mao era had condemned the peasantry to 'socialist serfdom' where they were tied to the land and considerable poverty, and that the policies of the first thirty years of the PRC had left a legacy of inequality to rural China that remains despite reform. The policies that have been followed since 1978 have built on and reinforced the earlier asymmetric relationship to such an extent that it is perhaps more useful to think of two linked social systems, though Whyte and others prefer to talk about China divided into 'two separate castes, rural and urban, with sharply different rights and opportunities in life' (Whyte 2010b: 13). Reform may have delivered decollectivization and freedom of decision in employment to rural residents, market reforms may have assisted many rural areas to improve their standard of living, but the persistence and elaboration of the household registration system ensures not only the continuation of discrimination against those with a rural registration but the continuation of a discrimination that works to the greater advantage of those living in urban China.

Two early policy changes in the reform era were clearly welcomed in rural China. The first was the dismantling of collectivized agriculture and its replacement by a household responsibility system, under which farmers had freedom of economic manoeuvre provided that grain procurements were met (and, until 2004, that taxes were paid). The freedom of economic decision-making led to the second policy change. Farmers could not only choose how to use their land, including whether to raise cash crops or develop a workshop, small factory or business, but they could also choose to go and look for work as wage-earners elsewhere, even in urban areas. In the event, this became the necessary labour boost for the development of the Special Economic Zones, and for small businesses generally, as many villagers were mobilized in this way. Urban rationing had been a necessary check on rural to urban migration for work before 1979 but this started to be phased out in the early 1980s, assisting the possibilities for labour migration. The economic results of these policy changes were extremely positive for rural China. The introduction of market principles to the urban economy did not begin until 1984 so that for a while there was a distinct narrowing, remarkably approaching equality, of the rural–urban per capita income gap (Yan Ye 2012: 186).

While the income gap may have temporarily narrowed, other aspects of the rural–urban difference actually worsened with reform, even in the short term. Health and education services in the rural areas had never been delivered at the standard of urban China before 1979, but there had been a basic state investment in and provision of schools, local clinics, networks of paramedical workers in the villages, and village cooperative medical insurance systems. Health and education now moved on to a user-pays system, which essentially led to the closure of the rural health system and undermined attendances at schools (Hannum and Adams 2009; Yip 2010).

The fragile financial viability of rural households was a matter of some concern to local and provincial governments. Starting in 2004, many provinces attempted to ensure a measure of relief by ending the collection of agricultural tax payments. At the same time, instead of taxes, rural households producing grain (usually the poorest) were able to benefit from newly introduced grain and agricultural production material subsidies. In and after 2005, a series of measures were taken to construct the 'New Socialist Countryside' (Ahlers and Schubert 2013). One of the first new policies to follow was the formal abolition of agricultural taxes, quickly followed by the abolition of school tuition fees. A third and even more dramatic policy was the extension of the *dibao* to rural China (Unger 2012a). In 2002, income support of this kind had gone to only 4 million people but, by 2007, the number had increased to 36 million, who on average each received 480 *yuan*, which was about 60 per cent of the minimum definition of rural poverty

(Gustafsson, Li and Sicular 2008). Inevitably, because of the expansion of the urban economy after 2002, the rural–urban income gap extended once again.

Without doubt, the single most important aspect of rural–urban relations in the reform era has been the emergence of rural migrants and their families moving to urban areas looking for work. Since the early 1980s, rural migrant workers have left the countryside, in large and increasing numbers, to fill the jobs produced by the expanding marketized economy to such an extent that they are estimated to account for 40 per cent of the urban workforce. Precise statistics are not easily obtained about rural migrant workers and their activities for obvious reasons: their household registration is other than where many of them permanently work and about half of them permanently live; and the remaining half are equally and necessarily peripatetic (Shi Xiuyin 2012: 155). Research, especially that based on household surveys, can and does adjust for these difficulties, but there must always be reservations (Li, Luo and Sicular 2012).

Construction, manufacturing, mining and haulage industries in particular are heavily dominated by rural migrant workers. In the service sector, domestic service, restaurants big and small, wholesale and retail sales, and street-level commerce of all kinds are largely staffed by rural migrant workers (Shi Xiuyin 2012: 155). Originally banned from certain kinds of employment that required urban household registration, (notably in state-owned enterprises and government agencies) since the late 1990s rural migrant workers have also come increasingly to be employed in state-owned enterprises and government agencies, though not on the same terms and conditions as urban natives and usually at far cheaper wage rates (Pun and Lu 2010b; Friedman and Lee 2010).

Rural migrant workers are now an important part of the urban workforce but they remain discriminated against in a number of ways. In the first place there is the legal and regulatory environment that restricts their ability to live and work in cities. The larger cities are necessarily often the largest magnets for migrant workers, and while they may effectively settle there they are excluded almost totally from access to housing, health, education and welfare systems for themselves and their families. Even the children of migrant workers, born and brought up in urban areas where their families do not hold the appropriate household registration, are also excluded from access to public services in this way (Solinger 1999a). Until about 2000, the ability of a rural migrant worker to change their household registration to an urban *hukou* was close to zero. Subsequently it has become possible for highly successful and wealthy rural entrepreneurs to acquire urban household registration; and in lower-order cities at sub-provincial levels it has also become possible for a rural migrant worker who has found employment and a sponsor to acquire an urban household registration (Carrillo 2011). At the same time, rural migrant workers are discriminated against through a whole range of urban practices, including social derision, being left under- or unpaid by their urban employer, being excluded from certain employment prospects open to urban natives, and harassment by police and local authorities (Chan and Buckingham 2008: 599; Guang and Kong 2010).

This description of rural migrant workers as a reserve pool of labour is a clear marker of the contemporary rural–urban relationship. Another is the expansion of urbanization at the expense of both rural residents and farmland. It is estimated that approximately 7 million acres of farmland were lost to agricultural use between 1987 and 2001, and that 60 million rural residents lost claims to the land they had previously worked (Zhang Jing 2009: 126). The development of farmland for industrial use or for real estate has clearly been aided by a financial environment that leaves local government with few alternative options for funding their expanding activities (Zhou Feizhou 2009).

REFORM AND INEQUALITY

The relationship between rural and urban China is obviously central to the examination of inequality as a whole, to some extent limiting any attempt to produce national statistics or statements. It is clear that a substantial proportion (probably about half) of the overall income inequality that has developed in the reform era is statistically solely derived from the large rural–urban difference (Chen Jiandong et al. 2010; Li, Luo and Sicular 2012). All the same, urban, rural and overall income inequality have all certainly increased since 1978 as, it would seem, have other forms of economic and non-economic inequality, particularly regional differences, ethnicity, gender, and the distinctions flowing from employment in the public as opposed to the market sectors.

In considering economic inequality, attention commonly focuses on the Gini coefficient, which strictly speaking is an index of income inequality and only marginally related to overall wealth, though it is often used as a proxy. Certainly, it would appear that the Gini coefficient for China has increased from the relative equality of 0.20 in 1978. According to the National Bureau of Statistics, it reached the considerably less equal level of 0.474 in 2012, having been even higher at 0.491 in 2009; levels which the NBS indicated gave cause for concern in terms of the developing inequality and its potential consequences (Xinhua 21 January 2013).

There are, however, several problems attending any further analysis based on these numbers, not the least of which is the doubt that has been cast on the NBS figures, especially for income. Research from a team based at the China National Economic Research Institute, UC Davis, and the Central University of Finance and Economics, suggests that there is considerable 'grey income' that is neither declared by its recipients nor included in NBS statistics. Their conclusion for 2008 was that the urban average income per capita was actually

32,154 *yuan* as opposed to the NBS figure of 16,885 *yuan* (Wang and Woo 2010). Research by another team, through household surveys for the China Household Finance Survey based at the Southwestern University of Finance and Economics and Texas A&M University, also claims that NBS income figures are incorrect. For 2010, they estimate that average urban per capita income was 24,688 *yuan* as opposed to the 19,109 *yuan* cited by NBS, and that average rural per capita income was 9,373 *yuan* instead of 5,919 *yuan* (Li Gan 2013).

In any case, there are statistical issues in the analysis of China's Gini coefficient. It is estimated that there are at least twenty different ways that the Gini coefficient could be calculated, providing often substantially different results (Chen Jiandong et al. 2010). For 2007, for example, the China Household Income Project (CHIP) organized by the CASS Institute of Economics calculated that the Gini coefficient was already 0.5 (Li, Luo and Sicular 2012). For 2010, the China Household Finance Survey calculated that the Gini coefficient was 0.61 (Li Gan 2012). There are further data problems: the NBS uses aggregate data rather than basing its calculations directly on its household surveys; it does not take the social benefits available and provided to the urban population into account; and there appear to be inconsistencies in its calculation of different categories, especially of income and residence (Bramall 2001; Khan and Riskin 2005; Gao and Riskin 2009).

Adding to these difficulties, it is clear that discussion of China's Gini coefficient has become a political issue, both domestically and internationally (Fang and Yu 2012; *Economist* 26 January 2013). From 2000 to 2013, no Gini coefficient was officially produced by the NBS, and when it did the Bureau made the telling comment: 'The recent release of inequality data . . . echoed the fact that an increasing number of Chinese people have become more vocal in recent years to demand for fairer distributions of incomes and opportunities, thanks in part to the penetration of the social media platforms such as the Twitter-like Weibo' (Xinhua 21 January 2013).

More interesting are the calculations of developments in economic inequality over time, and by sector. Especially interesting are those that use the China Household Income Project surveys conducted in 1988, 1995, 2002 and 2007, as opposed to NBS data. Growth in inequality has by no means been constant over time, even allowing for differences between rural and urban sectors. During the early 1980s, rural growth narrowed the gap with urban incomes. By the time of the 1988 household survey it appeared that 'The level of overall earnings inequality remains low in China and only slightly correlated with economic growth, in part because the tendency toward higher levels of inequality in faster-growing cities is offset by the lower returns to human capital variables in these cities' (Xie and Hannum 1996: 984).

This conclusion was strikingly at odds with later research that showed both that (particularly after 2002) faster-growing cities grew even more rapidly and that later returns to human capital, especially education, were high (Gong, Leigh and Meng 2010). A college degree earns a graduate 75 per cent more than a high-school education, and a master's degree brings a 73 per cent higher return – though a doctorate results in a 30 per cent lower income than a master's degree (Li Gan 2013).

It is generally accepted that both rural and urban inequality grew dramatically from the late 1980s to 1995, but then that rural inequality declined, though only to the levels of the late 1980s (Gao and Riskin 2009: 36). There has, however, been considerable debate over the impact of reform (and the market) on inequality in urban areas between 1995 and 2002. Those who include the hidden subsidies to urban residents, especially in terms of household finance with housing reform, argue that urban inequality declined somewhat (Khan and Riskin 2005), but those who do not attempt this calculation see inequality as having continued to increase (Ravaillon and Chen 2007). Since 2002, the evidence of the CHIP surveys is that overall inequality has increased, as has urban inequality, with the rich getting richer, helped no doubt by the development of a larger urban housing rental market. The 2002 and 2007 CHIP surveys were also able to include data on migrant-worker households for the first time, or at least those migrant-worker households that were temporarily settled in an urban area for at least six months. For this category of urban worker (estimated to be about half the total number of migrant workers), the surveys found that their incomes in cash terms (though not their real disposable incomes) were rapidly approaching parity with urban households (Li, Luo and Sicular 2012).

Given the size of China, and the scale of its constituent provinces and differences in their resource base and economic positioning, it would be surprising if there were no spatial aspect to economic growth and inequality. According to NBS figures, the highest-income provincial-level unit in 2011 was Tianjin (a city directly under the Central Government) with a GDP per capita of 85,213 *yuan* – just over five times more than that of Guizhou Province, the lowest, with 16,413 *yuan* (NBS 2012: 59). Interestingly, this comparison suggests a decrease in overall provincial inequality since 2000 when Guizhou Province had only 8 per cent of the GDP per capita of Shanghai, then the highest per capita provincial-level administration (Goodman 2004b: 320). Generally, it is the case that the Eastern seaboard provinces are wealthier than those in the West, though this is far from an invariable rule, with Jiangxi Province and Anhui Province, which are both next to the light industrial powerhouse of Jiangsu Province, being two of the poorest provinces.

The reform era's development strategy divided the country into an Eastern Region, a Central and a Western Region. Urban reform and the introduction of market forces led to higher growth and incomes in the eastern coastal provinces especially, first Guangdong, then Fujian, Zhejiang, Jiangsu and Shandong, as well as in the metropolitan areas of Beijing, Shanghai and Tianjin. Increasing disparities between the coastal provinces and the interior led to major regional development projects to first 'Open Up the West' (1999), then the 'Northeast Strategy' (2003) and the 'Rise of the Central Region' (2006) (Chung, Lai and Joo 2009). The evidence of CHIP surveys is that those development projects seem to have made some headway in reducing the increase in regional inequality, especially when consumption relativities are taken into account. It is considerably cheaper to live in, say, Gansu or Sichuan, than in Zhejiang or Southern Jiangsu. When income is adjusted for purchasing power parity (PPP), the increase in regional inequality since 2002 becomes less pronounced (Gustafsson, Li and Sicular 2008; Li, Luo and Sicular 2012).

At the regional level it would seem that income inequality has been increasing among the provincial-level administrations of the Eastern Region, and decreasing among the provincial-level administrations of the Central and Western regions. At the same time, there remains a greater incidence of poverty in the Western Region (Yan Ye 2012: 207). This is indicative of the greater inequality being that between rural and urban areas within each province and each region (Li, Luo and Sicular 2012). Unsurprisingly, the large urban areas are generally less unequal, with significant pockets of inequality in even the richest provinces such as Guangdong, Jiangsu and Zhejiang. The distribution of wealth across the country is thus extremely varied.

Ethnic inequality is part and parcel of the spatial distribution of wealth. China has fifty-five officially approved minority nationalities in addition to the Han Chinese majority. This 8 per cent of the population are based largely in the designated Western Region. Indeed, it seems likely that a large part of the logic for the campaign to 'Open Up the West' was designed to manage their development to the extent that minority nationality populations not physically located in the Western Region were incorporated into the new strategy (Goodman 2004b: 333). Almost all of the non-Han peoples are poorer than the Han

Chinese with whom they live, regardless of whether they are urban or rural residents (Freeman 2012). The CCP's stated policy on the minority nationalities is that differences among ethnic groups (including the Han Chinese) are not cultural in any sense but a function of economic development. Economic growth and the embrace of the PRC's current development strategy are promoted as panaceas to the perceived difficulties facing the various minority nationalities. In some cases, ethnic groups have indeed embraced the opportunities offered (Heberer 2007). In others, it is clear that there may be greater resistance: the Uyghurs, for example (in Xinjiang), would apparently prefer to be poor and follow their own customs (Zang 2012).

There is considerable evidence to suggest that in the early stages of the reform era, gender inequality did not increase in the PRC. More recent research suggests, however, that gender inequality has increased with marketization of the economy since the early 1990s. While this inequality remains muted in the public sector, it has grown substantially in the marketized sector of the economy, with the exception of foreign-invested firms (Cohen and Wang 2009).

It would be a mistake to think that there had been male–female gender equality in the Mao-dominated years of China's politics (Wolf 1985). At the same time, there was some form of political commitment to change, which resulted in a higher profile for women generally, as well as for some specific women in public service or in the ranks of the CCP. Trends since the early 1990s seem to have reinforced even earlier social norms that kept women out of sight and at home. Whereas in 1973 10.3 per cent of the CCP's Central Committee membership was female, in 2012 this figure had fallen to 4.9 per cent. This trend is reflected in employment and the economy, where there is not only a tendency for young middle-class women to leave employment in order to get married and have a family but, even when they do go on to establish their own business, for women to often register it under their husband's name, and make him the front person for the operation who entertains clients and deals with government (Minglu Chen 2011).

The most striking evidence of the increase in gender inequality is the increase in the 'gender penalty' – the difference between men and women's income where they have the same experience and seniority, identical educational qualifications, and hold the same position working in the same industry. This rose from 7.3 per cent in 1986 to 12 per cent in 1993, and to over 15 per cent by 1999 (Cohen and Wang 2009: 39). In 1990, female urban employees generally earned on average 15 per cent less than their male counterparts. By 2000, the difference had grown to 25 per cent. Research suggests not only that gender inequality increased substantially but also that women are more likely to take lower-paid jobs in lower-paid sectors of the economy, particularly in domestic service, in the textile industry, on light industry production lines and in the service sector. There is, however, variability to these findings by sector and by location. The public sector (state-sector enterprises and government and government-associated social activities, such as education and health) has somewhat less gender inequality at least in income; and there is almost none in foreign-invested enterprises. Conversely, there is greater gender inequality in income in the higher GDP per capita cities, though this is mediated somewhat by a high level of foreign investment (Cohen and Wang 2009: 51).

The difference between the public sector and the marketized sectors of the economy, which is so noticeable in terms of gender inequality, points to a further, more general inequality. Chinese people talk about the inequality between those who work and live 'within the system' (*tizhinei*, 体制内) or 'outside the system' (*tizhiwai*, 体制外). The 'system' in question is essentially the Party-state, though it might more usefully be described as the wider public sector. It includes all the institutions (and employees) of the government, the CCP and their associated administrations (including ministries, the military, the police and civil defence forces, transport and communications, education and health services) and at different levels of territorial administration (central, provincial, city, county and town), as well as all state-sector economic enterprises and all enterprises owned or controlled by SOEs or by Party-state agencies. Altogether, there are about 74 million people employed in the public sector: just short of 10 per cent of the working population (Wang An 2012). In many ways, the inequalities between inside and outside 'the system' are almost by definition impossible to quantify, especially in cash terms, though economists and social scientists all agree they exist (Gao and Riskin 2009: 21). Indeed, it may even be that in cash terms the distinctions are barely visible (Li Gan 2013).

Rather than economic capital, the distinctions are those of social and cultural capital. Those within the system have networks of influence, privileges and benefits that are not available to those outside. Not the least of the benefits is a greater permanency of employment. Though the 'iron rice bowl' is meant to have disappeared with reform, the extent of marketization in the public sector, especially in the state administration and associated functions (education and health services, for example) is very low. In addition to a higher security of tenure, the benefits include access to health services, education for children, and in particular highly subsidized housing.

Housing reform in the second half of the 1990s commercialized housing and led to the high levels of ownership now in place. But the better placed 'within the system' work-units were able to provide housing and subsidies that were not available to those outside (Tang 2013). It remains difficult to quantify this housing benefit precisely, though it is clear those within the system have gained substantially more than those outside the system from the housing-cost inflation of the last decade (Li Gan 2013).

A hypothetical example of such benefits and their contribution to rising inequality may explain some of the dynamics. University members of staff at the time of housing reform had the opportunity to buy the apartments they already inhabited at subsidized prices of between a third and two thirds of market prices. The apartments are located on campus but in a very pleasant, secure and convenient location with lots of open spaces, access to schools, clinics and other amenities. The only limitation on new purchasers of the apartments is that if they sell a property to another member of the university it has to be at the institution's subsidized rate (usually fixed annually at a cost per square metre). Purchasers are free to sell apartments on the open market for much higher prices than originally paid, though of course they would still have to find somewhere to live. Then the university in question decided, as many have done in the last decade with the expansion of higher education, to open a new campus somewhere else. The university will build not only new offices, teaching and administrative areas, but also new housing for its staff. New apartments were offered to all members of staff at the current subsidized rate, even to those who already had purchased an originally university-subsidized property: the new campus counts as a different place from the original campus, even though it may be next door or close by. The university members of staff in question can then buy the second apartments on the same terms as the first, realize their assets by selling the first on the open market, and still have somewhere to live.

Housing is an important fulcrum of this story of social change (Tomba 2004). With access to good housing in China, as elsewhere in the world, comes potential access to the 'right' schools (those that can deliver a good secondary education followed by university entrance) and the better health and community services. In part this is a legacy of the old state socialist system and its work-unit-centred development. Nonetheless, even the development of new housing estates has maintained these kinds of links, for sound socio-economic reasons from the point of view of their residents.

STRATIFICATION AND CLASS

A number of attempts have been made, both inside and outside China, to interpret the inequalities and changes of the reform era in terms of systematic schema of social stratification. They identify broad social groups and classes, for the most part recognizing, though often without providing detail, that these social categories themselves can and should be disaggregated further to adequately understand the processes of stratification and class formation (Wang and Davis 2010). Systems of stratification necessarily depend on their purpose, and a good many domestically derived accounts are not only related to contemporary political discussions about class, but are also critical of current trends. Most agree that gender, education, cadre status and occupations are the major indicators (Yan 2012: 208); and that whereas before 1992 hard work alone led to wealth, since that time the balance has shifted to organizational, economic and cultural resources (Lu Xueyi 2002: 16).

An early critical account of social change under reform came from Liang Xiaosheng, a popular writer and commentator, whose account of stratification remains a best-seller sixteen years after its original publication. Reacting against both the class politics of earlier times and the corruption of the present, he wrote a description of each of seven new strata he identified in Chinese society: capitalists, compradors, the new middle class, intellectuals, ordinary citizens, the urban poor, peasants and secret societies (Liang 1997). It has been suggested that Liang is essentially in search of a new morality to offset against rampant materialism (Lin and Galikowski 1999: 135).

A more trenchant critique was provided by He Qinglian who, as a result of the reception of her ideas, moved to the USA in 2001. In contrast to the dominant view of the class structure that places its emphasis on the growing middle class, He Qinglian argues that power and wealth has passed to a new class of bureaucratic capitalists who have hindered the emergence of a middle class through the monopolization of economic, social and cultural capital. In her view, the social structure has a small and socially narrow-based elite, a middle stratum of state officials and professionals, and an overwhelming majority of peasants and workers (He 1998, 2000).

On the other hand, there are many Chinese academics willing to follow the insistence of some CCP theoreticians that analysis should stay with a two-class structure, albeit that their two nominated classes (the workers and the peasantry) are actually occupational categories. There are essentially three variants of this approach to understanding current social stratification. All set about interpreting change in terms of identifying occupational groups: new categories such as small-scale business people, private entrepreneurs, managerial, technical and professional staff in private and foreign-owned businesses, and employees of social organizations, in addition to the pre-existing categories such as cadres, managers, peasants, workers, military personnel, teachers and students (Guo 2012). One approach attempts to group all occupations into one of the two designated classes, as did then President of the PRC and General-Secretary of the CCP Jiang Zemin, in the first years of the twenty-first century (Jiang 2001). The second identifies two classes and then a non-attached set of occupations which are not part of a class but do not in themselves form a class (Zhu Guanglei et al. 1998; Li Shenming et al. 2002; Yan Zhimin 2002). The third approach, essentially that of Lu Xueyi and the CASS schema, as already noted, sees classes by ideology and classes by occupation as separate issues (Li Peilin 1995; Yang Jisheng 2000; Li Qiang 2002; Li Lulu 2003).

Liu Xin, of Shanghai's Fudan University, has developed a sophisticated analysis of social differentiation, based on the changing relationship between the exercise of state power and property rights. The ways in which state power interacts with market operations determine distribution (and stratification) results from administrative (and political) decisions, from market decisions and from rent-seeking behaviour. He proposes a ten-category stratification, with basic distinctions made according to whether an individual or social category exercises public power, and whether they have direct control over public assets or are subject to market operations. Those who are in the public sector are further divided by their exercise of administrative decision-making, or technical competence; those in the market sector by their reliance on human or economic capital. Society is then described in terms of technocrats, bureaucrats, SOE managers, clerks, private entrepreneurs and managers, the self-employed, high-level professionals, low-level professionals (differentiated by market recognition), skilled workers and non-skilled workers (Liu Xin 2009).

Lu Hanlong, in examining the goal of *xiaokang* society, developed a five-class model of Chinese society based on occupation and life conditions. In all market systems, including the socialist market system, there will always be hierarchies of the rich and poor. In China's case, the rich class includes both 'capital owners and profiteers' and less well-off entrepreneurs and small business owners. The poor class are 'the poor, the unemployed . . . And those unable to be self-sustainable.' There are three middle classes: an elite class of political leaders, business executives and senior professionals; a mid-level class of the knowledge-service groups – government and office staff, white-collar workers in corporations and 'general professionals'; and a class of direct producers – self-employed business people, manual and semi-manual workers, retail service workers, self-employed workers and peasants (Lu Hanlong 2010: 116).

Li Chunling, in discussing the emergence and growth of the middle class, incidentally develops a five-class approach taking into account income, occupation, education and consumption. She explicitly acknowledges that her analysis is derived from the work of John Goldthorpe, and the East Asia Middle Class project led by Michael Hsiao (Goldthorpe 1980; Hsiao 1993). There is a capitalist class of private entrepreneurs; a new middle class of officials, professionals and managers holding positions of importance in the public and private sectors; an old middle class of small business people and the self-employed; a marginal middle class of low-level white-collar workers; and finally the workers. While Li recognizes that the emergence of a capitalist class and an old middle class are significant developments, she emphasizes greatly the growth of the new middle class, comprising senior officials, professionals and managers, and its political importance (Li Chunling 2010: 144–6).

Alvin So, of the Hong Kong University of Science and Technology, has provided a convincing and comprehensive account of class in China under reform, not least because he is able to start from the assumption of a 'class-divided society' rather than one that is haunted by its recent history of class struggle. Through a focus on the processes of 'class differentiation, class polarization, and class conflict', he identifies a capitalist class, an old middle class (small-scale business people), a new middle class (intellectuals, professionals and students), a peasantry and a working class. Crucial to this analysis is the emergence of a capitalist or cadre-capitalist class, formed by the merger of interests between the political leadership and private entrepreneurs, and their monopolization of economic, social and cultural capital. Cadres have been embourgeoised and private entrepreneurs have been brought into the orbit of politics and the state (if they were not already involved). At the same time, So notes the disempowerment and segmentation of the working class with the growth of a private sector, the depoliticization of the professional and managerial middle class, and the professionalization of middle-level cadres (So 2003a).

In complete contrast, from looking at consumption patterns in China in 2010, a group at the Boston Consulting Group (BCG) was able to develop a class identification based on lifestyle and purchasing potential (Silverstein et al. 2012). Some goods are purchased regardless of income and class; others increase in cost and imputed quality as income rises. Then there is a third category of discretionary expenditure that is class and income specific. There are three inflection points in rising income where people's consumption habits change dramatically. When household income reaches about 45,000 *yuan* a year, consumption moves to focus on fresh fruit and vegetables, ready-to-wear clothing and better housing. When household income reaches 75,000 *yuan* a year, people think about buying a car, they start buying health foods and the cheaper luxury goods, and increase their expenditure on beauty products, clothes and shoes, entertainment and alcohol. At a household income of 114,000 *yuan* a year, consumers move to spend money on travel, recreation, sophisticated household goods and non-everyday foods such as yoghurt, chocolate, coffee and wine. Expenditure on transport and communication, education and health increases dramatically above this final inflection point. From this analysis, BCG is able to identify class by consumption as indicated in table 2.1.

THE EMERGENT CLASS STRUCTURE

The model of the contemporary class structure developed by Lu Xueyi and his colleagues at the CASS Institute of Sociology is fast approaching orthodoxy, especially in the development of social policy. It has been derived from a series of surveys undertaken since 2000, and provides for ten strata or classes. The formal antecedents of the class approach adopted were drawn from the work of Anthony Giddens (Giddens 1973) and Erik Olin Wright (Wright 1997), highlighting class in contemporary society as being derived from the means of production, position in the authority structure and the possession of skills and expertise. The Institute of Sociology team used these three determinants and added a fourth – officials were differentiated according to the extent to which they were within or outside the Party-state system (Lu Xueyi 2002: 44). Table 2.2 provides details from the surveys, and from historical data of the distribution of the

Table 2.1 Class by consumption in the PRC, 2010

CLASS	PERCENTAGE	SUBGROUP	NUMBER OF HOUSEHOLDS MILLION	HOUSEHOLD INCOME PA YUAN
Upper	6%	Upper affluent	7	270,000 plus
		Lower affluent	16	139,300–270,000
Middle	28%	Middle class	22	90,000–139,200
		Emerging middle class	87	43,800–90,000
Lower	66%	Next generation	176	15,000–43,800
		Left behind	65	6,000–15,000
		Poor	20	Less than 6,000

Source: Compiled from Silverstein et al. 2012: 29.

Table 2.2 PRC Class Composition of Workforce (percentage), 1952–2006

CLASS	1952	1978	1988	2001	2006
State and social administrators	0.5	1.0	1.7	2.1	2.3
Managers	0.1	0.2	0.5	1.6	2.6
Private entrepreneurs	0.2	–	–	1.0	1.3
Individual business owners	4.1	–	3.1	7.1	9.5
Professional and technical personnel	0.9	3.5	4.8	4.6	6.3
Office workers	0.5	1.3	1.7	7.2	7.0
Employees of commercial services	3.1	2.2	6.4	11.2	10.1
Industrial working class	6.4	19.8	22.4	17.5	14.7
Agricultural labourers	84.2	67.4	55.8	42.9	40.3
Urban and rural unemployed and semi-employed	–	4.6	3.6	4.8	5.9

Sources: 1952–88 (Lu Xueyi 2002: 44); 2001 (Lu Xueyi 2004: 38); 2006 (Lu Xueyi 2012: 20, 403); 2001 data from national sample survey data; 2006 data from the 2005 sample survey of 1 per cent of the Chinese population undertaken by National Bureau of Statistics and the 2006 National General Social Survey of CASS, Institute of Sociology.

workforce, in terms of the class composition identified for selected years since 1949.

In detail, each of the ten strata is defined in the following terms (Hu, Li and Li 2012: 403–6):

+ State and social administrators – leadership cadres in the CCP, government, state administration and social groups; the high and mid-levels of the social structure; the white-collar managers of departments within the system; do not own but do control state and production resources.
+ Managers – high- and mid-level managers in both the public and market sectors; do not own means of production, but manage production and resources; high cultural capital through educational qualifications and professional experience.

+ Private entrepreneurs – owners of capital who invest for profit and employ labour; own economic resources; varying amounts of social and cultural capital and political status.
+ Individual business owners – largely small-scale business people outside the system; small amounts of private capital invested in real estate, production, distribution or service, or financially invested; self-employed; employ low-level office and manual workers.
+ Professional and technical personnel – high- and mid-level white-collar workers; do not own production resources but are relatively autonomous; intermediate or advanced professional and technical knowledge, training and experience; teachers, professionals and technical personal in the public sector; professionals and technical staff in the market sector.
+ Office workers – administrative staff and white-collar workers; mid- and low-level officials of the CCP, government and state administration; low-level managers of enterprises.
+ Employees of commercial services – largely blue-collar workers and self-employed outside the system; employees engaged in non-professional, non-manual and manual work.
+ Industrial working class – production workers, construction workers, miners and related employees; physical and semi-manual work; migrant rural workers in both urban and rural areas; urban working class.
+ Agricultural labourers – farmers who contract collectively owned land with agriculture as their primary source of income; self-employed, or employees with limited resources in the market.
+ Urban and rural unemployed and semi-unemployed – people of working age with no stable source of income.

As an explanatory device focused on occupation, this schema has some clear merits, but problems remain. In the first place, in its detail it is very focused on the upper and middle strata of society as well as on urban China. The working classes (urban and rural) and rural China are equally complex – particularly in their interactions with the market, industrial development and each other – and require further elaboration. Second, while the classification contains implicit suggestions about income and wealth, not least through its hierarchical presentation, these aspects are somewhat obscured. Third, and largely because the schema concentrates on occupations, some of the key inequalities that have been highlighted as having emerged during the reform era remain masked. While that is somewhat understandable for regional and ethnic inequality, the result is clearly problematic for gender inequality, which also has an occupational basis, and which requires further consideration. Moreover, the schema draws the boundary of 'within the system' too narrowly. There are also people who are not cadres – some managers, professional and technical personnel, and even office workers – who are certainly 'within the system' in the sense of having access to privileged benefits.

As already noted, a prime purpose in developing this view of the emergent class structure has been to promote the idea and the practice of an expanding middle class. While this is yet to be examined in detail, from the point of view of understanding the intent for the whole class structure it is worth considering where the middle class might actually be located. There are three major problems that attend such an exercise. The first is that in the politics of the PRC, with its ruling Communist Party and an ideology developed both from its own experience and a Marxist–Leninist heritage, the concept of a middle class sits sometimes uneasily despite the ideological developments of the last fifteen years. The second problem is that while a middle class is being encouraged and identified, there is no apparent separate identification of an upper class. Third, while there is always a tendency to see contemporary class in terms of income or wealth, even from this perspective the middle class is not readily visible. In particular, the lifestyle and consumption patterns associated strongly with the middle class seem to currently belong to the more affluent in society. As already

Table 2.3 Distribution of hidden income, urban residents, PRC 2008

PERCENTILE	NBS 2008 YUAN	NERI 2008 YUAN	PERCENTAGE OF HIDDEN INCOME
0–10	4,754	5,350	0.4
11–20	7,363	7,430	0.0
21–40	10,196	11,970	2.3
41–60	13,984	17,900	5.1
61–80	19,254	27,560	10.9
81–90	26,250	54,900	18.8
91–100	43,614	139,000	62.5

Source: Compiled from Wang Xiaolu and Wing Thye Woo (2010: tables 3, 5 and 6).

noted, there is considerable hidden or 'grey income' in Chinese society. The implication of research into urban incomes from 2008 (table 2.3) is, however, that this is not equally distributed by any means. Of the additional 14.7 million *yuan* of 'grey income', 62.5 per cent went to the top ten decile of income households, and 18.8 per cent to the next decile (Wang and Woo 2010).

The following comments from Yan Ye on the CASS view of the social structure may or may not be empirically verifiable, but they certainly offer a concern about the future:

> The top is characterized by having luxury and being vulgar. The middle is energetic and anxious, and the bottom works to the bone and is angry. In the pursuit of interests, the competition in the whole society is becoming more bitter. (Yan Ye 2012: 215–16)

Whether or not these comments present an accurate portrayal of China's class system is at least in part the subject of the following three chapters, which examine each in turn – the dominant class, the middle classes, and the subordinate classes.

3 | The Dominant Class ──────────

Economic development in China during the last three decades is often regarded as having resulted in the emergence of an essentially capitalist system. While capitalism comes in many forms and there is much to be said for regarding China as part of global neoliberalism, there are some specific characteristics that still set it apart, not the least of which is the obvious point that it remains a Communist Party-state, with a substantial proportion of its economy dominated by the remnant structures of state socialism (Harvey 2007; Huang Yasheng 2008). This has implications not simply for the evolution of the political system, but also for the country's socio-economic development, for stratification and for class formation. To be sure, the economy has become more marketized, and there is an emergent class of entrepreneurs. At the same time, in trying to identify and understand the social and political dynamics of the PRC's dominant class, the starting point has to be those who control and manage the resources of the state and not just the owners of economic capital – as the dominant class may be defined in other contexts. A socialist market economy still has allocative decisions made by the state and its political elite and, as in other emerging market economies, property is not so much about ownership as about the 'bundle of rights' that includes 'control, income and transfer' (Oi and Walder 1999: 4–5).

The purpose of this chapter is not to simply identify the various elements of the dominant class – drawn from the leading cadres of the Party-state; managers of state-owned enterprises, large-scale private and foreign-invested enterprises; and entrepreneurs – but to examine the interactions between the political and economic elites, and the extent to which they and their families form a coherent ruling class. The idea of a dominant class might be equated with that of a ruling class, but the two may also be differentiated by their degree of coherence, organization and permanence. One key question is whether the owners and managers of capital and the wielders of state power, on the one hand, overlap with and are coterminous with those in whose interests the major economic, social and political decisions are taken, or those who take those decisions, on the other hand. A second question is whether there is an intergenerational transfer of privilege.

The idea that there is now a new ruling class in the PRC, based on a combination of the earlier state socialist-era institutions of power and the more recent structures of wealth, has certainly grasped the popular imagination. Such views are far from uncommon in either the social or print media within China. For example, in February 2013, the noted artist and public intellectual Chen Danqing, interviewed in the *Southern Weekend*, identified the new 'ruling class' in terms of their privilege, wealth and power and criticized its members for their vulgarity and for nonetheless not actually being 'upper class' (Chen Danqing 2013). Colloquially, in certain parts of China it is common to hear those assumed to be the new ruling class described as 'the black-collar class' (*heiling jieceng* 黑领阶层) – in contrast to blue-collar (manual) and white-collar (office and middle-class) workers. They are described as black-collar because they are early middle-aged, corporate types: males with black hair, dressed in black suits, dark ties and black leather shoes; wearing dark glasses; engaging in shady (and sometimes illegal) collusion (from one side or the other) between officials and entrepreneurs; driving expensive and high-status, black (usually Audi) sedans, with no number plates (the number-plate holder thereby being black too), and never obeying traffic signs and regulations.

At first sight these popular views seem to echo the comments of He Qinglian and Alvin So (noted in the last chapter), and indeed the available evidence does seem to point to the emergence of a ruling class with its foundations in the Party-state and wealth creation. At the same time, uncertainties remain. He and So were not making an identical argument about the contemporary dominant class. He Qinglian focused on the monopoly power of the Party-state, and saw that monopoly power and the influence of the leaders of the Party-state extending to both management of the economy and wealth generation as well as to the exclusion of independent private entrepreneurship (He 2000, 2003). Alvin So, on the other hand, postulated a cadre-capitalist class that controls economic and political power. This class is not presented as just a categorical or paper combination of the newly emergent bourgeoisie and leading cadres at all levels of the Party-state. The point of the analysis is to suggest that the constituent parts of the 'cadre-capitalist class' (in his terminology), or however the new ruling class may be described, work closely together in both business and politics in the protection of their joint and mutual interests. So's argument is, quite explicitly, that cadres have become embourgeoised and that capitalists have been politicized (So 2003b).

Other uncertainties also remain, not least of which are the permanence of the trends that seem to have emerged. There was a major shift in the development of marketized sector enterprises and the relationship between entrepreneurs and the CCP, in and after 1992. While from the perspective of the present, future change in that relationship may seem unlikely, some adjustment is not impossible. The developments in China's political economy which have led to the perceptions of a new ruling class are fairly recent and the intergenerational transfer of wealth and power which they suggest is yet to be tested. While the

CCP has clearly to some extent been complicit in these changes, it has also, for reasons of both ideology and legitimacy, been somewhat reluctant to embrace the degree of inequality that has resulted and has certainly not abandoned its principled commitment to serving the interests of 'all the people'. As the CCP demonstrated by devoting a whole day to its discussion at its 18th National Congress in November 2012, it remains committed to the promotion of 'greater equity' (*RMRB* 12 November 2012). Moreover, the CCP has shown that it can act decisively to adjust socio-economic conditions, when it so chooses, as the introduction of the Minimum Livelihood Guarantee (1999), the Campaign to Open Up the West (2000) and the development of the New Socialist Countryside programme (2005) all bear witness. Difficult and sometimes inadequate though these attempts may be, adjustment and rebalancing has resulted. Similarly, while self-interested corruption sometimes seems to be the spectre haunting Communism, or at least the CCP, there also seems to be little doubt of the Party's determination to tackle the challenge, organizationally as well as politically (Landry 2008: 92).

THE POLITICAL ELITE

The exercise of state power in the PRC is in the hands of leading cadres appointed by and centring on the CCP. This is the essence of the PRC as a political system. The CCP ('the vanguard of the proletariat') exercises supervision over the work of the government through a parallel hierarchy and through the power of appointment at each level of the Party-state hierarchy (Burns 1989). The Party-state hierarchy is based on a series of territorial-administrative levels – from the centre to province, prefecture, county, township and village, with government administration and party organization equivalences for ministries, bureau, divisions and sections. Cities can and do exist at all levels of the territorial-administrative hierarchy at county-level and above.

SOEs are regarded as part of the government administration, usually at central and provincial levels, though there are some county-level SOEs.

The precise number of Party and government cadres at all levels of the PRC is unknown but is estimated to be about 40 to 42 million. Of these, about 500,000 are leading cadres at county (or division) level or above, while there are about 40 million local-level cadres. The entire cadre force is clearly not the political elite, but they do represent the pool from which it is drawn. The 500,000 leadership positions include about 900 in Central Party and government organizations, with the CCP's Political Bureau and the PRC's State Council at the apex of the system: 2,500 positions at ministerial and provincial-level (including the very largest SOEs); 39,000 appointments at prefecture and departmental levels; and a further 446,000 positions down to county-level (Burns 2006; Walder 2006b). While there have been some small changes in this overall pattern with the development of the reform era since 1978, on the one hand, the general statistical pattern has remained remarkably constant. On the other hand, the change in development strategy has meant significant changes not only in the career background of the political elite, their qualifications and social characteristics, as one might imagine, but also in the ways appointments have been managed.

In 1978, the political elite could largely have been characterized in exactly the same terms as that which came to power in 1949: its senior figures were veterans of the CCP's Long March (1934–5), and the overwhelming majority of the cadre force had been involved in the War of Resistance to Japan (1937–45) and the Civil War (1946–9). On the whole, they were generalists – former guerrilla soldiers and political activists whose political loyalty to the CCP was assured but who had little professional or technical training, including only accidentally in state administration (Zang 2004: 43). There are essentially two reasons for the similarities in elite profile between 1949 and 1978. The first is

that when the political elite came to power in 1949 they were still relatively young and, as a consequence, aged in office. Even Mao's Cultural
Revolution and the attack on leading cadres in the late 1960s did little
to change this characteristic – for the most part 'those in authority
taking the capitalist road' were replaced by others from the same generation. After Mao's death in 1976, those who had been removed
during the late 1960s were rehabilitated in large numbers. Their political reputations were restored, many were reappointed to similar positions as those they had held before, and all had their economic rights
(including pensions) restored. This is the second reason for a similar
profile to the political elite over a thirty-year span. In many cases they
were not just individuals of the same generalist profile; they were
exactly the same individuals.

Nonetheless, the new development strategy adopted in 1978 had
a need for greater specialization and a higher level of knowledge,
skills and qualifications in the political elite if its aims were to be
achieved. Retirement of the veteran cadres (even so briefly after reap-
pointment) was stressed, as was recruitment of younger and technically more competent individuals. A policy of the 'Cadres Four
Transformations' was adopted. This attempted to ensure that cadres
were 'younger, better educated, more specialized, and politically correct'
in an obvious echo of the then appeal to the 'Four Modernizations'
of the new development strategy. Compulsory retirement at age sixty
was introduced and new age limits were set for appointments: county
leaders could not be older than forty-five, division leaders no older
than fifty. Leading cadres were now expected to be college graduates
with some additional technical knowledge and expertise (Goodman
1985: 230).

Rejuvenation and increased levels of educational qualification have
indeed characterized the political elite over the last three decades, as
was almost inevitable given the eventual transition from the revolutionary generation of the political elite to those recruited to the CCP and

leadership after 1949 (Kou and Zang 2013). Recruitment to the CCP is through education, the workplace and the professions, with fast-trackers identified for leadership at an early stage. It is estimated that about a quarter of all CCP members go on to become leading cadres at some level. Since 1978, the average age at appointment has fallen dramatically at all levels, and for the most part retirement ages and age bars to appointment have been observed. One clear result of this change has been that the political elite is, with one exception, now more representative by any measure of the country as a whole. In earlier years the political elite was dominated by individuals from areas in Southeast and North China where the CCP had been active before 1949. The one exception to the greater representativeness of the political elite is in terms of its gender balance. There were never many women in the political elite even before 1978, but now there are even fewer (Shih, Shan and Liu 2010).

By 2012, the report rates on the education levels of the political elite were impressive. For members of the Standing Committee of provincial-level CCP Committees, for example, 74 per cent were said to have Masters degrees, and 22.8 per cent were said to have doctorates (Li Cheng 2012: 604). Andrew Walder's observations on the role of education in leading to appointment as a leading cadre are dramatic: 'A party member with a college education was 26 times more likely to become a cadre than a non-Party member with less than a high school education, and over four times more likely than a party member with only a high school education.' As he points out too, even in rural China the role of education in determining the appointment of cadres is crucial: each year of schooling increases the likelihood that an individual will become a cadre by a third, and someone with six years of schooling is six times more likely to become a cadre than someone without (Walder 2006b).

There can be no doubt that education has become a necessary condition for entry to the political elite, but the changes of the last three decades need to be put into some perspective. The role of education in determining elite status even before 1978 cannot be completely discounted. Even allowing for the Cultural Revolution, when schools and colleges were disrupted and formal education was derided in some circles, education was still an important pathway to elite success. There were two segmented paths to elite status: one determined by ideological conformity and political appropriateness leading to political appointment; another generated by educational qualifications and leading to a professional position (Walder, Li and Treiman 2000). One of the consequences of the elite dualism of the Mao era is its persistence, albeit in a modified form. There is a difference in political elite appointments between CCP and government positions, supported by two different career paths. Everyone is required to have educational credentials and political capacity. At the same time, human capital is emphasized when government leadership appointments are made, and political loyalty for appointments to the CCP hierarchy. In appointments to leadership in the CCP party, seniority is more important, whereas professional and administration experience count more for appointment to a government position. University education is a particular determinant of advance to a leading position in government (to such an extent that professionals and intellectuals may be co-opted), whereas particularistic ties seem more important for appointments to the CCP hierarchy (Zang 2004).

The operation of the CCP's control of appointments to the political elite has changed dramatically since the early 1980s. The system of control of appointments in the PRC is usually still called *nomenklatura* (table of ranks) when discussed in English, after the Russian of the Soviet Union from whence it originally came. (For some reason it is rarely called *bianzhi* (编制), the Chinese equivalent, though one example is Brodsgaard 2006.) The essence of the system is that each position in the Party-state hierarchy is assigned a rank, and each individual is graded similarly by rank, through regular periods of study at a Party school (Pieke 2009). An individual can only be appointed to a position for which they have the qualified rank. Each CCP committee at each level has a list of positions for which it is responsible. The list has two sections: those positions that can be filled by the CCP committee in question directly, and those that must obtain an additional approval from the CCP's Organization Department.

Before 1984, the CCP *nomenklatura* was highly centralized, with appointment to a position at a given level a matter of report to the Organization Department of the CCP Committee two levels above the decision being taken. One of the important reforms of 1984 was to replace this injunction so that reporting was only to the one superior level of CCP committee Organization Department. Another equally important reform was a large reduction in the number of positions being supervised in this way by the Organization Department of the Central Committee, the senior Organization Department in the system (Burns 1994). At the start of the reform era some 13,500 positions were under review by the Central Organization Department. This has now been reduced to about 4,000 positions, including those in the Central Party and government, the 2,500 elite positions at ministerial and provincial level, and an unspecified number of appointments to the leadership of SOEs. Although appointment to the leadership of universities was removed from Central Organization Department responsibility in 1990, it was returned to this category in 1998 as the decision was taken to expand university education (Burns 2003).

As John Burns argues, when there is political stability and strong internal Party discipline the CCP's control of appointments is very effective in selecting competent and politically loyal leaders (Burns 2006). There have, however, been times when it does seem to have broken down or become impaired. One of these was during the late 1980s when there seemed to be a loss of self-belief to some extent in the system, both before and after the Tiananmen Incident of 1989.

A survey of 1,700 central and provincial leaders found that their 3,100 children held official positions at that time at or above bureau level, and that another 900 of their children were the leaders of large and medium-sized SOEs (Li Cheng 2001: 128–9). There has certainly been a high degree of political institutionalization that has created greater political stability, particularly in comparison with the first thirty years of the PRC (Zhao 2010). But not all political institutionalization may have the desired ends. For example, corruption clearly presents a challenge to the CCP's legitimacy, yet there is evidence that the introduction of compulsory retirement at sixty leads some cadres not only to look for employment in the private sector at fifty-nine, but also leads others to engage in corrupt activities (Li Cheng 2012: 603).

Remarkably, the extent of decentralization that has characterized the reform-era PRC has not challenged the CCP's control of appointments, even though only 38 per cent of the local-level cadres are also members of the CCP. Additionally, 70 per cent of government expenditure is now the responsibility of local government: a high proportion for a decentralized or federalist liberal democracy let alone a centralized Party-state. Pierre Landry's path-breaking study of local elites demonstrates how the CCP continues to control its local cadre force through a performance management and appraisal system. Cadres are rated according to a range of social, economic and political indicators which are assessed variably according to whether they are crucial, hard or soft targets. There is also an element of peer and subordinate review included in the assessment. A high level of performance, especially the economic growth of the area being led, may lead to promotion. At the same time, Landry suggests that poor performance brings few adverse consequences, thereby encouraging the coherence of the system as a whole (Landry 2008: 261). On the other hand, the CCP's control of local appointments seems to have done little to counter the possibility of local corruption which to some extent has been exacerbated by decentralized control over local resources, especially land (Smith 2009; Zhang and Liu 2010).

THE ECONOMIC ELITE

The economic elite that has emerged from three decades of reform is a sometimes bewildering mixture of business people, enterprise managers and private entrepreneurs, as well as (particularly at the most local of levels) leading political cadres from a variety of political, social and cultural backgrounds. There are several reasons for this complexity: change has grown over three decades out of state socialist structures, with political contestation at almost every stage and with a high degree of local variability. Marketization has developed intermittently in consequence, and has also led to the shaping of different generations of entrepreneurs. There is a significant divide between the early years of reform up to 1992 and after, which has bequeathed different kinds of enterprise development and markedly different members of the economic elite. Moreover, this difference has been exacerbated with the passage of time and the arrival into positions of economic leadership of those who were too young to have experienced either the era of state socialism or even the early part of the reform era in China (Wright 2010).

Though often described as 'privatization', change has come through the introduction of market forces into economic and enterprise management, not for the most part through the large-scale sale or transfer in other ways of state assets, as has happened in other reforming state socialist systems (Walder 2006a). Although it may sometimes seem otherwise, particularly in the state's discussion of such distinctions, there remain imprecise boundaries between the public and private sectors (Dickson 2008: 60). As of 2013, the public sector consists of perhaps as many as 110,000 SOEs at different levels of the territorial-administrative hierarchy, and an unknown number of collective sector enterprises, responsible in total for about 25 per cent of GDP (2013). The largest SOEs – the 117 considered the most strategic to the development of the economy – are under the State-owned Assets Supervision and Administration Commission (SASAC) under direct line of control to the State Council. Everything outside the public and foreign-invested sectors is sometimes equated with a 'private sector': 10.59 million large and medium-sized enterprises and 39.85 million smaller-scale individual businesses at the end of 2012; a sector said to be responsible for just over 60 per cent of GDP (Xinhua 2 February 2013; Ying Yiyuan 2013). The distinction between the public and the private sector is, however, hard to maintain in practice. In 2012, Zong Qinghou was China's wealthiest individual with a net worth of 82 billion *yuan*. He is the founder and CEO of the Wahaha Corporation, the country's largest drinks company, a nominally collective-sector enterprise which he founded, based on an 'open-door schooling' economic activity that had been created in a primary school during the Cultural Revolution. The economy is characterized more by hybrid public-private enterprises like Wahaha: there is a bewildering range of enterprises based on combinations of share-holding, collective, state and private ownership, with elements of foreign investment and ownership occasionally involved. To take two contrasting examples: SOEs apparently own 25 per cent of all private enterprises, and SOEs themselves may have private shareholders (Garnaut, Song and Yao 2006; Naughton 2010).

At the apex of a hierarchy of wealth, there are the extremely wealthy. As of early 2013, China had 212 dollar billionaires – with wealth of at least US$1,000 million each – and 1,020,000 millionaires, or rather what is called a millionaire in China: someone with wealth of at least 10 million *yuan* RMB. Rupert Hoogewerf, who annually compiles the *Hurun Rich List* on China, acknowledges that these figures underestimate the numbers of the rich (Wang Zhuoqiong 2013). There are apparently a total of 7,500 *yuan* billionaires, with net worth of at least

1,000 million *yuan* RMB, but 5,000 are described as having 'hidden income'. In a recent study of the top fifty names in the *Hurun Rich List* and the *Forbes Rich List of China*, Lu Peng patiently pointed out that many significantly rich people choose for various reasons to keep their wealth hidden (Lu Peng 2013). Senior leaders of the CCP and PRC Government are forbidden from engaging in sideline economic activities, but there seems to be little check on their close relatives, many of whom would appear both to be more than considerably wealthy and not have their wealth advertised in public, particularly not by inclusion on the *Hurun Rich List*. In 2012, then soon-to-be-retired Premier of the State Council, Wen Jiabao, was the subject of articles in the *New York Times* suggesting that his family, including his wife, controlled assets of US$2.7 billion. Part of this was one investment by his ninety-year-old mother worth US$120 million in 2007 (Barboza 2012).

The average Chinese millionaire is thirty-nine years old (2012 figures); 60 per cent are male, and 46 per cent of them smoke. They spend on average only 3 per cent of their personal wealth each year, with travel, their children's education, 'daily luxuries' and entertainment their largest items of expenditure. Strangely, the *Hurun Wealth Report* claims that 21 per cent of millionaires do not use a single Apple product. They travel internationally three times a year (France, the USA and Australia are the top three destinations) and plan to send their children overseas for education (preferably to the US, UK or Canada). Half of the millionaires are business owners and a fifth are professional investors. Another 15 per cent are real-estate investors and 15 per cent are senior executives, with 16 per cent already being citizens of other countries (the PRC does not permit dual nationality) and up to half also contemplating moving overseas (Canada, the US and Singapore are the favoured destinations) (Hurun 2012).

While not every entrepreneur is a millionaire, the PRC's economic elite has emerged from a history of business development that has passed through several distinct stages since 1978 (Dickson 2008: 32–65; Zhang Houyi 2012). The first stage was the development of Town and Village Enterprises (TVEs) as part of the early reform-era opening up of rural China. In 1984, the attention of reform in economic management turned to urban China and the opportunity arose for small-scale individual businesses to be established. Particularly after the Tiananmen Incident of mid-1989, there was confusion and reluctance on the part of some in the CCP to proceed further with private business development. This confusion also extended to the role of foreign investment in developing joint-venture enterprises in China. Starting in 1992 and at the insistence of the then Paramount Leader of the CCP, Deng Xiaoping, the development of private enterprises was put back on the agenda, though Nee and Opper have recently argued that this decision was largely a recognition of a significant economic trend already under way (Nee and Opper 2012: 32). The fourth stage, in the mid-1990s, was that large numbers of TVEs were restructured, becoming private enterprises, shareholding collectives or corporate entities of other kinds. The fifth stage started in 1995 with the decision to restructure SOEs, a process which, while reaching its height in the subsequent decade, still continues. A simultaneous development was that of the growing systemic confidence that came with the expansion of the private sector, and the restructuring of public-sector enterprises permitted from the mid-1990s, based on more open and unrestricted opportunities for foreign investment, first in joint ventures then in wholly owned companies.

The emergence of TVEs during the 1980s was a reaction in the rural areas to villages and households being able to operate in the market, to utilize what was seen as underutilized labour and other forms of capacity, and to develop rural economic activities. They developed fastest and in greater numbers in the suburban and peri-urban areas of cities and in the coastal regions, rapidly becoming major adjuncts to the state sector. In many such urban cases, the development of rural industry also rapidly ensured that villages ceased agricultural activities altogether. Though all were designated as collective-sector enterprises – enterprises technically owned by the people who live in a given area or work in the enterprise – there were in practice different kinds of TVEs (Alpermann 2006; Zhang Jianjun 2007). One type was indeed that of a TVE collectively owned and developed by local government. This is often referred to as the Sunan Model, named after Southern Jiangsu, the area of the Lower Yangtze River Delta where it originated, centred on the cities of Suzhou, Wuxi and Changzhou (Oi 1995; Whiting 2001). A second variety of TVE was actually a private enterprise. Private entrepreneurs in the last thirty years have always had more difficulties obtaining access to loans, labour and land than state- and collective-sector enterprises. In the 1980s and early 1990s, this was particularly acute for both ideological and political reasons, and so many private entrepreneurs became what have been known as 'red hat' entrepreneurs: collective-sector managers in name but private entrepreneurs in practice. Private enterprise TVEs are also sometimes spoken of as the Wenzhou Model, after the town in Zhejiang Province where the practice was both prevalent and particularly successful (Liu Y. 1992; Parris 1993). Official estimates in 1996 calculated that about half of all TVEs were 'collectives' of this kind (Lau 1999: 64). The third variety consisted of TVEs that were essentially cooperative ventures between villages in Guangdong, Fujian and, to a lesser extent, Zhejiang Provinces, and Chinese investors from Hong Kong and Taiwan, often though not exclusively by any means returning to their ancestral homes (Chan, Madsen and Unger 2009; Saich and Hu 2012: 73).

As might be imagined, the varied development of TVEs generated a wide variety of entrepreneurs and managers with different social backgrounds and experiences, ranging from those who had been at the centre of local communities before 1979, sometimes with substantial education and training, to those who had been completely on the outer, with 'black' class labels, only now able to participate more fully in public life. This second extreme was certainly a characteristic of those who started developing individual urban businesses in the 1980s. Those who chose in the 1980s to start individual household businesses were almost exclusively the earlier dispossessed: those with bad class labels during the Mao era, and those who had been urban youth rusticated to the countryside during the Cultural Revolution and deprived of education and training, but now allowed back into urban China (Gold 1989; Davis 1992).

In and after 1992, the number of private enterprises started to expand. While it is clear that a debate will continue for some time over whether this growth was led by an 'endogenous shift to capitalism' (Nee and Opper 2012: 37) or political actions by the leadership of the CCP (Wright 2010: 42), the result has been a massive growth in small and medium-sized enterprises. Many of those who became entrepreneurs in the 1990s came out of the Party-state. Subsequently, it has become more usual for graduates to move into business, both working for others and for themselves. Backgrounds and educational levels have changed dramatically. Before 1992, 37 per cent of entrepreneurs were former peasants or factory workers; by 1996, only 7 per cent came from these backgrounds. In the 1980s, only 40 per cent of entrepreneurs had more than a junior high-school education; by 2002, 88 per cent had at least graduated from high school (Nee and Opper 2012: 36). A study of local economic elites in Shanxi Province during 1996–8 found that more than half of entrepreneurs had previously worked in the Party-state, and 40 per cent of them were university graduates (Goodman 2001). With the restructuring of TVEs and SOEs that followed, these characteristics of entrepreneurs were intensified. A survey of private entrepreneurs in five coastal provinces during 2006–7 found that 51 per cent had formerly worked in the state economic sector and 19 per cent had previously been a Party or government cadre (Chen and Dickson 2010: 37).

Changes in the private sector during the 1990s inevitably brought pressure for change to both TVEs and the state sector. In both cases, investment was short, despite state assistance through the banking system, which was not so readily available to the private sector, and competition was increasing. Privatization was introduced to TVEs through turning most of them into shareholding companies, largely through management buyouts (Sun Laixiang 2005; Naughton 2007: 291–2). One survey found that by 1999, 86 per cent of TVEs in Jiangsu and Zhejiang had at least partially privatized in this way and 57 per cent had completed the process (Li and Rozelle 2003). Often, however, while the companies were being turned into share-based operations, either a portion of the shares or a commitment to future profits was reserved for local government. Indeed, in Shanxi Province, a common complaint from entrepreneurs in the 1990s was that they were being required to surrender equity to local government as a condition of being granted permission to proceed in business. Often too, in this process of turning TVEs into shareholding companies, it seems that there was sometimes room for side deals and collusion between local officials, on the one hand, and buyers, friends or family, on the other (Zhang and Liu 2010). On the surface this might seem to suggest that economic power has fallen prey to local government and its cadres. This may have occurred in some areas, but in others it would seem to be a misrepresentation of the power of local elites, who have used the development of the shareholding system and (in the words of research from one study):

> wrested control of collective assets from the public sector. It is clear that property rights subversion is taking place. Those in control of the corporation are gradually taking away the power (control of resources) from the local government and, at the same time, keeping it from the workers . . . These corporate leaders wear several hats. They are simultaneously corporate executives, Party secretaries, and

village administrators. It is clear, however, their primary role is as corporate leaders. (Lin and Chen 1999: 168)

The restructuring of the SOEs was considerably different, not least because in many cases the enterprises concerned were substantially larger and had been an essential part of the socio-economic structure of state socialism. An SOE was not only an economic unit, but also a social and political organization. They were not only saddled with often inefficient and outdated equipment but also with debt and increasing numbers of retirees, all of whom remained the company's responsibility. Lack of investment funds and competition were also important issues for SOEs, but they had been exacerbated by the attempts of SOE managers to meet reform imperatives by setting up subsidiary companies that effectively moved former company assets and staff elsewhere, usually into the collective and private sectors, while retaining a share of the equity in the new enterprises (Lin and Zhang 1999; Ding 2000).

In 1994, a corporate restructuring programme for SOEs was introduced with the explicit intent of ensuring the continuation of the leading 1,000 or so large-scale SOEs, and that the state remained economically active in those areas considered the most strategically important – such as energy, telecommunications, public utilities, transport and anything related to security issues – but not in other areas where non-state enterprises were already active and successful. This has necessarily been a slow process of implementation as the CCP has been concerned at the considerable scale of worker redundancies and unemployment that has followed. Restructuring has led to some bankruptcies, as well as to the public offerings of shares, employee and management buyouts, development of leasing arrangements, and the establishment of joint ventures with foreign investors, and this has seen SOEs replaced by shareholding companies, private enterprises and limited liability companies (Zeng and Tsai 2011). A 2004 survey found that some 37 per cent remained public-sector enterprises, 32 per cent became corporate enterprises, 24 per cent became private enterprises and 5 per cent became foreign-invested enterprises (Oi and Han 2011: 23).

In addition to drawing attention to the various kinds of private and hybrid public-private entrepreneurs who have emerged since 1978, this survey of enterprise development has also indicated that some managers should also be regarded as part of the economic elite. The leaders of the largest private enterprises and foreign-invested firms, as well as of SOEs, act in many ways as entrepreneurs, by virtue of their responsibilities and decision-making functions. The profile of all three of these groups is very similar, and almost identical with that of the political elite, and particularly that component of the political elite employed in government positions. They are mostly university- or college-educated, usually with work experience in the Party-state, and almost always members of the CCP. Since appointments to senior levels in SOEs and in government are recruited in the same ways and from the same pool, that particular profile should be no surprise. Managers of the largest private enterprises and foreign-invested firms are further characterized by their high level of foreign-language competence, usually English (Pearson 1997: 65–99; Wright 2010: 46).

POWER AND WEALTH

The relationship between political and economic elites that has emerged during and after three decades of reform is, then, complex. At the national level the political and economic elites are certainly not coterminous, but they do intersect and occasionally overlap, as in the case of SOEs and the management of the public sector. At local levels, the evidence for coterminousness is somewhat contradictory, with some indications of considerable overlap and regional differences complicating the picture still further. Walder's research on the rural economy suggests that entrepreneurs do not seek to become cadres, and that cadres do not leave official positions to become entrepreneurs (Walder 2006b). On the other hand, there is also evidence that in some places, such as villages in Tianjin Municipality (Lin and Chen 1999: 145) and Guangdong Province (Saich and Hu 2012: 176), politics have been captured by local economic elites, and that in other places, such as Taiyuan (Goodman 2007) and some localities in Jiangsu (Zhang Jianjun 2007), economic leadership rests largely with political elites. Under all circumstances, though, there are likely to be close links between political and economic elites, particularly given that about half of all private entrepreneurs are estimated to have worked in the Party-state previously, and that an unknown but substantial proportion of the economic elite are still based in the public sector, and others occupy positions in hybrid public-private enterprises.

The emphasis on economic development that came with the start of the reform process in 1978 has meant that for many of the political elite, and especially those in territorial administration at local levels, the business of government is business, or at least encouraging its development. Conversely, members of the economic elite, or at least those wishing to engage in business on any scale beyond the very smallest enterprise, need to have good political connections. These bring not only business and contracts, but also access to land, labour and loans. This is particularly true for those members of the economic elite not in the public sector. Public-sector managers and entrepreneurs have privileged access to the Party-state, as well as to the banking and finance system, access that often remains denied to private entrepreneurs (Chen and Dickson 2010: 80–1).

The CCP's response to the development of economic activities alongside the public sector has changed in stages. Individual household businesses were accepted as 'non-exploitative' from the beginning.

TVEs were understood as collective-sector developments, and as such to present no challenge to the notion of public wealth. In the 1980s, private business was accepted as 'a necessary and beneficial supplement to the public economy' but at the 15th CCP Congress in 1997 it was recognized as 'an important component' of the national economy. At the 17th National Congress in 2007, the CCP pledged itself to 'unswervingly encourage, support and guide the development of the non-public sector', essentially giving private enterprises, corporate entities and businesses based on shares or other notions of equity the same status as that granted to SOEs (Xinhua 21 October 2007). 'Both public and non-public sectors of the economy are important components of the socialist market economy and significant bases for economic and social development' was the perspective emphasized by the Third Plenum of the 18th Central Committee of the CCP in November 2013 (Xinhua 12 November 2013).

Certainly, it became clear in and after the mid-1990s that, especially in cities and at county-level, the development of the local economy was rapidly becoming the main task for the political elite. Blecher and Shue's landmark study of Shulu County in Hebei Province detailed the central role of local political leaders in navigating the change in direction from the 1970s into the reform era as the county developed an industrial and commercial infrastructure outside its immediate organizational control and direction (Blecher and Shue 1996). Jean Oi's research across ten provincial-level jurisdictions goes further, seeing the emergence of 'Local state corporatism' in the ways in which counties, townships and villages each operates as a corporate entity on its own, and together as a system. For Oi, county government is essentially the corporate headquarters for local economic activity (Oi 1999: 99). Landry's more recent study shows how important management of the local economy remains to the careers of local cadres: together with other factors, success in this area often leads to promotion (Landry 2008). Interestingly, while this relationship may apply at the local level, it seems not to be of continued importance as a cadre moves up the political hierarchy. A 2012 analysis of members of the CCP Central Committee shows (inter alia) that political advance is not related to performance in economic management (Shih, Adolph and Liu 2012).

Understandably, the corporatization of politics at the national level appears to have taken a different form. Here the emphasis is inevitably on policy, strategy and government settings, the ways in which the corporate world attempts to influence these areas, and the ways in which government and the CCP interacts with the business world and economic interests. Some commentators have seen the development of an interest-group mechanism that extends not only to individuals campaigning for initiatives within the senior levels of decision-making but also leads to external lobbying, much the same as that known in parliamentary and congressional systems. Provincial and local governments have long-established liaison offices in the capital, major metropolitan centres and other cities in a practice that dates from imperial times. Historically, these liaison offices not only represented the interests of their locality around China, but also provided a place where natives could come and stay and find people who spoke the same language and ate the same food – important in a continental-scale political system. The contemporary liaison offices now include newly formed proactive corporate and industrial interest agencies – notably those representing the state monopolies of banking, oil, electricity, coal, telecommunications, aviation, rail, tobacco and shipping – the function of which is solely to interact with government and the CCP. There are also important lobby groups that have been formed for state, foreign and private firms on a sectoral basis, one of the most important of which is for real-estate development (Sun Liping 2006). In 2010, Central Government issued regulations on the establishment and activities of these various lobby groups and liaison offices (Li Cheng 2012: 614).

While these developments suggest that politics may have become increasingly more corporatized with reform, they do not of themselves indicate that the political elite has become embourgeoised, as Alvin So suggested might occur. However, according to many commentators in the PRC, there is evidence that this has indeed begun to occur (Pieke 1995; Wu Xiaogang 2006). Zhou Xiaohong, of Nanjing University is one such commentator:

> the upper 'capitalist class' and a fraction of the middle class in Chinese society . . . are derived from the former power center or, at least, have something to do with it. Part of their wealth is acquired through unfair competition or utilization of the loopholes in the state system and policies. More importantly, this group of people, while small in number and proportion, owns a great part of the social wealth. (Zhou Xiaohong 2008: 11)

Certainly, the dismissal of Bo Xilai, the leading cadre in Chongqing Municipality and a member of the Political Bureau in 2012, gave further credence to such beliefs. Despite his appointment as a leading cadre with a comfortable but not considerable salary attached, Bo Xilai, his wife and his family were revealed to be amongst the very wealthy and to be active in economic activities on the global stage (Garnaut 2012). A survey of CCP and government officials undertaken in 2005 by the CCP Organization Department revealed that cadres often approached private entrepreneurs with three aims in mind: to gain economic benefit for themselves and their families; to look for opportunities for themselves to leave a party or government position and find a job in the business world; and to seek political support from the private sector due to its increasing political importance (Zheng 2006).

One of the most spectacular ways in which cadres have involved themselves in individual wealth creation is the buying and selling of

official positions. Under most circumstances these are not uncondi-
tional sales or purchases: a candidate also needs to have the right
training and experience, and even additional connections to ease the
persuasion. Nonetheless, the practice appears to be not uncommon.
The cases that have come to light on dismissal of the officials concerned
suggest not only that selling offices is profitable, but also that holding
office clearly leads to the acquisition of further wealth (Smith 2009).
One of the most spectacular cases appears to be that of Liu Zhijun,
Minister of the Railways 2003–11, who was accused of trying to buy
his way into the CCP's Political Bureau and to appointment as a Vice
Premier (of the State Council) by using 2 billion *yuan* in bribes (Li
Cheng 2012: 605). Liu had received 64.6 million *yuan* in bribes himself
between 1986 and 2011, and had conspired with Ding Shumiao (a
railway contractor) for her to handle 4 billion *yuan* of a facilitating
payment on his behalf (Wang Xiangwei 2013). At the more local
level, a 2001 report from the CCP Organization Department reported
(after disciplinary measures had been taken) on a number of cases:
in Guangxi a former deputy general-secretary of the provincial government had bought his appointment as the head of an urban district
with a transfer of 270,000 *yuan* to the wife of the former provincial
governor; in Hebei a former county Party secretary took 10,000 *yuan*
for each appointment he delivered to applicants; in Shanxi, the former
deputy head of a county government bought his re-election by sending
500 *yuan* by courier to each member of the county people's congress
the day before the election (CCP Organization Department 2002:
211–12).

These activities are clearly corrupt, but helping one's family might
under some circumstances be seen more as morally reprehensible or
even politically imprudent than necessarily illegal. There is considerable difference between assisting one's children with better education
and improving their life chances, and corrupt behaviour. One internal
report by the CCP's Organization Department recorded that in 2012,

of 8,370 senior executives in the major SOEs directly under the SASAC, 6,370 had immediate family members who live overseas or have foreign citizenship (Li Cheng 2012: 617). A publicly available study from 2013 suggests that the children of cadres earn 15 per cent more in their first employment than do the children of other people (*Global Times* 7 May 2013). At the local level, a study of cadres in Shanxi revealed a three-generation pattern. The parent, usually a father, is born a peasant, becoming a cadre as an adult, but the children become business people (Goodman 2000). Another internal report by the CCP's Organization Department recorded that 90 per cent of millionaires in 2006 were the children of high-ranking officials (Dickson 2008: 23): an allegation which, if correct, might lead to further questions about political propriety at the very least.

In terms of class formation, it is clear that many of the current economic elite have their origins in the Party-state. This includes not only those still working in the state sector but also the majority of those identified as private entrepreneurs. More interesting perhaps, in terms of the intergenerational transfer of privilege, is research which suggests the continuation of specific family influence from the pre-1949 local elite, through the establishment and development of the PRC's political elite into the contemporary economic elite in both Shanxi (Chen Minglu 2012) and Yantian, in the Pearl River Delta (Saich and Hu 2012: 182). Research on emergent market economies in Eastern Europe during the 1990s revealed the phenomenon of 'interrupted embourgeoisment': the families of people who had been business people before a Communist Party-state was established (in the second half of the 1940s) became business people themselves later, once political change permitted, despite their lack of direct business experience in the intervening period (Szelényi 1988). Lu Peng's study of the exceptionally wealthy, and a wider study of just very rich entrepreneurs based on Qingdao, Taiyuan, Lanzhou, Kunming, Zhongshan and Nanjing, suggest a different pattern in China. Many of the contemporary economic elite meet two conditions: they or one or both of their parents was in the Party-state before 1979, and they had a parent or grandparent who was a member of the pre-1949 local elite (Lu Peng 2013; Goodman 2014).

It would be misleading to describe the economic elite as having been politicized during the reform era, since many actually started out from within the Party-state. A better indicator of the politicization of the economic elite is the private entrepreneurs' near-universal membership of Chambers of Commerce and business associations that are organized by and through local government (Chen and Dickson 2010: 45). Certainly, the CCP has moved to ensure close relations in general with private entrepreneurs (Dickson 2007). For their part, private entrepreneurs repeatedly say (through regular surveys) that they feel a need to be in 'the system' (Dickson 2008: 94–5). Access to financing and business opportunities, and concerns about tax and industrial and commercial management policy, are usually given as the main reasons for their wanting to be involved (Zhang and Ming 1999: 50). A large number of private entrepreneurs have reported that they feel discriminated against in comparison with the public sector's relationship with the Party-state (Tsai 2007: 84).

A 2007 survey found 37.8 per cent of private entrepreneurs to be members of the CCP, though there were significant regional variations. Party membership was considerably higher in Shandong, Zhejiang and Jiangsu Provinces and lower in Guangdong and Fujian Provinces, though it is noticeable that entrepreneurs in Guangdong Province are generally less likely to participate in any form of political activity (Chen and Dickson 2010: 43). CCP membership is, however, a low-level indicator of political participation. More significant are the numbers of entrepreneurs who become deputies to people's congresses and people's political consultative conferences. The people's congress is the legislature and representative assembly at different levels of the territorial-administrative hierarchy. The people's political consultative conference meets alongside the people's congress and is an advisory body for entrepreneurs, professionals, local notables and the democratic parties. The people's political consultative conference works through scrutinizing the work of government and making recommendations to it about new initiatives. At the highest levels of the political system, in 2013, thirty-one billionaires were elected representatives to the National People's Congress, along with a further 210 entrepreneurs, and another fifty-two billionaires were appointed to the Chinese People's Political Consultative Conference (Anderlini 2013). In 2004, more than 9,000 entrepreneurs were delegates to people's congresses at county, provincial and national levels, and a further 30,000 had been elected to various people's political consultative conferences (Zhang Houyi 2004: 318). If the aim (from the side of entrepreneurs) was to ensure easier access to factors of production for their projects, then certainly those private entrepreneurs who engaged in such activities were successful: studies of private entrepreneurs and their level of political embeddedness have showed that those who participated in formal institutions in these ways were more likely to obtain bank loans and financing (Zhou Wubiao 2009; Talavera, Xiong and Xiong 2010).

Assessing the size of the dominant class in terms of the interactions of economic and political capital is bound to be imprecise. At the barest minimum, 500,000 leading cadres and just over a million Chinese-defined 'millionaires' have to be included in the equation, but clearly the privileges of wealth and power extend further into the wider pool from which the most narrowly defined political and economic elites are recruited. Somewhere between 3 and 4 per cent of the population are estimated to have an annual income at or in excess of 500,000 *yuan* a year (Wright 2010: 7); and the cadre force extends to some 40–42 million people in total, though clearly many administrative cadres should be considered more part of the middle than of the dominant class. As a working figure, it would seem reasonable to estimate that a total of up to about 3 per cent of the total population constitutes the dominant class.

In their original description of class in contemporary China, the CASS Sociology team had attempted to group the ten occupational classes they had identified into five broad categories, referred to as 'upper, upper middle, middle, lower, middle, and lower' with most related to more than one (Lu Xueyi 2002: 9). The designation of anyone as 'upper' class disappeared soon after in their published work and did not appear in their later reports following up the initial research. By 2010, the broader categories had been reduced to 'upper middle, lower middle, and workers', and by 2012 these broad categories had disappeared altogether (Hu, Li and Li 2012: 403). As will be seen in the following chapter, and as has happened in other countries (Parker 1972), for a variety of reasons the dominant class's existence is masked by the discourse of the middle class.

4   The Middle Classes

The embrace of the middle class as a policy setting has been one of the more remarkable developments in the PRC since 2002, and not only because of the ideological particularities (Guo 2009). Cadres and workers have been briefed, in the words of a handbook from China's Police Academy, that the middle class is 'the political force necessary for stability . . . the moral force behind civilized manners . . . the force necessary to eliminate privilege and curb poverty. It is everything' (cited in Tomba 2011). In 2005, the official news agency announced that the middle class would be 40 per cent of the work-force by 2010 and 25 per cent of urban households (Xinhua 15 September 2005). In 2007, it was reported that 55 per cent of the population would be middle class by 2020: 78 per cent of the urban population and 30 per cent of rural residents (Wu Jiao 2007). It has become commonplace for officials and strategic documents to acknowledge that in the conceivable future 'the middle class will be the dominant class'. Much is provided for, and expected of, the middle class. 'The Chinese government has put forth policies to increase the proportion of the middle class, improve residents' property income and expand higher education' (Lu Xueyi 2012: 59). The State Council's Development Research Center, in its report with the World Bank, stated that the explicit goal is to emulate the experience of other industrial countries in ensuring 'a large middle class that acts as a force for stability, good governance, and economic progress' (World Bank 2012: 16).

The goal is clear, but the meaning of the middle class in this context and the ramifications for both social policy and stratification considerably less so. There are definitional problems and the measurement of the middle class sometimes defies belief. It is, for example, far from clear that when the CCP talks about the middle class, or even the middle classes, they have in mind the intermediate class (as described in the wider sociological literature) of those who possess skills, knowledge and organizational experience as opposed to economic capital (the dominant class) or their labour power or nothing (the subordinate classes).

Uncertainty about the identification of the middle class is reflected in the discussion within the PRC not only about its size and wealth, but also about whether it exists at all. Estimates of both the current size of the middle class and its future prospects vary greatly. A large and heterogeneous range of people are referred to as middle class in the PRC and the variety certainly includes elements that would more normally be regarded as part of the upper or dominant classes. Regardless of the precise definition of the middle class employed, it is also clear that, despite the rhetoric about its growth, the middle class is currently more limited in size if not profile. Certainly the emphasis on the middle class as an agent of consumption and an arbiter of public style highlights the aspirational nature of these politics. In short, in the PRC 'the middle class' is a very uncertain term, which may well explain its application as the new universalizing class: it has considerable mobilizing potential precisely because it is less precise and so more inclusive. Indeed, it is hard to escape the conclusion that the Party-state's middle class is more a discourse than a social structure.

All the same, there may well be an intermediate middle class of those whose place in society flows from their possession of skills, knowledge and organizational experience. A professional and managerial middle class developed as part of the modernizing state during the 1950s, and has expanded further with the changed development strategy since 1978. In addition, some of the private entrepreneurs and self-employed constitute an entrepreneurial middle class, so that altogether it is possible that as much as 12 per cent of the population might be considered middle class in these ways.

CONSIDERING THE MIDDLE CLASS

The 'middle class' is a very broad concept that has been used historically to cover a wide range of social phenomenon (Robison and Goodman 1992). The middle class of the early Industrial Revolution were the bourgeoisie, the first captains of industry and the owners of capital; middle because they were a new force in between the court and the burghers. For both Marx and Weber, the middle class figured very little, treated for the most part as residual categories for other social forces. For Marx, the middle class was by definition largely irrelevant given that it played no central role in the process of class polarization and historical change. For Weber, the middle class even included the peasantry. By the middle of the twentieth century, the term had come to be applied to the managerial and professional classes generated by industrial society to support the evolution of the nation-state, supporting both the citizenry and economic development, as well as being applied to the professions and managers engaged in the process of development of economic enterprises (and particularly of new forms of economic enterprise). By the later part of the twentieth century, particularly in North America and Europe, 'middle class' came to refer more generally to those who enjoyed a comfortable lifestyle, characterized by homeownership and higher education, held to be the aspiration for the majority of the population. More recently still, this comfortable lifestyle has even been quantified, with the middle class identified as those who have an income of at least US$10 a day (Kharas and Geertz 2010).

It is entirely understandable that a middle class in European terms might be sought with the changed economic strategy in China after 1978 and the resultant dramatic economic growth, as elsewhere in East Asia (Hsiao 1993; Ravaillon 2009). All the same, before new social classes in Asia, and particularly in China, are identified as middle class, it is probably prudent to enquire as to the differences as well as the similarities between the earlier European and the later Asian experiences, not least of which is the central role of the state in class formation in the latter (Jones 1995).

Within the PRC, the determination of the importance of the middle class may have resulted from political leadership, but nonetheless a number of academics have been involved in the discussions, and not only those at CASS. The list of PRC scholars who have written about the contemporary middle class in China is a roll call of the country's leading social scientists. As already noted, a sizeable group is indeed based at the Institute of Sociology, Chinese Academy of Social Sciences, originally led by Lu Xueyi (who died in 2013). It includes Li Peilin and Li Chunling. At Tsinghua University, Li Qiang and Sun Liping are well-known academics and social commentators. Others well known for their writings on the middle class include Zhou Xiaohong (Nanjing University), Li Youmei (Shanghai University), Li Lulu (Renmin University), Lu Hanlong (Shanghai Academy of Social Sciences), and Liu Xin (Fudan University) (Anagnost 2008: 504–7; Cheng Li 2010: 60).

For these scholars, there is a degree of agreement about the general characterization of the middle class, despite differences in detail. They see the middle class as employed in particular high-status occupations, and recognize the advantages as well as status that flow from appointments 'within the system'. The middle class is also seen as holding positions involving supervisory obligations and the exercise of managerial authority. In addition, there is an expectation that those in the middle class are higher-education graduates, though allowance has been made for those from generations in which education was adversely affected by the politics of the Cultural Revolution. Most importantly, though, there is a general agreement that consumption and lifestyle are significant to the identification of the middle class, particularly as expressed through housing and homeownership. To quote Zhou Xiaohong:

> what's more, to the Chinese middle class, private housing and a car not only represent consumer goods with which they can build their self-identity and win social recognition but also practice fields for molding new notions of consumption. (Zhou and Chen 2010: 94)

The differences in scholarly discussion centre on how these general principles lead to identification of the middle class and, in particular, which social groups should be included in any analysis. Lu Xueyi's initial class categorization allowed for every one of the ten recognized strata but one (the 'urban and rural unemployed') to be capable of contributing to or becoming part of the middle class (Lu Xueyi 2002: 9). Others have been more restrictive in their identification of the middle class. A key point of dispute is whether to include private entrepreneurs in the definition of the middle class. Zhou Xiaohong, on the one hand, does not, regarding managers (but not owners) of TVE, SOE, and even private-sector and foreign-funded enterprises as part of the middle class, alongside professional and technical staff and small-scale business people (Zhou Xiaohong 2008). Li Chunling, on the other hand, does include private entrepreneurs, identifying four subgroups in the middle class: private entrepreneurs (whom she describes as the 'capitalist' middle class on the grounds that the PRC as a socialist market economy does not have a fully formed capitalist class); the professional and managerial middle class; self-employed and small-scale business people; and white-collar workers (Li Chunling 2010: 144–5).

Generally, though it might seem unusual in other contexts to include business people, particularly those associated with large-scale enterprises, their inclusion has certainly become normal practice in the definition of China's middle class (Li Lulu 2003; Li Chunling 2013; Yang Jing 2013). This inclusion, or at least the homogenization of business people as a class (Chen and Matlay 2006), must by the same token be one of the main causes of uncertainty in describing social stratification within the PRC. Entrepreneurs and business people come in different occupational shapes and sizes. Very large-scale private entrepreneurs are more often than not part of the economic elite, though some private entrepreneurs may certainly be regarded otherwise as part of the middle class, not by virtue of the size of their economic activities so much as their restricted access to capital and their use of skills, knowledge and experience. Some of the self-employed and small-scale business people might conceivably be middle class because of their supervisory and managerial roles but, equally, the vast majority are likely to be part of the subordinate classes: individual petty traders, itinerant artisans, stall-holders and small shopkeepers (Huang 2013).

The early scholarship on the middle class led to a barrage of criticism within China, some of which not only objected to aspects of what was being claimed but went on to doubt the existence of a middle class at all (Shen Hui 2005; Liu Changjiang 2006). There was clearly reaction to Lu Xueyi's early predictions that the middle class would grow to 40 per cent by 2025 (Liu Jun 2005), and some of this would seem to have been generated by those who were more ideologically conservative. An article in the *Global Times* accused those who claimed the middle class was growing, and would become the dominant class, of being more than a little premature: 'the so-called middle class in China is no more than a myth invented by media reporters and scholars' (Cai 2004).

There were essentially three objections expressed against the developing ideas of the middle class. Perhaps the most potentially serious objection was not one of observation but of interpretation. Ideologically, there could be no middle class and, if there was to be one, then it could not possibly become dominant (Wang Yi 2003). Second, the predictions of middle-class dominance have been criticized. One such objection was on grounds of practicality, since two thirds of the workforce are either industrial workers, migrant workers or agricultural workers and peasants; another was the even more trenchant observation that the growth of the wealthy has hampered the expansion of the middle class (Sun Liping 2006). While change might occur, the possibility of the middle class ever becoming the majority was seen as unlikely (Liu Changjiang 2006). Third, while there might appear to be a middle class, it was argued that in fact the middle class constituted several groups with widely different agendas and no shared values (Chen Yiping 2005; Cheng Li 2010: 68–71).

Zhou Xiaohong has mounted a stout defence of the existence of the middle class on several occasions. In particular, he has argued that the middle class is not about politics and so not a social structure in the way that classes have previously been understood in the PRC. Indeed, he points to the continued existence of the PRC as a Communist Party-state as proof that the middle class can have no political impact. But, as he argues, the impact of China's accession to the WTO and the globalization of its economy have meant that the middle class has become 'the vanguard of consumption and the rearguard of politics' (Zhou and Chen 2010: 85). This is a view echoed by Shen Hui, who acknowledges that for most people, and especially for the young, the 'middle class' implies houses, cars and aspirations. In this interpretation, the 'middle class' is more a cultural than a social construct (Shen Hui 2005).

As might be expected, there is also a distinct regional variation to the conceptualization of the performance if not the existence of the middle class. A study of class in Shanghai, for example, identified the middle class in terms of private entrepreneurs, private enterprise executives, public officials with 'hidden income', senior technical staff and celebrities in the performing arts. Members of the middle class were typically said to own an automobile that cost between 100,000 and 200,000 *yuan*. They would only on rare occasions use the Shanghai Metro, preferring private transport, and the majority are also said to be in the process of paying off their own homes. The survey goes on to paint a somewhat cynical if not jaded picture of the local middle class:

> Most of them are married, but some regret it. Either they already have extra-marital affairs or are prepared to have extra-marital affairs. The single men have girlfriends but keep changing them. The single women want boyfriends but are not interested in them. The elders closest to them are not their parents. The women closest to the men are not their wives. Their mobile phones are either busy or cannot be reached. They could be in a meeting, driving, or in the air. . . . After a period of being meat-eaters, they become vegetarians. After a period of driving their own cars, they turn to jogging instead. The native Shanghainese do not like using their own language, and speak in English instead. The outsiders, on the other hand, do not like to use Modern Standard Chinese, and attempt to speak in Shanghainese. (Baoru 2010)

On the other hand, another study, of the middle class in Beijing, emphasizes the role of the state in the formation of the middle class. For those of the new middle class who are 'outside the system' – white-collar workers in foreign-invested enterprises, owner-operators in small and medium-sized private enterprises and individual business people – state connections have proven crucial. Those 'within the system' – white-collar workers in state-owned work-units of all kinds – 'form the most influential group and the most stable elements of the new middle class' (Li and Niu 2003).

SIZE AND WEALTH

The uncertainties about the Party-state's embrace of the middle class are amplified when the attempt is made to assess its size and wealth. A number of studies have been undertaken that have attempted to measure the size and wealth of the middle class. The results of some of these are summarized in table 4.1, which also includes details of when the research in question was undertaken or the date of the data referred to by the source, the percentage of the population estimated to be in the middle class, an indication of the minimum threshold income for inclusion, the conceptual framework for understanding the middle class and the location of the study.

The studies reported on in table 4.1 were published between 2005 and 2013 and relate to research undertaken in that period. (A summary of earlier studies may be found in Li Cheng 2010: 67.) Income is, of course, not the same as wealth, but where the information is available, income is the data recorded. Three of the sources listed are of studies based on survey work undertaken by PRC-based scholars (Zhou Xiaohong, Lu Xueyi and Li Chunling), two are studies commissioned by and for multinational consultancy companies (Boston Consulting Group, McKinsey), one is the approach of the National Bureau of Statistics, and two are the research of scholars based outside the PRC, but based on material derived domestically in the PRC (Jie Chen and Teresa Wright). Income is provided as either per capita or per household. In the PRC (and specifically the NBS statistical system) households currently have 3.1 people. The surveys that underlie these studies are based on different kinds of research instruments, including census samples, household surveys, telephone surveys, or combinations of all of these, and various configurations have been used on different occasions. All statistics must be used with care, but those based on NBS data-sets especially so, for reasons already discussed.

Table 4.1 Size, wealth and definition of China's middle class

SOURCE	DATE OF RESEARCH	% TOTAL POPULATION ESTIMATED TO BE MIDDLE CLASS	MINIMUM INCOME THRESHOLD FOR MIDDLE CLASS DESIGNATION YUAN PER YEAR	DEFINITION OF MIDDLE CLASS RESEARCH LOCATION
Zhou Xiaohong (2008)	2004	11.9	60,000 per capita	Occupation, income, position, self-ascription. Beijing, Shanghai, Nanjing, Guangzhou, Wuhan
NBS (2005)	2005	5	60,000 per household	Income. All China
Li Chunling (2010)	2006	10–12	60,000 per capita	Occupation, income, position, self-ascription. Urban China
Lu Xueyi (2012)	2006	23	53,700 per capita	Occupation, income, position, inside/outside system. Urban China

Table 4.1 (Continued)

SOURCE	DATE OF RESEARCH	% TOTAL POPULATION ESTIMATED TO BE MIDDLE CLASS	MINIMUM INCOME THRESHOLD FOR MIDDLE CLASS DESIGNATION YUAN PER YEAR	DEFINITION OF MIDDLE CLASS RESEARCH LOCATION
Teresa Wright (2010)	2007	12	60,000 per capita	Income. All China
Jie Chen (2013)	2007–8	24.4	n/a	Self-employed labourers, professionals, managers, office workers. Beijing, Chengdu, Xi'an
Silverstein et al. [BCG] (2012)	2011	28	68,250 per household	Consumption. All China
Barton, Chen and Jin [McKinsey] (2013)	2012	14 upper middle 54 mass middle	106,000 per household 60,000 per household	Less than 50% expenditure on necessities. Urban China

Sources: Zhou Xiaohong (2008: 1); Lu Xueyi (2012: 19–20); Jie Chen (2013: 157); Wright (2010: 7); Li Chunling (2010: 154); Silverstein et al. (2012: 29); Barton, Chen and Jin (2013).

The various studies reported on in table 4.1 are clearly not statistically comparable, even though all are acknowledged to have an urban bias. They have been compiled, for the most part, on the basis of different ideas of the middle class, and often in different environments. Zhou Xiaohong and Li Chunling, for example, define the middle class by a combination of income, occupation, hierarchical position and self-ascription, whereas Lu Xueyi proceeds by reference to occupation, income, position, and whether the individual works within or outside the Party-state and its agencies. Jie Chen defines the middle class in terms of four specific groups: self-employed labourers, professionals, managers and office workers. Zhou Xiaohong's study was conducted through a telephone survey in Beijing, Guangzhou, Shanghai, Wuhan and Nanjing. Li Chunling's study was derived from the National Census, a 1 per cent population survey, a household income survey, a national survey on social structure, the China General Social Survey, and the Beijing Middle Class Survey. Despite differences and variety of approach, the information provided and the table's obvious disparities in the dimensions of the middle class provide food for thought.

A major concern is the calculation of middle-class income. There can be no doubt that some commentators in the PRC would prefer to see the middle class as no more than a middle-income category and stop any further analysis, largely for ideological reasons (Li Qiang 2001). The middle-class-by-middle-income category is usually identified in terms of the middle 20 or 40 per cent of income distribution: that is to say from either the 40th to the 60th or the 20th to the 80th percentile. The NBS determined in 2004 that the middle class would be defined in income terms as between 60,000 and 500,000 *yuan* per household (of three people) per year. This was nowhere near the middle percentiles of income distribution (as detailed by NBS) in 2004 or subsequently. In 2004, only the top 8 per cent of the population had an income of at least 60,000 *yuan* per capita; by 2009, this figure had grown to 16 per cent (Cheng Li 2010: 71). In 2012, while the wealthiest 10 per cent of the population by household income had an average household aggregate income of 101,848 *yuan*, the next wealthiest 10 per cent had an average household aggregate income of only 58,039 *yuan* (NBS 2012: 349).

At the same time, it is clear that, with the exception of Lu Xueyi, the studies by PRC scholars (as opposed to consultancy companies operating in the PRC) have accepted the NBS definition of a minimum threshold of 5,000 *yuan* per capita (and not per household) a month for entry to the middle class. This is additionally strange as a signifier of the middle class for two further and fairly obvious reasons. The first is that this figure appears to have stayed constant despite economic growth and inflation since 2004; between 2009 and 2012 alone, GDP per capita doubled in the PRC to 38,354 *yuan* (Song 2013). The second is that China is a continental-scale economy. There are obvious variations in purchasing power across the country, so that material standards of living vary greatly. To take a simple example: one would pay almost twice as much to rent a relatively new two-bedroom apartment in Suzhou, Jiangsu (in the East China economic heartland) as its approximate equivalent in Lanzhou, Gansu (in China's West), and probably more than twice as much if one wanted to buy the place. Housing apart, 5,000 *yuan* a month in Suzhou would generally buy a lot less than in Lanzhou. In the Shanghai survey of class, discussed in the previous section, individual and household income and assets were reported as being well at the top range of the NBS scale. Base annual salaries for a middle-class individual in Shanghai are said to be 150,000 to 400,000 *yuan*, and annual incomes 200,000 to 500,000 *yuan* for a household, with overall assets between 1 and 10 million *yuan* (Baoru 2010).

These figures highlight one particular glaring problem with the attempt to assess the size and wealth of the middle class: the lack of identification of a group above the middle class. Teresa Wright addressed this problem by removing the 3 per cent that earned over 500,000 *yuan* a year from her calculations, but this has not been universal practice. Studies by PRC scholars simply report the minimum threshold for middle-class entry. While the surveys by multinational consultancy companies operating in the PRC also identify the richer, upper-income group or groups, the NBS generally downplays the profile of these groups.

Li Chunling and Li Peilin, both from the Institute of Sociology at CASS, have each separately attempted to develop schema to more accurately assess the size of the middle class. Li Chunling identified four dimensions of the middle class – income, occupation, consumption and self-identification – each of which she calculated separately from her survey work (undertaken in 2003). She found that by these measures, 24.6 per cent could be considered of middle-income categories, 15.9 per cent were in middle-class occupations, 35 per cent followed middle-class consumption patterns, and 46.8 per cent considered themselves to be middle class. Bringing these four measures together revealed that an estimate of only 4.1 per cent of the workforce, and 2.8 per cent of the total population, could meet all the criteria of middle classness (Li Chunling 2005: 485–99). Li Peilin attempted a similar exercise based on data from a 2006 survey of households across China. Li Peilin identified three dimensions of the middle class – income, education and occupation. He created an index based on meeting the criteria for all three of these dimensions, for only two, and for just one. Someone who met all three criteria was said to be part of the middle-class core, someone who met two criteria was regarded as semi-core middle class, and someone who met one criterion was identified as marginal middle class. The calculation was that 3.2 per cent were core middle class, 8.9 per cent semi-core middle class, and 13.7 per cent marginal middle class (Li and Zhang 2009).

These observations are more than somewhat at odds with the oft-repeated mantra that 'the continually expanding size of the middle class is the outstanding feature of China's social class structure', let alone a claim that the middle class was already 23 per cent of the population in 2007 (Lu Xueyi 2012: 19–20). Indeed, they represent a challenge to all that those comments would seem to imply. It would seem more likely that the PRC's social structure is not developing on the lines of a country with a few very wealthy people, a small but substantial strata of the relatively poor, and a large middle-income majority. There is a real possibility, now seen as a danger, that instead of developing an olive-shaped income distribution, the PRC's social structure is becoming more shaped like the cross-section of a railtrack, with a wide wealthy top, a narrow middle class, and a solid and substantial working class underneath that is a base of very poor people (Hu, Li and Li 2012: 429).

The overgeneralization implicit in a claim of 'the expanding middle class' also completely misses the necessary unevenness and regional variation in the development of the middle class. While there may be a rural component to the middle class, it is largely an urban phenomenon. Moreover, the larger metropolitan areas, centring on Beijing, Shanghai, Guangzhou and the Pearl River Delta, South Jiangsu, and Hangzhou, have a disproportionate number of the country's rich and middle classes, and far greater concentrations than other urban centres (Hurun 2012; Barton, Chen and Jin 2013). These areas may not each have a middle-class majority population but they surely have a substantial middle class, as well as generally a lower degree of inequality. It is, for example, estimated that in South Jiangsu – centring on the cities of Suzhou, Wuxi, and Changzhou – a third of the working population has a monthly income that (as of 2012) was at least 5,000 *yuan*. By the same token, though, there are large areas of the country where the middle class is far less numerous. Jiangsu Province is another good example: while the south of the province is very wealthy, the north of the province (north of the Yangtze River) is very poor.

The likelihood of continued and almost unending expansion of the middle class, even with sustained economic growth, seems low. For the middle class to become the majority, a greater number of the urban working class, migrant workers and even peasants will have to transform themselves into largely urban white-collar workers, and there are clear structural and behavioural reasons mitigating against that. These include not only the household registration system, but the lack of access to higher education that has become the access point to the middle class. Urbanization by 2013 has ensured that about half the population live in urban-administered local authorities, though by no means half live in urban communities.

Moreover, the statistics do not seem to add up. The CASS Institute of Sociology research does not relate its identification of the middle class (specifically in terms of percentage) to its distribution of the population by strata. It was claimed that (as of 2007) 23 per cent of the total population was middle class. From the same data 29 per cent of the workforce was identified as being cadres, officials, entrepreneurs (large-scale and small), managers, office workers, professionals and technical staff. Clearly, not all of these could be identified as middle class, even without worrying which of them might really be considered either upper or ruling class. Many entrepreneurs, small business people, and white-collar workers without much in the way of supervisory functions or managerial responsibilities could not be considered middle class.

It is hard to reconcile the figures provided with the notion of either a continually or dramatically expanding middle class. In the first place, there is the question of the growth of the middle class since 1978. Growth there has certainly been. Table 4.2 provides comparative information for 1978 and 2006 from the CASS Institute of Sociology research on the six strata that are most likely to include elements of the middle class. In total, these six strata expanded from 6 per cent of the population in 1978 to 29 per cent in 2006. Yet, of that 29

Table 4.2 CASS Institute of Sociology – dimensions of the PRC middle class, 1978–2006

CLASS	YEAR	
	1978	2006
State and social administrators	1.0	2.3
Manager	0.2	2.6
Private entrepreneur	–	1.3
Professional and technical staff	3.5	6.3
Office worker	1.3	7.0
Small business person	–	9.5

Source: Compiled from Hu Jianguo, Li Chunling and Li Wei (2012), p. 399 (for 1978), and p. 403 (for 2006).

per cent, 7 per cent are office workers, 1.3 per cent are private entrepreneurs, and 9.5 per cent are small business people, most of whom are marginal (if in different ways) to any possible calculation of the middle class.

Then there is the question of the possibility of future growth so that the middle class becomes about half the population; 29 per cent of the workforce may be estimated to be about 19.7 per cent of the total population. Even assuming that as much as 23 per cent of the total population were indeed already middle class in 2006, the additional 27 per cent of the population to be recruited as future middle-class members would have to come from the transformation of some of those who were then industrial workers (14.7 per cent of the workforce), employees of commercial services (10.1 per cent of the workforce), and agricultural labourers (40.3 per cent of the workforce) and their families. Change may indeed come, but it is worth bearing in mind that, according to the same data-set, from 1990–2005 the proportions of agricultural labourers in the workforce decreased by 13.6 per cent, industrial workers rose by 2.7 per cent, employees of commercial service rose 6.8 per cent, office workers rose by 1.8 per cent, and the proportion of those who might be regarded as automatically to be included in any consideration of middle-class occupations (state and social administrators, managers, professional and technical staff) rose only by 3.19 per cent (Hu, Li and Li 2012: 416). The predicted dramatic growth of the middle class seems unlikely under these circumstances. Of course, this is not to argue that more people will not get wealthier and enter the middle-income ranges as the economy grows, or that the goal of being or becoming middle class is not individually significant.

THE ASPIRATIONAL MIDDLE CLASS

While the precise identification of the Party-state's middle class is clearly problematic, there can be no gainsaying the aspirations of middle-class politics. There is a powerful state-sponsored discourse of the middle class designed to encourage economic growth, consumption and a rising standard of living. It is also designed to mediate the increasing social inequality, including even to some extent to mask the emergence of the extremely wealthy. One reason for this focus is presumably that an appeal to the 'middle' anything is almost certainly less psychologically threatening than other approaches to public policy. Equally, there is a wide understanding in Chinese society of a desirable international middle-class lifestyle that reinforces and is reinforced by Chinese nationalism. Certainly, in repeated surveys most people regard themselves as either middle class or aspirational middle class (Bian and Lu 1996; Li Chunling 2003; Zhou Xiaohong 2005).

The state-sponsored discourse of the middle class grew out of and has been associated with the idea of *suzhi* (素质) – a concept which is concerned with the formation of human capital but is difficult to define precisely, not least because of confusion over the difference between quality and qualities, over differences between the individual and societal determination of *suzhi*, and over the role of nature and nurture in its development. In simple terms, *suzhi* is often translated as 'quality', though possibly 'human qualities' would be more accurate. *Suzhi* was originally a term referring to the individual's inherited qualities, which are then cultivated to achieve excellence. Starting with state campaigns to introduce birth control (in the 1970s) and then education reform (in the 1980s), the idea of *suzhi* was added to each of those concerns to encourage individual development for the public good. In the process, the idea of *suzhi* lost any idea of inherent quality and became instead a matter only of cultivation, with an emphasis on the hierarchical distinction between high and low *suzhi*, with improvement now a national goal (Kipnis 2006).

Starting in 1999 and with the substantial reform and expansion of higher education, the use of *suzhi* spread rapidly from the realm of public policy into more popular usage. Various goods and services – notably housing, but also clothing, automobiles, white goods, clothing, holidays and travel – were advertised as being beneficial to increasing *suzhi*. Books, newspapers, magazines, television programmes and the like were all dedicated to providing advice to parents on how to ensure that their children had a high *suzhi*. As Ann Anagnost has pointed out, *suzhi* has become a description of the 'minute social distinctions defining a "person of quality" in practices of consumption and the incitement of a middle class desire for social mobility' (Anagnost 2004: 190). The middle-class fundamentally positions itself in society in this way and in the process also clearly differentiates itself from others considered not to have the appropriate *suzhi*, for example, by establishing themselves in gated communities where the lower orders only have access in service. Interestingly, as Anagnost also highlights, the very difficulty of defining *suzhi* (as with the difficulty of identifying the middle class more precisely in structural terms) is an advantage: 'it is this very insubstantiality of *suzhi* that allows it to stand in for a differential separating the middle class from its other' (Anagnost 2004: 197). The 'other' in question is not just the lower orders in general, but quite specifically the migrant worker.

The discourse of the middle class is most apparent in the marketing of lifestyle issues and the development of a consumer society. Private automobiles and private housing are merely the start. A middle-class lifestyle extends to: advanced technology purchases; shopping in malls with international brands; eating out two thirds of the time; consuming foreign food and drink; spending leisure time in activities such as golf, sauna and teahouses; learning and speaking foreign languages; engaging in tourism and foreign travel; and providing foreign education for one's child (Gerth 2003; Davis 2005). While these seem fairly universal middle-class activities, there are also some particularly Chinese characteristics. The Chinese consumer is considerably more brand conscious than consumers elsewhere, 70 per cent preferring to purchase a branded rather than a non-branded (but otherwise identical) product, compared to 30 per cent in the USA. Foreign brands are preferred for clothing and consumer articles, but domestic brands for home appliances (Cartier 2008; Silverstein et al. 2012: 40).

Middle-class values have been particularly highlighted in the development of both higher education and private housing. The focus on the middle class has been very visible in the reform of higher education. University and college graduate status is the entry point to the middle class. Yet in 1978 there were less than a million undergraduates attending universities, with only 165,000 graduating annually. As table 4.3 indicates, by the end of 1998 and beginning of 1999, when the decision was taken to expand higher education, the PRC's universities still had limited capacity. The sector has subsequently grown dramatically, with 7 million students graduating in 2013 (Xinhua 25 June 2013), the number of universities and colleges more than doubling and a huge increase in state investment in higher education, rising from 33.4 billion *yuan* in 1997 to 290.2 billion *yuan* in 2011 (NBS 2012: 20–40).

Table 4.3 PRC undergraduate enrolments in higher education

YEAR	UNDERGRADUATE NUMBERS	TOTAL POPULATION	NUMBER OF COLLEGES	GRADUATING UNDERGRADUATES
1978	856,000	962,590,000	598	165,000
1984	1,703,000	1,043,570,000	1016	316,000
1989	2,082,000	1,127,040,000	1075	576,000
1992	2,184,000	1,171,710,000	1053	604,000
1999	4,134,000	1,257,860,000	1071	848,000
2001	7,191,000	1,276,270,000	1225	1,036,000
2003	11,086,000	1,292,270,000	1552	1,877,000
2005	15,618,000	1,307,560,000	1792	3,068,000
2007	18,849,000	1,321,290,000	1908	4,478,000
2009	21,447,000	1,334,500,000	2305	5,310,000
2011	23,085,078	1,347,350,000	2409	6,082,000

Source: Compiled from *China Statistical Yearbook 2012*, tables 3–1; 20–5; 20–8; 20–9.

This increase in higher education has been heralded quite explicitly as providing increasing access to the middle class. To quote researchers at the CASS Institute of Sociology:

> the expansion of college enrolment has enabled millions of students to enjoy opportunities for higher education, the opportunities for social mobility has gradually increased and each year the several millions of college graduates directly create a reserve force for the expansion of the middle class characterized by high academic qualifications. (Hu, Li and Li 2012: 419–20)

The expansion of higher-education capacity has also been heralded as providing opportunities, especially for women, rural residents and minority nationalities, all of whom have long been recognized as being under-represented in higher-education places. Rural women in particular have been targeted for recruitment on equity grounds. The potential for social engineering in the expansion of higher education is clear, as is its role in the state-sponsored discourse of the middle class. The argument is neatly summarized by Jing Lin and Xiaoyuan Sun:

> a potentially massive middle class is being created through higher education expansion. The expansion allows the new middle class to come from all sectors of the society, broader in scale than ever before and potentially affecting every family and community in China. (Lin and Sun 2010: 222)

Unfortunately, the evidence is that these hopes have not been realized. On the contrary: higher-education expansion has only benefited the already privileged. As Teresa Wright has pointed out, higher education provides the main path to good jobs. Good jobs are of course not guaranteed, but without higher education, and often a

Masters degree as well as a first degree, high-status employment is less likely (Bai 2006). Secondary schools provide the access to higher education and so parents attempt to position themselves through housing and in other ways to ensure their children can attend a school that has a good track record of university entrance. Almost all such schools are located in the neighbourhoods of the already wealthy and educated. Even so, admission often also entails payments to the school by parents to ensure their children can enrol (Lee 2009: 220). Wright concludes:

> since the early 1990s in China, more university students have come from financially privileged families who have benefitted from economic reform. Fewer qualified students from average and low-income homes have been admitted, and fewer have had the financial capacity to enrol. (Wright 2010: 66)

A specific research project looking at four leading universities in Shaanxi, Sichuan and Anhui during 2009 reinforces the view that higher education has become the preserve of the upper and middle classes. The project was designed to see whether recruitment to higher education in these relatively poorer provinces was able to ensure positive outcomes in favour of previously less-privileged groups in society. The conclusion was that it had not. Women and those from rural areas were under-represented in enrolment to university. Rural women were significantly under-represented, though urban women were not. The children of rich rural individuals were not under-represented but those from poor areas were. Poor, rural women from minority nationality groups were found to be the most under-represented of all. According to the researchers, 'College is still a rich, Han, urban and male club' (Wang, Liu, Zhang, Shi and Rozelle 2013: 469).

The discourse of the middle class is also highly visible in the development of housing since the late 1990s, though in different ways from the development of higher education. For a start, homeownership may be a necessary part of the definition of the middle class, but it cannot be sufficient. Housing reform since the late 1990s has meant that most people now live in their own home. The homeownership rate for the PRC is 89.7 per cent (2012), with a rate of 85.4 per cent even in the urban areas (Li Gan 2013). Homeownership, like higher education, is a symbol of social standing, though it is also clearly a differentiator of wealth and status. There has been considerably less direct public investment in housing, though local governments have often worked closely with real-estate developers. Moreover, the booming real-estate market was fuelled by the privatization of public housing and the development of commercial housing after 1998 to such an extent that prices rose significantly and threatened a degree of housing unaffordability (Man 2010: 186–7). Partly in consequence, and partly from concerns of inequality, after a decade local governments started to provide low- and middle-income housing, to encourage real-estate developers to build smaller units, to support the development of rental housing, and occasionally even to require developers to provide for a social mix on specific estates (Tang and Tomba 2008).

Though all of the new housing is advertised to potential buyers in terms of a comfortable lifestyle, it is the gated community – with security and the variable provision of other services – which is presented as the epitome of middle-class living (Youqin Huang 2005; Pow 2009). Some of these gated communities can be extremely luxurious, with detached villas standing in their own ground (Hu and Kaplan 2001; Bosker 2013). At the same time, there are many more gated communities with more modest blocks of apartments and townhouses (Zhang Li 2010: 130). Homes in these lesser-ranked gated communities are bought on the open market by private purchasers or supplied by state agencies and enterprises to their employees as subsidized housing (Zhang Li 2010: 113; Tang 2013:

56). In researching the representation of the middle class, Ann Anagnost came across a newspaper supplement advertising a gated community in Chengdu that defined the middle class for the reader, before assuring them that they too 'belonged' in terms of income, car ownership, demeanour, leisure-time activities and interests. The supplement (presented as reportage) then continued:

> This reporter interviewer interviewed a number of homeowners. Almost all were of a high educational level or had high-income levels. When they were looking to buy a home, their first concern was to see what the environment was like; then they looked at price; the next important issue was to assess the 'quality' [*suzhi*] of the neighbours, followed by functional issues, property management, and finally the architectural style of the home. (Anagnost 2008: 509)

The middle-class appeal of the gated community is manifest not least in the behaviour of those individual residents who deny that they are in fact middle class (Anagnost 2008: 507; Tang 2013: 69).

THE INTERMEDIATE MIDDLE CLASSES

The state-sponsored discourse of the middle class plays an important role in the PRC. It is designed to encourage consumption and hard work. It is intended to be inclusive, drawing attention away from the extremes of inequality and potential class conflict. At the same time, though, it is a blunt tool for social analysis. Outside of that context it is possible to see the middle classes as defined by their access to knowledge, skills, expertise and experience, between the dominant class and the subordinate classes. Of course, that approach is also by no means precise since the identification and cohesion of the intermediate middle classes is also inherently contested elsewhere (Abercrombie and Urry 1983). Nonetheless, the understanding of the intermediate middle classes as including both an 'old middle class' of small-scale entrepreneurs and the more successful self-employed, and a 'new middle class' of (largely urban) professionals and managers, provides a useful explanatory device (Edgell 1993: 62–73).

As elsewhere, in China the intermediate middle classes are fragmented and heterogeneous, and include a variety of entrepreneurial, professional and managerial classes. As might be expected in a reforming once state socialist system, the relationship between the intermediate classes and the state is close. Many of the professional and managerial middle class are either state officials or state-sector employees (including large numbers in the education, communications and health sectors), and many of the entrepreneurial middle class have close institutional and associational relations with the Party-state.

The entrepreneurial middle class is particularly difficult to identify in the PRC. There is an unfortunate tendency to treat the 10 to 11 per cent of the working population identified as business people (private entrepreneurs, small-scale business people and the self-employed) in the CASS schema as though they were a single, homogeneous entrepreneurial class. Many, if not most, of the self-employed are essentially part of the subordinate or working classes, with whom they have most in common in terms of their occupation, responsibilities and life chances. By no means are all private entrepreneurs members of the economic elite and, while some could be justly regarded as middle class in terms of their responsibilities and resource base, many would also be better seen as members of the subordinate classes (Huang 2013: 353–8). There are distinct echoes here of Marx and Engels's disparaging description in *The Communist Manifesto* of the entrepreneurial middle classes as 'the lower strata of the middle class'.

The entrepreneurial middle class is also particularly difficult to identify because of the extent to which the Party-state still plays a role in the economy beyond the state-owned sector. It is estimated that about a quarter of enterprises registered as 'private' are owned by SOEs; an undetermined number of additional enterprises are hybrid public-private concerns. Classification of the entrepreneurs responsible for these enterprises, all of whom may regard themselves as 'owners', is bound to present difficulties (Goodman 1999).

Between 1955 and the early 1980s, the PRC had no entrepreneurial middle class outside the Party-state. In the post-1978 re-emergence of business activities, 1992 was a clear watershed. Those who were business people before that date were considerably less educated than those who came later, and their links with the Party-state were almost non-existent. After 1992, business people increasingly came from the same social background as middle-level cadres, where indeed they had not served in those roles themselves beforehand. They were well educated, many as graduates of higher education, and often either experienced managers, the children of cadres, or both. Interestingly, many were natives of the localities in which they became entrepreneurially active (Goodman 2001).

The professional and managerial middle classes were very much part and parcel of the socio-political system before 1978. There was a need for ordinary (as opposed to leading) cadres and minor officials to run the new bureaucracy after 1949: managers to operate the state and collective sectors of the economy and a variety of professionals and technical staff for state agencies (in media and communications, health and education, for example). There was a dramatic change in CCP policy in and after the Hundred Flowers Movement of 1957, but the result of this was to emphasize training for political reliability rather than to reject the need for professional, technical and managerial staff.

The numbers of those in the professional and managerial classes grew considerably after 1978, probably doubling as a proportion of the workforce. Certainly this was fuelled by the growth of the non-state sector, but the state sector itself, both in state administration and sectors like communications and education, also increased. In the process, the range of occupations expanded to include professions previously excluded (notably lawyers, but also a range including market researchers, management consultants and service providers) or that had not previously existed (information technology), or became more professionalized. The resultant professional and managerial classes have been variously conceptualized by scholars outside the PRC. Wang and Davis, through an analysis of the China Household Income Project (CHIP) data for 1995 and 2002, differentiated elements of the middle class according to education and occupation. They identified cadres, an upper-middle class of managers and professionals with a college education, and a lower-middle class comprising ordinary white-collar workers and non-cadre managers and professionals without a college education (Wang and Davis 2010: 159–62). Jie Chen saw the middle class in urban China as comprising self-employed labourers, managers, professionals and ordinary office workers (Jie Chen 2013: 41). Teresa Wright concentrated on a range of different professions: intellectuals, lawyers and accountants in particular (Wright 2010: 70–83).

From the CHIP data for 2002, Wang and Davis found that cadres were 6 per cent of the urban working population, the upper-middle classes in their definition were 8 per cent, and the lower-middle classes were 44 per cent (Wang and Davis 2010: 161). From data for 2004, Jie Chen calculated that mangers were 1.5 per cent of the population, professionals were 5.1 per cent, and 4.8 per cent were ordinary white-collar workers (Jie Chen 2013: 56–7). As with the work of Li Chunling and Li Peilin, these figures suggest severe limits to the size of the urban middle class. Without any high degree of certainty, an estimate of around 12 per cent of the population as the intermediate middle class (as more widely understood outside the PRC) would seem to be reasonable. This is based on a number of assumptions, including that about 1 per cent of the total population is entrepreneurial middle class;

that 1 or 2 per cent are middle-class office workers; that 6 per cent are the professional middle classes; and that about 3 or 4 per cent are middle-class cadres and managers. These figures are consistent with those provided in table 2.2 (p. 60).

Wang and Davis's distinction between the upper- and lower-middle classes has a sound analytical basis as well as suggesting that those identified as lower-middle class are more aspirant than middle class. Not only are the upper-middle classes better educated, but they also earn more, have larger financial assets and better housing, and are healthier; over the period of the study (1995–2002) upper-middle-class salaries grew rapidly, and actually grew faster than those of cadres and workers (Wang and Davis 2010: 163–70). Wang and Davis also point out very clearly the extent to which the middle class is an essential part of the state system. In 2002, well in excess of four fifths of the middle classes were employed directly by the state. This included not only white-collar workers in the state administration and the SOEs, and managers and professionals in the state sector of the economy, but also a sizeable number of professional and technical staff in the state utilities and service agencies.

Since 2002 there have been changes, but none too substantial, in the relationship between the professional and managerial middle classes and the Party-state. There have, for example, been changes in the legal profession. State legal workers started to be replaced by professionally trained lawyers in 2003, and Bar exams were introduced in 2001. By 2004 there were 150,000 lawyers, and only 15 per cent of law firms were state-owned. Nonetheless, their distancing from the state should not be exaggerated. A high proportion of lawyers are CCP members, as might be expected, and CCP attention on their work is close (Michelson 2007). There have also been areas of activity in which the state's employment of the professional and managerial middle classes has increased. Most notable is the expansion of education, which has meant that from 1998 to 2011 just under an extra million full-time staff were appointed to teach in universities alone, and another million administrators were also appointed in higher education (NBS 2012: 20–6).

Before 1978, cadres had been selected for their political reliability, and professionals for their educational qualifications, with the two principles leading to two separate recruitment and career channels. After 1978, this dualism was maintained, though increasingly cadres were also asked to meet higher-education qualifications as well as tests of political reliability (Walder et al. 2000). Higher education is clearly the single most important determinant of the professional and managerial classes in the PRC, but family influence is also not negligible. In particular, there is a middle-class cycle of reproduction. Access to a professional or managerial appointment comes mainly from higher education, and access to higher education is a function of direct parental influence (Gong, Leigh and Meng 2010: 6). At the same time, professional employment practice reinforces this trend: there is a high level of inheritance in the professions with children usually following their parents (Buckley 1999: 68).

This chapter has indicated that there would appear to be limits to the size and growth potential of the middle classes. Nonetheless, it is equally clear that the discourse of the middle class presents lifestyle and consumption patterns which the subordinate classes are encouraged to emulate, even if their economic wherewithal does not permit them to match the experience of the entrepreneurial, professional and managerial middle classes. Chapter 5 examines how the urban working class, peasant migrant workers and the peasantry have experienced the reform era.

5   The Subordinate Classes

The overwhelming majority of China's subordinate classes – the unskilled and semi-skilled in the workforce that rely mainly on physical labour for their income – are to be found in the informal economy. In general terms, the informal economy is that part of economic activity 'unregulated by the institutions of society, in a legal and social environment in which similar activities are regulated' (Castells and Portes 1989: 12). In China, though largely ignored by state statistics, most of the country's working population are employed in the informal economy (Huang 2009). Using the methodology suggested by Philip Huang to calculate the size of the informal economy during 2006–10 (Huang 2009: 409; 2011a: 22; 2012: 602; 2013: 359), in 2011 the informal economy accounted for about 60 per cent of the urban working population and about 80 per cent of the total working population. The informal economy includes all those who work without the protection of state labour laws and regulation, without the benefits that flow to regular employees, and usually for much lower pay. It includes all those who are engaged full- and part-time in farming, workers in rural industries, migrant workers who stay in rural areas and those who move to the cities, the self-employed, casual and fixed-term workers in the private and public sectors, and unregistered workers. The statistics are difficult to interpret and not always reliable (Solinger 2001b), yet estimates can be made by reference to the data presented by the NBS and the ways in which numbers do not add up. For 2011, it appears that the rural informal economy was 53 per cent of the total working population (405.06 million people) and the urban informal economy was a further 28.6 per cent of the total working population (218.20 million people) (NBS 2012: table 4.1).

The size of the informal economy is one compelling reason why, for the conceivable future and almost certainly beyond, the subordinate rather than the middle classes will constitute the majority of China's working population. Workers in the informal economy do not receive the benefits, or have the opportunities, that would enable them – or even in most cases their children – to become middle class in material or occupational terms. Another reason is due to the scale and place of farming in the Chinese economy, and its particular socio-economic configurations. About a quarter of the working population is still engaged predominantly in agricultural production, with another quarter spending time in agricultural production as well as some other economic activity, often working in the TVE sector. A further fifth of the working population has rural household registration, while living and working as migrant workers in the cities.

The predominant pattern for China's twenty-first-century peasant is that of half agricultural cultivator and half industrial worker, and 'virtually every peasant household has someone employed off-farm' (Huang et al. 2012: 163). As of 2013, there were about 300 million migrant peasant workers, roughly half in the rural areas and half in the cities. To some extent the rural agricultural economy effectively subsidizes the urban working and middle classes. Remittances from the migrant worker to the family help support the low returns obtained from agriculture. At the same time, the family farm is the security blanket for the migrant worker and represents both their fallback in case of unemployment and their plan for retirement. Peasants do not own their land but have only usage rights, which are sometimes reallocated in order to ensure a high degree of egalitarianism. Moreover, in order to ensure an egalitarian distribution of land within a village, it is often the case that a peasant household is allocated plots of land that are not coterminous. Economies of scale are thus all but impossible to achieve in agricultural production. Another result is then the continuation of an extremely dominant (in terms of population) small-holding peasant economy. Peasants may improve their standard of living, but without further and major structural change it is hard to see how they may become middle class.

These observations underline the complexities that attend analysis of the approximate 85 per cent of the population that constitutes the contemporary subordinate classes in the PRC. At a cursory glance, it is possible to identify a vast range of social categories that include urban-resident workers in state-owned enterprises and in the collective, private and foreign-invested sectors of the economy, migrant workers in both urban and rural areas, workers in unregistered businesses, office and service workers in urban areas, small business people and the self-employed in both urban and rural areas, the urban poor (largely those made redundant through industrial restructuring, the long-term unemployed and the unemployable), peasants who live and work in rural areas, peasants who live and work in urban and peri-urban areas, and agricultural labourers. As noted in chapter 2, two fundamental inequalities in Chinese society are the rural–urban divide (related to but not completely coterminous with household registration distinctions) and that between work in the public sector on the one hand, and the new economy of the non-state, private or marketized sector on the other. The PRC's subordinate classes thus form three broad (and to some extent porous and overlapping) social categories defined by those inequalities: public-sector workers, workers in the marketized sector of the economy, and peasants in both rural and urban areas.

These three broad groups have had different trajectories since the start of the reform era and not surprisingly, given the dramatic changes in life chances and experiences that have occurred, there has often been friction between those from the city and those from the countryside. 'Peasants . . . can work hard, eat worse food, carry heavy things. They're fierce competition,' complained one urban worker, laid off from his SOE and looking for work (Solinger 2002: 314). 'Why do the local people never treat us as human beings? – now that I'm out in the world, I find myself a hundred times more worthless than in the village,' a young female migrant worker wrote despairingly to her boyfriend from Shenzhen (Pun 1999: 12). This friction has persisted even though some urban workers would not take on certain tasks, especially in the construction industry: 'City people would rather do nothing than this,' said one urban resident of construction work (Solinger 1999a: 48). One result has been the essential monopolization of work in construction by migrant workers (Pun and Lu 2010a). The harassment of migrant peasant workers coming to the cities has been particularly acute. They have had trouble renting housing, been faced with taxes and arbitrary charges, and been frequently rousted by local security forces (Solinger 1999a: 65, 135–6). This harassment has been particularly severe when they have competed for jobs against laid-off urban resident workers (Lee 2007: 114). Riots at the Foxconn factory (a major Apple component manufacturer) in Taiyuan in 2012 were well-reported worldwide as an example of labour activism, but less so in terms of the friction between local urban resident workers and migrant peasant workers from other provinces that had caused it (Barboza and Bradsher 2012; Perlin 2013).

Differences and tensions apart, there are commonalities in the ways each of the three broad social categories has developed. Local conditions are extremely varied and have determined social change to a remarkable extent. The restructuring of the state sector was universal in and after 1997, but the ways in which it was carried out, and the impact on former workers and the continuing public-sector workers, depended on the specific circumstances of the local economy. Jean-Louis Rocca identified the proportion of SOE workers in the workforce, the scale and scope of redundancies, and the strategic importance and financial capacity of the location as the key determinants of regional variations (Rocca 2003: 81). Opportunities for migrant workers in the marketized economy were almost inherently variable, as one study concluded: 'One of the defining characteristics of China's emerging market economy is the large variation in local labour markets. Rates of foreign investment, employment, economic growth, and change in standard of living all vary dramatically from city to city' (Cohen and Wang 2009: 53). For the peasantry, the ways in which land has been allocated (Brandt et al. 2002: 79) and in which development has been followed, especially in terms of non-farm work, has been locally determined (Parish, Zhen and Li 1995: 728) – as too was the introduction of the rural tax reform, heralded as bringing major change (Linda Li 2006).

Another commonality across these broad categories has been the considerably increased level of social activism and public protest, even allowing for their greater possibility in the changed political environment since 1978 (Chung, Lai and Xia 2006; O'Brien and Li 2006). Work stoppages and strikes have become commonplace in the public sector, involving not only workers who felt threatened by or were undergoing restructuring, but also those campaigning for better pay and conditions (Feng Chen 2006; Lee 2010). While workers in the marketized sector of the economy are almost by definition lacking the organization available to workers in the public sector, there is some evidence of an escalation in the scale and extent of organized protests by migrant workers, at least in the Pearl River Delta (Chris Chan 2012; Leung and So 2012). Perhaps even more remarkably, particularly before the introduction of rural tax reform and associated measures in and after 2004, there was a high degree of protest and violence in the countryside. There were many reported cases of attempts to establish autonomous peasant organizations separate from government influence and to take control of local resources (Bernstein and Lu 2000).

A final commonality is the role of the understandings of class as a general shaper of social activism. Despite the regime's attempts to downplay the language and politics of class, especially in reaction to the Mao-dominated years of the PRC, it is clear that ideas of class often shape the ideas of activists, and sometimes are even explicitly used as part of their language of politics. While many regard the Cultural Revolution's approach to class as dysfunctional, there is an understanding of class and class struggle that is never far from the surface of their activism. As Yan Hairong put it somewhat poetically in her analysis of migrant women workers: 'Class . . . as a spectre, exists between absence and presence' (Yan 2008: 248). Certainly there is evidence, particularly from instances of protest, about the language of class being used. For example, in 2004, workers protesting the restructuring of a SOE in a city in Central China put out a leaflet arguing that:

> The Chinese working class joined the revolution in order to control the means of production, factories and equipment. The working class' control over the means of production has determined the nature of our country . . . Now [those officials] want us to give up the factory and give the means of production to capitalists and then still call this social-ist. It is a gross deception. (Feng Chen 2006: 48)

In 1997, township and village cadres in Jiangxi Province protesting the tax and fee structure that was being imposed on them raised banners saying 'Down with the urban exploiting class,' 'Divide the wealth of the new rural despots' and 'establish peasant political power' (Bernstein and Lu 2000: 759).

PUBLIC-SECTOR WORKERS

As of 2011, China's public sector had 73 million regular employees: 67 million in SOEs and 6 million in urban collective enterprises. On the surface, these figures seem to indicate that the major change has been in the reduction of the urban collective-sector workforce: in 1978, there were 74.5 million workers in the state sector and 20.5 million in urban collectives (NBS 2012: table 4.2). In fact, these figures mask a major shift in industrial structure and employment practices. In 1978, state- and collective-sector employees constituted 99.8 per cent of the urban workforce, as opposed to 20.3 per cent in 2011. The figures for 1978 include everyone who worked in SOEs and urban collectives, whereas those for 2011 only record workers employed on fixed-term contracts of more than three years, and do not include the large numbers of migrant workers and those employed casually who now make up a significant proportion of even the public sector's workforce. Moreover, and possibly most dramatically, where in 1978 every public-sector employee assumed they had a job for life, and in most cases the possibility of a job for their children too, employment is now considerably more contingent. In the industrial restructuring that occurred between 1997 and 2004, some three fifths (30 million) of SOE staff were retrenched (Taylor and Qi 2010: 412), and it is estimated that 60 million people lost their jobs in the state and collective sectors between 1993 and 2006 (Hurst 2009).

Change did not occur easily or all at once: it came in stages after the introduction of urban reform in 1984 and, as might be expected, in the process the relationship between the Party-state and public-sector employees moved well away from one in which SOE workers were treated as some form of 'aristocracy' (Mok and Cai 1999: 79). Remarkably, though, not least because of the turnover in individual employees, workers in the public sector still retain a sense of entitlement, a sense of being the 'leading class' under socialism, and have not developed a discourse of opposition to the regime, or even for the most part to the reform project which has so dramatically affected their lives (Blecher 2002; Qiu and Wang 2012).

There can be little doubt that the position of all urban workers (and SOE workers in particular) was extremely privileged in the PRC before 1978. In the words of Joel Andreas, 'Workers did not own the factories in which they worked . . . Workers did, however, own their jobs, and these entitled them to consumption guarantees. They were lifetime members of their work units, which were responsible for providing for their welfare' (Andreas 2012: 107). Benefits included not only ill-health and retirement provisions for themselves and their family, but the possibility and well-established practice of a child replacing a parent in the workforce (*dingti* 頂替). Benefits even extended to providing home and sustenance should an individual be released from prison after a criminal conviction. Contemporary accounts were telling:

> State enterprises provide almost total security for their employees: virtually guaranteed lifetime employment, complete disability compensation, paid sick leave, fully paid medical care for employees and subsidized service for dependents, generous retirement pensions, death benefits for surviving family members, loans for employees in financial trouble and payment of funeral costs. State enterprises, further, often provide housing for significant percentages of their employees, usually have plant hospitals, medical clinics, or referral services to nearby hospitals, and usually provide meal halls, kindergartens, and day care centres. (Walder 1984: 25)

The provision of housing and other welfare through the work-unit was both generous and expensive. It is estimated that it cost 527 *yuan* per state-sector worker in 1978, or 82 per cent of the average state-sector wage that year (Walder 1984: 25).

The centrality of the work-unit system was one reason why some commentators, notably Andrew Walder, were reluctant to see urban workers before 1978 as a working class. The argument is straightforward: the relationship between management and workers was one of mutual dependency, where production essentially took second place to employment (Walder 1986). Workers relied on enterprise leaders for patronage, and leaders relied on workers because they were all permanent members of the work-unit, without whom nothing could be done (Andreas 2012: 108). In any case, as Walder also pointed out, being a public-sector worker was the result of residence and birth brought about through state action. There had been no process of proletarianization for the rural population, and no development of class consciousness: 'the revolution has ushered in the *unmaking* of the Chinese working class. The process of growing political unity, collective organization, and consciousness of common interests in opposition to other classes . . . was effectively reversed after 1949' (Walder 1984: 41–2).

The system began to change in 1984 with the introduction of measures to abolish lifetime tenure, the so-called 'smashing the iron rice-bowl'. Public-sector employees were encouraged to surrender their status in return for a one-off payment and new limited-term work contracts. This enabled enterprises to divide their workforce into two: the more or less permanently employed management, technicians and skilled workers, and casually employed process and manual workers. In some cases, enterprises have gone even further, outsourcing manual labour to subcontractors. From an early stage in the reform period, this has particularly been the case in both mining and the construction industry, where manual labour is now provided by young, migrant peasant workers (Solinger 1997; Tomba 2002; Wang Shaoguang 2006). Enterprises also moved quickly to stop responsibility for welfare provisions, including clinics, schools and entertainment facilities (Tomba 2012).

The move to economic efficiency was not totally successful, as public-sector enterprises had only reduced their current account costs and not their inherent financial liabilities. A classic example of this problem was the rise in retirees, all of whom, under the work-unit system, formed a work-unit cost. This problem would have occurred anyhow, given the ageing population, as the number of urban retirees grew from 2.1 million in 1978 to 100 million in 2005 (Wright 2010: 96), but was clearly exacerbated by the processes of reform (Hurst and O'Brien 2002; Frazier 2004). It has been estimated that by 1995 very few SOEs were profitable in any sense. The largest 500 SOEs provided 63 per cent of state profits, but 44 per cent of all SOEs and 72 per cent of the smaller SOEs were not at all profitable (Garnaut et al. 2006: 38). At the same time, SOE workers were becoming increasingly disconcerted, not least because during the 1980s reform was accompanied by inflation. According to one survey of workers in 1991–2, they had 'high expectations and decreasing social status' which resulted in a sense of relative deprivation, strikes and protests (Tang, Parish and Feng 1996: 367).

The longer-term solution came at and after the 15th Congress of the CCP in 1997. Although some SOEs had been allowed to close in the early 1990s and there had been some experimental restructuring – particularly with the introduction of shareholding cooperatives (Gu and Luo 2004) – privatization now became a national policy. With the exception of SOEs regarded as strategically important, SOEs and urban collectives were essentially put on an open market for domestic and foreign investment. In some cases, domestic investment took the form of management-led buyouts where future profits would be taken as the basis for loans to secure the investment.

The result was a massive number of workers being laid off and essentially put out of work as employment practices changed, and as economic efficiencies were introduced into enterprise management. As *The People's Daily* had warned in its 1997 May Day editorial, 'It's possible the benefits of some workers may be temporarily affected. Seen in terms of long-term benefits though the pain is worth enduring.' In 2001 alone, it is estimated that 15 per cent of the total urban workforce lost their jobs (Garnaut et al. 2006: 50). Li Peilin, from CASS Institute of Sociology, has estimated that between 1998 and 2002 the number of workers needing income support through being laid off rose from 1.84 million to 20.6 million (Li Peilin 2004: 76). Interestingly, these laid-off workers were not regarded automatically as redundant, unemployed or 'looking for work.' Technically, they had just been laid off temporarily. Not only do laid-off workers not show up in the unemployment statistics, but they have to remain out of work for at least three years to be regarded as unemployed (Liu Jieyu 2011). In 1999–2000 the NBS found that 53 per cent of laid-off SOE workers remained out of work after four years (Appleton et al. 2006a: 37), and by 2002 that figure was estimated to have increased to 74 per cent (Qiao 2004: 285).

The Party-state has attempted to take measures to deal with the problem of large-scale unemployment, but as Dorothy Solinger details, the results have been woefully inadequate (Solinger 2004). Workers have been encouraged to find jobs through the market, most enterprises and authorities have been encouraged to set up specific re-employment projects to assist laid-off workers, and a social security net has been introduced based around the Minimum Livelihood Guarantee. Especially through her work in Wuhan, Solinger provides serial examples of the failures of these measures (Solinger 2011). For example, in 1998 Wuhan's textile trade re-employment centre was charged with finding work for 10,000 laid-off workers and succeeded in 400 cases (Solinger 2002: 309). There was a lack of available placements, of services for laid-off workers, and of promised subsidizing payments to make the scheme more than perfunctory. The result has been the creation of a new category of the urban poor, approximately 23 million people (as of 2011) 'whose per capita family income falls below a locally set poverty line . . . rendering them eligible for a monthly allowance that is pegged to compensate the household – but just up to the income level necessary for the barest survival in a given city'. While comparisons of this kind are invidious, as Solinger points out, these urban poor are 'in fact *worse off financially* than are the rural-born migrants who now reside in the metropolises' (Solinger 2012).

Severance, negotiations over pay and conditions, restructuring and the threat of restructuring or being laid off have resulted in high levels of protests and strikes by public-sector workers (Feng Chen 2003; Lee 2010). There certainly was a dramatic decline in the provision of service and standard of living that they experienced. In the words of one commentator: 'State-supplied housing, medical care and education have declined in quality and availability, and increased in cost to workers' (Blecher 2002: 284). It is little surprise that old workers expressed a feeling of betrayal by the CCP: 'We gave our youth to the party and now it has abandoned us, we ask our children for help; but they have been fired' (Rocca 2003: 89).

At a fairly early stage in the reform process, the Party-state took measures in recognition of the need to manage change. Under the 1988 Enterprise Law, which also made provision for businesses to close, public-sector companies were required to establish a Staff and Workers Representative Congress. A replacement welfare system was put in place to provide old age, health and unemployment protection to replace the former work-unit system. This was based on enterprises and workers contributing to funds established by local authorities, though often in the event with little or no contributions from enterprises and poor fund management (Rocca 2003: 82). In 1987, the National Labour Dispute Arbitration System had been reinstated (it had been in abeyance since 1955) to handle the termination of permanent employment in SOEs. In 1993, its scope was extended to include urban collective and private enterprises, and concerns including wages, benefits and safety (Lee 2010: 62). A study of the grievances taken to arbitration committees by public-sector workers showed that 58 per cent were concerned with severance issues, 25 per cent were complaints about unpaid wages, 10 per cent related to work accidents and work compensation, and 7 per cent to claims of unpaid childbirth allowances (Thireau and Hua 2003: 91).

When the concerns of public-sector workers moved to more open protests, strikes and industrial action, as they have done in large measure, commentators have been struck by the extent to which these are backward-looking and do not seek to challenge the regime and its policies, despite challenging immediate and specific actions. There has been a certain acceptance of restructuring as a principle, although obviously not in each and every case, and particularly not those enterprises where the protestors were based. Workers seemed to prefer not to protest and certainly not against the system: 'We don't demand fish, meat and eggs – we only demand a mouthful of rice.' 'What do we workers hope for? We hope there will be another Cultural Revolution and all those corrupt cadres will be killed' (Blecher 2002: 294–5). The justification for protest and action was that of a moral economy appealing to the past, and the goal was defensive and restorative, wanting (as to some extent in the pre-reform era) to be part of the decision-making process. 'Give the factory back to me!' proclaimed one union newspaper in 2000, protesting the sale of an enterprise to a private owner. The proposed sale of the Shanghai Zhentai Rubber Company was protested in similar terms: 'They cannot just sell the factory like this. The factory is not theirs. It belongs to all workers. I have worked here for about thirty years. They cannot just send me home like this' (Feng Chen 2003: 248).

The emphasis by public-sector workers on infringements to the moral economy has led most commentators to argue that public-sector worker protests should be seen as reactive rather than programmatic, not opposed to the Party-state and not class-based (Cai 2002; Wright

2010: 113). Certainly, it does seem that the public-sector workers prefer to see their relationship with management in the same dependency relationship as existed before. On the other hand, it is far from clear that the new management of public-sector enterprises has quite the same perspective on enterprise management.

At the same time, it is far from always the case that class is absent from the messages being delivered by protesting public-sector workers. In his examination of the privatization process in SOEs and the reactions of public-sector workers, Feng Chen has detailed how class consciousness has been heightened. He describes a conversation on one occasion in which the new owner of an SOE told protesting workers off for 'carrying out class struggle'. 'What's wrong with class struggle? What you are doing is class vengeance,' one of the protestors replied. And another labour leader stressed, 'Our struggle [against privatization] is a manifestation of class struggle. Oppression and polarization inevitably lead to class struggle.' In another instance of protest against privatization, Jiang Zemin's theory of the 'Three Represents' was described as 'a betrayal of the working class'. Elsewhere another worker activist commented, 'All government agencies are serving the capitalists . . . What the government wants to do now actually is not to improve SOEs, but to install a capitalist system' (Feng Chen 2006: 49–50). Unfortunately for the workers, on those occasions when protests of this kind were successful in halting or reversing privatization, the realities of the reform-era economic environment inevitably meant that the enterprise in question was no longer viable, with the result that it went out of business completely (Feng Chen 2006: 55).

WORKERS IN THE NON-PUBLIC SECTOR

The marketized sector of the economy is very different from the public sector, not only in age but also in size, in variety, in its industrial relations, and in the participation and reactions of the workforce to conditions. Much attention in its development has understandably fallen on the emergence of large numbers of migrant peasant workers who have moved to the cities looking for employment. At the same time, however, the marketized economy also includes urban residents: older ones who have found employment having once worked in the public sector, and younger workers entering the workforce for the first time. It is difficult to estimate the number of workers to be found in this sector of the economy, not least because of the way the NBS records statistics. For 2011, official statistics record 123.4 million employees outside the public sector: 20.75 million working in limited liability companies; 7.9 million in shareholding companies; 45.8 million in private enterprises; 6.8 million in enterprises funded from Hong Kong and Taiwan, 9 million in foreign-invested enterprises; and 33.1 million people who are self-employed (NBS 2012: table 4.1). Alongside these statistics, Philip Huang estimated that there were 153 million migrant workers in urban areas in 2010 (Huang 2012: 602). Given that it is estimated that no more than a third of migrant workers has formal employment contracts (Ching Lee 2007: 164), the 2011 total workforce of the marketized economy was perhaps as many as 230 million people (or 64 per cent of the urban working population), which is consistent with the numbers provided by the NBS.

Despite the range of enterprises and activities in this sector of the economy, its unskilled and semi-skilled labour force all work under an industrial relations regime described by one commentator as 'brutal and insecure employment conditions' (Wright 2010: 116–17). Many workers are simply casually employed, at low rates that do not include allowance for overtime or holiday working, for long hours, in poor conditions, and rarely with insurance or retirement benefits. Often too, workers remain unpaid, for long periods, and without any redress. Where public-sector workers are able to access a more formal arbitration process, workers in the new economy are more likely to discuss their concerns with local authorities through the latter's Letters and Visits Office, the function of which is to precisely receive public complaints. An analysis of the topics raised by workers from the marketized economy petitioning local authorities in this way has found that 65 per cent of the concerns involved unpaid wages; 40 per cent involved excessive overtime; 15 per cent had been caused by the employer's refusal to offer a contract; and 10 per cent resulted from claimed arbitrary dismissal (Thireau and Hua 2003: 91).

Contracts, where they are available, are fixed-term, usually up to three years, despite the intent of the 2008 Labour Contract Law (Becker and Elfstrom 2010). Even the supposedly more respectable, and definitely the more established, of the large-scale enterprises in the marketized parts of the economy share the standard approach to industrial relations. In 2007, the world of international business was somewhat surprised to hear of the resignation of Ren Zhengfei, the astute and charismatic founder and CEO of Huawei Technologies, one of the leading telecommunications equipment companies anywhere. The resignation was apparently occasioned by the new Labour Contract Law, due to come into effect in the new year. This legislation stipulated that anyone who had been working for a company for ten years (or more) had to be appointed to an open-ended continuing appointment. Ren's resignation was intended as the model for another 7,000 who had been working for the company for eight years and more. They were asked to resign, provided with compensation (at a cost to Huawei of 1 billion *yuan* RMB) and in 6,500 cases rehired on new contracts. It was a procedure rapidly copied by other established companies (Wang, Appelbaum et al. 2009: 492–3).

As in the public sector, but on a far larger scale, contracting out in the non-public sector has also become common. The construction industry provides a complex and well-established example. In the early 1980s, the State Council announced that in future all construction work would be outsourced through contracting companies: government agencies would no longer employ their own construction workers. A system has emerged in which, by 2010, 40 million construction workers were part of a multi-tier labour contracting system. The top-tier contractors bid for projects with local authorities and property developers. They seek to make a profit by laying off the investment risk as well as outsourcing the actual construction. They subcontract raw material and labour supplies to separate contractors. These subcontractors in turn further subcontract, especially for labour. A labour-supplier contractor is contracted to provide labour management and to facilitate labour-use, and they in turn contract construction workers in variously sized construction teams. Understandably, margins are very tight for the subcontractors, and given their lack of access to either capital or credit facilities, the practice of not paying workers is readily explained (Pun and Lu 2010a: 146–50).

In the foreign-invested sector, labour dispatching has become the norm. This is a practice where enterprises employ workers through dispatching agencies, such as FESCO (Beijing Foreign Enterprise Human Resource Service Company) or CIIC (China International Intellectech Corporation). Originally approved (in the 2008 Labour Contract Law) as a provision for temporary and auxiliary employment, by 2011, 37 million workers had come to be employed in this way. It had become a means for foreign-invested enterprises to reduce costs by not employing workers on continuing contracts, or at the same pay rates as directly employed workers, and without the same benefits. In December 2012, the State Council announced a 'Decision of Revising the Labour Contract law', to come into effect on 1 July 2013 and designed to tighten up such practices by increasing legal and financial requirements for labour-dispatching agencies, by limiting the proportion of contract labour that can be employed and by emphasizing the principle of 'equal pay for equal work' (China Briefing 2013).

Labour in the marketized sector of the economy is highly gendered. Construction and security work are almost totally male; light-industry production lines and the textile industry are almost totally female, as is domestic service. Retail activities are disproportionately female, as are hotel and restaurant activities. Women are also over-represented in the health and social welfare services (Liu Jieyu 2007; Guang and Kong 2010). One result has been that in those industries and occupations where women dominate, wages have been generally lower, and overall female urban employees earn about a fifth less than men (Cohen and Wang 2009: 46). Moreover, gender stereotyping in the workplace is acute. Pun Ngai, who spent half a year on a production line in Shenzhen, reports on the ways in which her women co-workers were encouraged to be girls and to be obedient: 'They were induced to fear any evidence of their own gender ambiguity or perversity. Gender became a means of discipline and self-discipline, invoked so that they would learn to police themselves' (Pun 1999: 15).

Eileen Otis, in her ethnography of life and work at a Beijing luxury hotel, details how jobs were determined by gender and generation. Young women were waitresses, hostesses and in reception. Young men undertook security work and physical labour. Middle-aged workers undertook cleaning and behind-the-scenes labour. Women staff were drilled to be congenial and welcoming, but not regarded as suitable for managerial roles. Men were expected to be strong, silent types, not assessed (as were women) for their emotional suitability. Interestingly, the workers themselves defended the gender stereotypes within which they worked. Both the male and female members of staff expected men to do the shifting and lifting because they were considered stronger than women. Young women accepted that they were best placed to act with emotional intelligence about client needs, and their male managers explained that women were best for these roles because they were 'soft, mature, and cooperative', or at least until they reached the age of thirty, when they were considered too old to be engaged in work that involved customer interaction. The result, in Otis's words was that 'Workers gain a stake in constructing and defending the gender and generational boundaries enclosing their work, even when those boundaries consign them to lower status and insecurity' (Otis 2009: 55).

There was one female member of the security staff (seeking to cross the gender boundary), but she was continually being pressured by her male co-workers (despite being an established martial arts master) to move to more 'gender appropriate work' such as being a waitress or in reception. She found their hints that she might be getting tired from standing up and might need a replacement tiresome, not least since their concerns did not extend to other female workers in the hotel.

Migrant peasant workers are the heart of the labour force in the new marketized sectors of the economy and their integration has been the benchmark that has determined working conditions in the sector (Solinger 2001a). Unfortunately, the bar has not been set very high. The CASS social stratification group has acknowledged the serious problems that result from 'the unsecured rights and interests and awful living conditions of peasant-workers' (Lu Xueyi 2005: 361).

As already noted, the precise number of migrant workers is difficult to establish. It is estimated that as of 2011 there were 153 million migrant workers in the cities, of whom about half had been settled there for at least six months – a distinction that the NBS adopted for the first time in 2000 for the census. A 2006 report by the State Council's Research Office on 'China's Migrant Worker Problem' reported that of the then 120 million migrant workers, 36.4 million (30.3 per cent) were in manufacturing, 27.5 million (22.9 per cent) in construction, and 56 million (46.7 per cent) in services with 12.5 million (5.7 per cent) in the 'social services' (domestic service, security, delivery services, massage and beauty services, refuse collection, cleaners and janitors), 8 million (6.7 per cent) were service personnel in hotel and restaurants, and 5.5 million (4.6 per cent) in wholesale and retail activities (Huang 2009: 408).

Almost necessarily, migrant workers are not equally distributed around China's cities, nor are they drawn equally from different parts of the country, even allowing for differences in the size of populations. As of 2007, most migrant workers were to be found in Shanghai (where they number 45.7 per cent of the workforce) Beijing (38.5 per cent), Guangdong Province (36.7 per cent), Zhejiang Province (22.4 percent), Fujian Province (21.4 per cent), Tianjin (18.7 per cent) and Jiangsu Province (13.9 per cent). Fewest migrant workers were to be found in Henan Province (1.6 per cent of the workforce) and Gansu Province (2.1 per cent). The highest proportions of local rural residents who had at some time moved for work were to be found in Jiangxi Province (88.3 per cent), Henan Province (84.3 per cent), Chongqing (83.6 per cent), Anhui Province (83.5 per cent), Guizhou Province (80.5 per cent), Hunan Province (79.7 per cent) and Sichuan Province (79.5 per cent). The lowest proportions of local residents who had moved for work were to be found in Guangdong Province (5.4 per cent), Shanghai (9.0 per cent) and Beijing (11.9 per cent) (Lu Xueyi 2012: 157). These figures include all rural to urban migrations and not just migration to the bigger cities of the eastern seaboard. There is often a dramatic contrast between the plight of migrant workers in the bigger cities and conditions for those who have moved to smaller county towns which are often more accommodating (Carrillo 2011).

Conditions for the migrant workers are a testament to the scale of the rural–urban divide (Loyalka 2012). In the 1980s and 1990s, migrant workers were frequently faced by difficulties in moving to the cities for work even temporarily. They were harassed by security forces, denied accommodation and subject to additional and arbitrary fees by local authorities (Solinger 1999b; Li and Duda 2011). Still they came for construction, for manufacturing, for textiles, and to populate the small-scale, self-employed urban economy that needed street-side food and convenience stalls, household services and transport. Female work-forces were recruited in large numbers to work on production lines, initially in South China (the Pearl River Delta) and then in East China (Zhejiang and Jiangsu Provinces and Shanghai) where they lived, ate and were regulated in company on-site dormitories. With State Council acknowledgement in 2006 of their often precarious circumstances, some conditions have improved marginally, but not by much. Migrant children are often refused entry to local schools or forced to pay exorbitant fees. For anything requiring residence or proof of household registration (access to health care, college entrance examinations, welfare support), migrant workers must return to their point of origin, regardless of how long they or their children have lived elsewhere (China Labour Bulletin 2013).

The 2006 State Council research reported that only 12.5 per cent of migrant workers had employment contracts of any kind, only 10 per cent were covered by medical insurance and only 15 per cent received retirement benefits. It was also reported that migrant workers worked 50 per cent more than regular workers in return for 60 per cent of wages (Huang 2009: 408). A later (2009) survey by the NBS found that (the by then) 145 million migrant workers in total worked an average of 58.4 hours a day, 89 per cent worked more than a forty-four-hour week, only 12.2 per cent were covered by health insurance and that only 7.6 per cent received retirement benefits (Huang 2009: 408; 2012: 602). Unpaid wages have been a major concern for migrant workers. At one point in the early part of the twenty-first century, Anita Chan reported that 72.5 per cent of migrant workers had suffered a degree of wage default, and that in the first eight months of 2004 alone, state-regulated construction work was 367 billion *yuan* RMB in arrears with wage payments. Sometimes local governments were enlisted to chase unpaid wages of this kind. In Guangdong Province in 1998, the government was chasing up a total of 5.6 billion *yuan* RMB (Chan 2005).

At the same time, the hostility of the urban environment aside, there are several ways in which migrant workers are clearly not typical of others in the new economy. Probably the most important, and the most obvious of these, relate to their relationship to the countryside. As Lei Guang notes from his study of migrant workers:

> The village, not the city, is the final point of accounting of a migrant's income, and thus his success. Thus the goal of successful migrants is to spend their hard-earned money on building a house, contracting a marriage, contributing to a family member's education, or starting a business in the rural areas. (Guang 2005: 499)

A migrant-worker family's smallholding is in many ways its social security, though perhaps not to the extent that is often articulated by some urban residents who claim that migrant workers have both more disposable income and more assets, without appreciating the dislocation and the costs that migrant workers also face. Migrant workers also have significantly lower expectations and feelings of entitlement than other urban workers. Local ties may help an individual get to the city but they may not help them find or keep work. As the workers Lei Guang interviewed said, their mantra was 'work competitively, expect little, and take care of family' (Guang 2005: 497). Description of this intense adaptation to market forces characterizes the ethnographic research on migrant workers.

PEASANTS

The third broad social category of the subordinate classes is the peasantry: some 405 million of whom (as of 2011) live and work in rural areas, in addition to the 150–60 million migrant peasant workers who live and work in the cities, and an indefinable number (at present) who live in urban areas. Given the number of peasants and the varied conditions across each province, let alone across China as a whole, generalizing about their socio-economic conditions is by no means a simple affair (Yeh, O'Brien, and Ye 2013). Peasants who live in areas of the coastal economies that have become thoroughly integrated with the global economy (the Pearl River Delta region in Guangdong Province, the southern part of Jiangsu and the northern part of Zhejiang Provinces, for example) clearly have different experiences from those in the north and west of the country where market conditions are less developed as well as less internationalized. Peasants living in urban and peri-urban areas are similarly considerably better off than those living elsewhere simply because they have easier access to both inputs and markets (Fan 2012).

The task of generalizing about peasants is made somewhat easier in that there is a basic continuity of rural organization, despite name and political changes, that characterizes village and township life, not only from 1949 up to the present but also, to some extent, from before the establishment of the PRC (Unger 2002). The communes and production brigades of earlier years, when agriculture was collectivized, were replaced by townships and administrative villages, with natural villages reappearing in the administrative space that had once been occupied by production teams (Unger 2012a: 23). Against that there is an almost inherent variability to the rural political economy. Relations between government, society and the economy at the village level are very varied even within each economic region. On a village-by-village basis there may be differences in the balance of capacities and power. Tony Saich and Biliang Hu (from their examination of an administrative village in Dongguan) identified the causes:

> Three major factors are important in determining the nature of authority at the local level: the capacity of the local authority to generate revenue and how it is redistributed, the relationship with higher levels of government, especially the political contracting system, and the structure of the local society and the degree of community organization, its homogeneity or heterogeneity. (Saich and Hu 2012: 14)

The categorization of someone as a peasant is essentially determined by their relationship to the land, together with their household registration, a system which is extremely complex. At its simplest it divides agricultural from non-agricultural households, residents in urban areas from residents in rural areas, and those with and without a household registration for where they live and work. Anyone with an agricultural household registration is technically a peasant, assumed to be able to provide food for themselves, regardless of whether they live in an area designated as an urban or a rural area (Kam Wing Chan 2009).

The relationship to the land is almost as complex. In the first place only a minority of peasants are engaged solely or even predominantly for most of their working time in agricultural work. Indeed agricultural labour is often not regarded as 'work' but as a family-based household activity, much like housework is also regarded in many places in the world. Farming is a function of the peasant household, but the peasant family extends well beyond the farm. It is more usual to find male members of the household engaged in off-farm work on a more regular basis, with farm work as such left to women and senior family members (Huang 2011b). There are few peasant households without at least one member engaged in off-farm work, as might be expected, given that there are some 150–60 million migrant workers in the cities, an equivalent number in rural areas (in TVEs), and (as of 2011) some 34.42 million workers in rural private enterprises and 27.18 million self-employed trades people, pedlars and others engaged in commercial activities (NBS 2012: table 4.1).

The relative lack of individual peasant involvement on the land with which they are associated is readily explicable. Since decollectivization and the allocation of land use and residual income rights through a household responsibility system between 1979 and 1983, landholdings have inevitably been small and disparate. It is calculated that on average a peasant household has about 7–10 *mu* of land to farm. Land has not been privatized and remains in collective ownership. It is allocated on lease to peasant households, originally for periods of fifteen years, but subsequently the lease period was extended for a further thirty years. Moreover, because land was redistributed on the basis of an egalitarian entitlement, in most places there was a fragmentation of farmland on grounds of equal quality. Land was also not redistributed according to the number of labourers in each household but initially according to the size of the peasant household and the numbers in the workforce, and after 1985 by the size of the household alone (Cheng and Tsang 1996).

Land-use allocations are complex in themselves, with households permitted by national regulation to hold land-usage rights in a number of different types of tenure. The largest amount of land (usually in excess of 80 per cent) is designated as 'responsibility land' allocated in return for delivery of grain or some other commodity to the state at below-market price. 'Grain ration land' is allocated to ensure that each household can feed itself and is provided on a per capita basis. A small amount of land is permitted as private plots, as was the case even under the collectivized system before 1978. 'Contract land', where it is made available, is rented commercially by households; and previously uncultivated land can be farmed, usually at no cost (Brandt et al. 2002: 73–4). These differences apart, the decisions about land-use allocation are all made locally, as are the processes by which determinations and allocations are made. As might be expected, some local authorities are more interventionist than others. In the majority of villages, households are freely able to decide on their crop mix, but this is not always the case. Similarly, there are villages where general land use is determined by the village. And probably of greatest importance, some places have had regular land-use reallocations to equalize distribution (Kong and Unger 2013).

The uncertainty inherent in repeated allocations, land-use and property ownership ambiguities are additional reasons off-farm activities are favoured. Moreover, the situation is exacerbated by the low returns on agricultural production. There is a shortage of the wherewithal for peasant households to move beyond agricultural production, worsened still further by the pattern of land-use. Migration and indeed off-farm work provide additional capital for investment and ideas for development, as well as supplementing incomes. As Rachel Murphy points out from her study of the impact of migrant workers on their home villages, 'Migration provides rural households with access to off-farm earning opportunities that lie beyond the limited resource base and patronage networks of the home areas' (Murphy 2002: 217).

Still, peasant households require political contacts, negotiating skills and (preferably) two or three pairs of hands to really benefit from the opportunities provided from migration. Murphy found that the richer households had at least two migrant workers, and that the very wealthiest had both off-farm workers and migrant workers.

Peasants do not have access to the benefits of urban living, or the public welfare provided to urban residents. On the other hand, the system assumes that their social security is assured through the family's land-use rights and collective ownership of the village. Despite uncertainties and ambiguities, then, the peasants' relationship to their village, family and land remains close. Indeed, research has found somewhat counter-intuitively that migration is not the preferred option for peasant households. There can be no doubt that the economic returns from migration are clearly higher than staying in agricultural production at home. All the same, analysis from a 1996 survey concluded that on the whole peasants would prefer to work off-farm or migrate to another part of the rural economy rather than to try their luck in the cities. This was particularly the case for those with relatively high levels of education and those with good political connections, who preferred to stay in their home village and establish private enterprises rather than move elsewhere (Guang and Zheng 2005). Certainly, from the early 1990s on, a discourse of localism – of assisting in the development of one's native village or township

– became an important factor of production for rural entrepreneurs (Goodman 2004a).

The scale and range of the PRC's subordinate classes clearly makes it all but impossible to simply summarize their experience. Nonetheless, it is equally clear that they have all been dramatically affected by the reform era and the processes of socio-economic change it has set in train. The logical next set of concerns is about how those processes continue: possible future change and the prospects not only for each class and their interactions, but also how these may influence the overall political economy.

6   The Political Economy of Change

The transformation of the PRC's politics, economy and society since 1978 has clearly been substantial and there can be little doubt that change will continue. But how this will occur and what will transpire remain fairly open questions. The CCP in November 2013 (at the 3rd Plenum of its 18th Central Committee) committed itself to the continued dominance of the public sector of the economy and the coexistence of other (marketized) sectors, as well as the maintenance of the Party-state. Commentators outside of the PRC have examined the various challenges the current regime faces as a result of the socio-economic changes of the reform era, and have attempted to highlight the possible checks on the continued operation of the Party-state in its current form. These include the impact on the dominant class from the introduction of the market; the increased political activism of entrepreneurs and the urban middle classes; the mobilization and organization of a new working class; the impact of increased peasant activism; and the threat to regime legitimacy from increasing inequality. The following examination of each of these suggests that while the challenges to regime maintenance may not be negligible, they also do not indicate the likelihood let alone the inevitability of revolutionary change, or at least not in the short to medium term and not without further conditions being met.

MARKET TRANSITION

The greatest challenge to the Party-state would seem to come from the introduction of the market, and its impact on both class formation and the exercise of power. The comparison of the PRC's post-1978 development with the experience of Eastern Europe, especially the Communist Party-states of Hungary and Poland during the 1980s, has led to a substantial body of research, led by Victor Nee, focusing on the changing nature of the dominant class and arguing that China was in the throes of a 'market transition' (Nee and Matthews 1996; Nee and Cao 1999, 2002). The technical side of the argument begins with the earlier work of Ivan Szelényi who pointed out that state socialism produced a 'redistributive economy' in which state-owned resources were distributed by the political elite, leading to politically determined inequalities (Szelényi 1978). As market reforms are introduced into a redistributive economy, the key question is whether political capital retains its power as the major determinant of inequality and stratification, or whether the forces of the market replace political capital with skills, knowledge and enterprise. In Nee's view, a market transition would lead to a 'transfer of power favouring direct producers over redistributors' (Nee 1989: 666). Nee followed up his initial statement with a series of studies showing amongst other things that rural stratification has moved to market determination (Nee 1996), that cadres have incentives to move into the private sector because of the market transition (Nee and Lian 1994), or out of SOEs and into private enterprise (Nee and Su 1998). The analysis of market transition is predictive: 'the spread of markets erodes commitment to the party and paves the way for regime change' (Nee and Lian 1994: 285).

Against this view of a market transition, a 'power persistence' theory has also been proposed. In this interpretation 'politically based privilege' is regarded as 'more permanent and more deeply embedded in the economic situation' (Bian and Logan 1996: 741). Interestingly enough, this too was derived from Nee's work. While he had based his ideas of market transition on analysis of rural China, he accepted that change might happen more slowly in urban China, dominated as it was by the public sector: there the market creates a hybrid system with the work of the existing bureaucracy (Nee 1991, 1992). More generally, and later, Nee also developed ideas about how the path-dependent influence of political capital remains part and parcel of the market transition (Nee and Cao 1999).

There is research other than that done with or by Nee himself, especially on the local level in rural China, which seems to support his hypothesis about market transition. In some places, as already noted, local politics have been subsumed one way or another by economic elites. On the other hand, there is also research, also as already noted, that shows both the continued and sometimes increased influence of local political leaders in economic decision-making. Nee himself has argued that, inevitably in a system undergoing such change, there will be residual state power acting alongside the market transition until a 'tipping point' is reached: 'Market transition theory is not a theory of radical change; instead it turns on the cumulative causation of decentralized market processes in promoting discontinuous change at the margins of the pre-existing stratification order' (Nee and Cao 2002: 36).

Moreover, as Nee has also pointed out, one clear consequence is that the process of change is highly localized with different impacts on the changing power of state and market respectively, according to the economic environment and political structures. In this process he identifies differences between the maritime provinces (impacted by foreign investment) and the inland provinces, as well as differences in the emergence of specific hybrid local economies where industrial production is dominated by either the state sector, the collective sector or the private sector, though containing elements of each (Nee and Cao 1999).

Nee's argument has been met with claims that it is methodologically tautological since there was no market before 1978 (Walder 1996), and considerable scepticism that the returns to political capital are declining compared to the development of the market. A series of studies has indicated the relative importance of political capital (for example, class background, CCP membership and political position), while accepting that market factors (for example, education, skills, enterprise) also play a role in determining inequality (Xie and Hannum 1996; Walder 2002, 2003; Bian and Zhang 2004; Gustafsson and Sai 2010). Against the theory of market transition, the majority position favours the coexistence of redistribution and the market as principles in the determination of inequality, stratification and ultimately elite position (Walder 1996; Bian and Logan 1996; Parish and Michelson 1996; Walder, Li and Treiman 2000; Zang 2001, 2004). This dualism is also the view of Szelényi and Kostello, who bring to the interpretation of the PRC a perspective that differentiates strongly between a socialist mixed economy, such as now exists in the PRC, and the contemporary capitalist economies of post-socialist Eastern Europe. In particular they argue, from the experience of Eastern Europe, not only that the economic elites cannot replace the political elite while the Party-state still exists, but also that, if the regime was to change dramatically, then under those circumstances it would be 'the technocratic fraction of the former *nomenklatura*' who would become the new system's political and economic elite, not the current private entrepreneurs (Szelényi and Kostello 1998: 318).

The controversy and debate is bound to continue. Victor Nee and Sonja Opper published *Capitalism from Below* in 2012, continuing the research into market transition by focusing on the development of the private sector. Through a study of firms in East China, they argued not only that private enterprise grew despite political opposition, but that the market has replaced redistributive power and that political capital does not lead to economic success (Nee and Opper 2012: 255). This conclusion contrasts with that of Ivan Szelényi who denies the prospects for 'capitalism from below' and characterizes China as a form of state capitalism (Szelényi 2008); or that of Bruce

Dickson who describes the development of the private sector in terms of 'crony capitalism'. This he defines as 'a system of interaction between economic and political elites that is based on patrimonial ties and in which success in business is due more to personal contacts in the official bureaucracy than to entrepreneurial skill or merit' (Dickson 2008: 22).

DEMOCRATIZATION

The discussion of market transition is related to but not identical with arguments about the prospects for democratization resulting from new class formation. In chapters 3 and 4 it has been argued that, although the entrepreneurial elite and the intermediate middle classes have grown in numbers during the reform era, they remain limited in size. Nonetheless, they clearly have advantages by virtue of their economic, social and cultural capital which provide the potential for interest articulation and organization. These capacities speak to a wider literature about socio-political change elsewhere that highlights the roles of the entrepreneurial and urban middle classes in heralding liberal democracy. This possible political consequence of the emergence of entrepreneurs and the growth of the middle class is certainly recognized within the PRC by both scholars and (with somewhat more concern) the Party-state (Rocca 2008; Li Chunling 2013).

Barrington Moore's observation of the relationship between social and political change – 'no bourgeois, no democracy' – has become a starting point for almost everyone (from outside the PRC) investigating the potential for China to become a liberal democracy (Moore 1967: 418). The logic of this proposal is that new social groups with growing economic strength but less access to political power and influence pressure for change because they want political support for their activities. Those who speculate that the PRC's entrepreneurs might head in that direction have essentially argued in this way

(Glassman 1991). As already noted, 'private enterprise' is now said to produce more than 60 per cent of GDP, and entrepreneurs often do express concerns about the direction of government policy and regulation.

This particular argument about the inevitability of liberal democracy in China exists without any evidence that entrepreneurs actually want the political system to change, and indeed the weight of evidence does not currently support the case. In the first place, the evidence is that entrepreneurs do not speak with one voice, not even private entrepreneurs, or have a single view on anything. To quote Kellee Tsai:

> The empirical analysis demonstrates that class formation has not occurred among China's capitalists because they have different social identities, draw on different networks and resources, and do not share similar types of grievances against the state. (Tsai 2005: 1135)

In the same way it is also clear that many have no desire to see a competitive electoral system replace the current Party-state (Tsai 2011). On the contrary, as many studies have determined, there is a close relationship that has developed between the new economic elites and the CCP. The relationship between entrepreneurs and the Party-state has been described as 'socialist corporatism' (Pearson 1994) and in terms of 'allies' (Chen and Dickson 2010).

As Chen and Dickson suggest, the lack of conflict between the Party-state and entrepreneurs should really be no surprise. In other authoritarian regimes where support is provided to the interests of the economic elite, and where there are concerns that a change of regime might adversely impact their economic position (the introduction of taxes, labour regulation and market controls, for example), there is not likely to be a difference of strategic-level political opinion and a push for change, even if there might be discussion and debate over specific issues (Chen and Dickson 2010: 4). Moreover, there are obvious institutional links between the Party-state and all non-public-sector entrepreneurs. A substantial proportion of these have emerged from the Party-state, and in turn the Party-state has moved to incorporate others in various ways. Some are even directly supervised by Party-state and public-sector agencies. Compared to the development of liberal democracy elsewhere, there seems to be much less political space between the established authority (the Party-state) and the (non-public-sector) entrepreneurs. It does seem, in Kellee Tsai's words, that 'capitalists have never had better access to the political system in PRC history' (Tsai 2007: 201). As Teresa Wright points out, the Party-state certainly seems to take their interests to heart. She provides a telling statistic: in 2005, the private sector produced 50 per cent of GDP and paid 7.1 per cent of the total taxes paid by enterprises; by contrast, the public sector produced 37 per cent of GDP but paid 63 per cent of the taxes (Wright 2010: 44).

Samuel Huntington's observation that liberal democracy is a consequence of the increasing social complexity that results from the development of the entrepreneurial, professional and managerial middle classes (Huntington 1991: 74) has also been taken up by commentators on social and political change in the PRC. It has been argued that the rise of China's middle classes presents the Party-state with a complexity that the latter will not be able to adequately manage (Li He 2003; Tang, Woods and Zhao 2009). While there clearly is increased social complexity, especially in the development of different elements of the middle class, it has not so far led to demand for radical political change. On the contrary, the PRC's intermediate middle classes are fundamental supporters of the contemporary Party-state, even if at times some are also the most articulate critics of specific actions and policy settings of the Party-state, particularly wanting it to be more efficient and just. As might readily be expected, they demand property protection and support for higher-educational expansion, but are also outspoken critics of the wider inequalities in society, of the lack of government accountability and of public-sector excess.

The lack of a desire for regime change is not hard to understand. As Zhang Li points out, the middle class is characterized by its 'heightened sense of security' (Zhang Li 2010: 7). Partly, but not exclusively, because of their increasing wealth and investment in housing (amongst other things) there is a fear of radical change. Particularly for the older members of the middle classes, these fears are heightened by residual concerns from the political past. House ownership in urban China on a substantial scale only started during the 1990s. Enterprise ownership has evolved greatly since 1992, but is still often substantially dependent on local institutional arrangements (Hendrischke 2013).

The Party-state still plays a role in most activities that involve members of the urban middle class, and indeed a substantial proportion of the professional and managerial middle classes owe their position and standing to the state. Overall, the proximity to the Party-state determines the extent of each element of the middle classes' support for the current regime. Repeated surveys have demonstrated that the closer members of the middle class are to the institutions of the Party-state, the more those individuals do not wish to see regime change (Wang and Davis 2010: 172). To quote Jie Chen on the politics of the PRC's middle class: 'the value and material bonds between the middle class and the state significantly affect the orientation of the middle class toward democratic change' (Jie Chen 2013: 90).

In addition, it is also clear that the Party-state has acted where necessary to ensure a closer relationship with social groups that might otherwise present challenges to the regime. The Party-state's accommodation of private entrepreneurs and the latter's increasing embeddedness in the political system is a good example of this process. Another example is the development of the Party-state's policy towards university teachers. At the start of the reform era, university teachers were rapidly becoming dissatisfied. Compared to others with similar educational and social backgrounds, their salaries seemed to be going backwards, and many were forced to take second jobs. A small but vocal minority were involved in reform activity during the 1980s that stepped beyond the Party-state's acceptable limits (Wright 2010: 72). In the wake of the events of 1989 in Beijing where both students and academic staff served in leadership positions, the government moved to improve salaries and conditions for university teachers. A new relationship with the Party-state was established, particularly during the late 1990s when university staff, as members of the state sector, were privileged through the processes of housing reform. As Tang and Unger conclude from their survey of university teachers during 2007–9: 'The Chinese educated middle class has, as a whole, become a bulwark of the current regime. As a consequence, regime change or democratization should not be expected any time soon. The rise of China's educated middle class blocks the way' (Tang and Unger 2013: 109).

There remains a small group of university academics advocating regime change in their writings and activities, but the vast majority, including the additional almost a million new university teachers appointed since 1998, are regime-supporting. Many are CCP members; others serve in government and state agency positions (Zheng Yongnian 2006: 250; Wright 2010: 76), though it nonetheless remains the case that they may be disproportionately in favour of political reform within the current system (Li Chunling 2013: 32).

Lawyers are another element of the middle classes distinctly in favour of political reform but not apparently seeking dramatic regime change. Lawyers certainly articulate a demand for the development of a rule of law, and their rhetoric is occasionally extremely liberal. At the same time, lawyers are most concerned about their own vulnerability in a system where rights between lawyers, clients and the state are not clearly delineated, or even often knowable. Their requirement is protection of their rights as lawyers, and the protection of others in their dealings with the state rather than regime change (Michelson and Liu 2010: 328).

Alongside this general acquiescence to the political system, the various sections of the middle classes have been both active in defence of their own interests and even to some extent critical (if variably) of wider issues, such as social policy, government accountability and the role of the state sector in economic development. A good example of the middle classes acting in defence of their own interests has come in the development of homeowners' movements (Cai 2005; Chen Peng 2009). As might be expected, given that the commercialization of housing has led to new gated communities, a whole new set of relationships has emerged involving local governments, real-estate developers, homeowners and a whole range of contractors involved in their construction and maintenance. A new political calculus has emerged in which homeowners have necessarily had to act and to organize in order to ensure a measure of control over the living environment that they have paid for. From his study of homeowners' movements, Rocca argues these changes may well be more significant for political change in China than any attempt to create a liberal-democratic revolution. Homeowners' movements:

> have allied with some powerful people and ruling groups, they promote liberalization, which is the objective of the vast majority of the population, they are able to convince the political apparatus to adopt new laws, and they increase their influence on the decision-making process. It is probably less exciting for observers than to wait for 'big change' but it may be more efficient in a long-term perspective. (Rocca 2013: 132–3)

Research into the core social values of different classes suggests that there is a range of satisfaction and happiness, with current conditions largely determined by the level of benefits received. Unsurprisingly, there is a high correlation between those who consider themselves the beneficiaries of the reform era and those who view the system as fair (Han and Whyte 2009: 206; Li Chunling 2013: 28). But this is not a simple, linear relationship. In particular, the professional and managerial middle classes have developed a concern with both social injustice and the extent of inequality. Those who are more educated tend to emphasize the 'external and unfair' explanations of inequality (Han and Whyte 2009: 204–5).

As Ching Kwan Lee details from her interviews in Beijing, members of the middle class are highly critical of examples of social injustice, and particularly the imbalances created by political power. As she concludes:

> even the upwardly mobile professional and middle classes, the 'winners' in the reform process, do not always find a just society. Expressing discontent about inequity in the legal system, they point to corruption and subordination of the court to the government, and usurpation of central government regulations and laws by local government. (Lee 2009: 227)

The injustice of socio-political settings is a theme explored often by the intermediate middle classes, particularly those elements who are or have been cadres or in the professions. Professor Sun Liping of Tsinghua University is just one such commentator who has written repeatedly in a high moral tone for over a decade, criticizing not the fact of the Party-state but its excesses, the dysfunction of the state sector of the economy and the path dependence of political power (Sun Liping 2002, 2006, 2013).

A NEW WORKING CLASS

Although the emphasis in explaining regime maintenance and change usually focuses on the elite, the working classes play an equally important role. How the working class reacts and interacts with the dominant class will greatly impact regime maintenance, not least by virtue of facilitating or hindering economic activities (Savage 2000: 153). In the case of the PRC, where the working classes have legitimacy and authority to act by virtue of the CCP's ideology, any additional movement or organization of the working class may have the potential to be even more politically significant.

China's contemporary working class has been the subject of much debate but little agreement. As was noted in chapter 5, there has been debate over whether SOE employees in the Mao era should have been regarded as a class or a status group because they were defined by their residence and employment. There remains doubt about whether public-sector workers remain a status group of that kind, still dependent on their relationship with management rather than having developed an independent class consciousness and activism. There is also debate about whether workers in the marketized sector of the economy, and the migrant workers in particular, are a new working class in the making: a class in itself or a class for itself (Leung and Pun 2009). This is a debate within Marxism that reaches back to Marx and the middle of the nineteenth century. A distinction is made between working-class action and proletarian consciousness, with only the latter being able to deliver revolutionary social change and universal liberation. The weight of opinion from published research is that while the old working class (in the public sector) has been considerably disempowered by the changes of the reform era, the new working class (largely migrant workers in the marketized sector of the economy) has yet to become sufficiently organized to pose much of a challenge beyond local activism, and the prospect of cooperation between the two segments of the working class remains low.

The possibility of two different trajectories for public-sector and other workers has led some to argue there are essentially two different labour movements (Anita Chan 1995: 36), if not two working classes, reinforced by regional variation (Rocca 2003: 93). Of course, there is always the possibility that in the longer term the two labour movements may find that their circumstances and interests merge. In the short term, however, this seems unlikely, not only because public-sector workers still see themselves as superior, but also because workers in the marketized sector of the economy, especially migrant workers, may not see any necessary unity of identity with public-sector workers. As one migrant worker in Beijing commented, on the difference with public-sector employees:

> They have [welfare] guarantees, but we have the freedom. They go to work in the morning and come home in the afternoon. Our situation is different: we work when there are projects for us to do, but play when there is none. We're not under any constraints [to work everyday]. (Guang 2005: 498)

Moreover, as Dorothy Solinger has pointed out, public-sector workers (employed and otherwise) and migrant workers see themselves as in competition: while the latter group is upwardly mobile, the former is in decline (Solinger 2002: 311). As the number of laid-off workers increased during the late 1990s with the restructuring of the public sector, newly available jobs were reserved for the laid-off former public-sector workers, and migrant workers were excluded from employment (Solinger 1999a: 115). Migrant workers, for example, were excluded from thirty-five types of job in Beijing and twenty-four in Wuhan (Solinger 2002: 314). Although public-sector and migrant workers may have sensed competition, there is evidence that the urban labour market has to date been more segmented than competitive, with three tiers: non-retrenched urban workers, re-employed urban workers and migrant workers (Appleton et al. 2006b).

Given the development of the marketized sector of the economy and the role of migrant workers, the question arises as to whether the labouring classes outside the public sector have become or are becoming a new working class. The structures of labour exploitation certainly exist, protests and industrial action by workers have increased, and there are many willing to describe the new industrial relations that have emerged (if not the system) as 'capitalist' (Wang, Appelbaum et al. 2009: 486). Commentators outside the PRC are divided on this issue, from those who regard labour protests as solely enterprise specific, to those who argue that there is not only emerging class conflict but even a heightened class consciousness and class activism, even though class organization is restricted by the Party-state's agenda.

Ching Kwan Lee, in her studies first of migrant women in South China (Ching Kwan Lee 1998) and then later of labour protests in both the North-east and the South (Ching Kwan Lee 2007), sees no evidence of class formation in any way. Her argument is that migrant workers have considerably less class consciousness than the laid-off public-sector workers and are more concerned with the development of their citizenship rights (Ching Kwan Lee 2005). Indeed, to the extent that they have class consciousness, she argues that this is as peasants rather than workers. Moreover, she emphasizes that migrant workers focus on individual action and rarely take collective action to improve working conditions. They focus on economic issues and do not have a political agenda (Ching Kwan Lee 2007: 315). The view that the migrant working class remains a class in itself, and has not yet become a class for itself, is a view on the whole shared by many others. At the same time, there is also a recognition that the ties that bind migrant workers to the Party-state are thinner than for other workers, and that economic growth and development may not guarantee the maintenance of that relationship. In other words, migrant workers may have been major beneficiaries of reform policies, but still more reform (particularly, for example, household registration reform) will be required to ensure continued regime support from migrant workers (Rocca 2003: 90; Wright 2010: 133–5).

Perry Leung and Alvin So, through an examination of protests in the garment and textile industry of South China, agree that the industrial action of the migrant workers tends to be focused on the enterprise or the local authority responsible, rather than on a wider political agenda. As they point out, the migrant workers do not call themselves workers, but 'peasant workers' (*nong gong* 农工), not least because they and their families do not have an urban household registration (So 2012: 87). Nonetheless, Leung and So still argue that 'the migrant working class will inevitably transform itself into a more militant, active agency to shape the development of China in the twenty-first century and beyond' (Leung and So 2012: 78). This argument is based on the events of 2010, which they see as suggestive of a qualitative increase in class activism. There was a series of high-profile and fairly large-scale strikes, some of which led to riots in May and June, and four of which took place in Honda factories. One result of these industrial actions was that workers received approval for their request to establish an independent trade union (independent of the All-China Federation of Trade Unions (ACFTU) and the Party-state) which would be democratically elected. The minimum wage was raised considerably in South China and factory subcontractors were required, after a number of legal judgments, to pay (or repay) wages, deposits and a number of charges that had been levied and that were now regarded as 'unreasonable'.

Chris Chan and Pun Ngai, both separately and together (Chris Chan and Pun Ngai 2009; Chris Chan 2012, 2013), have been most positive in their assessment of the emergence of a new working class.

Their research is based on the analysis of industrial activism by migrant workers (also) in the Pearl River Delta of South China. The argument is that increased activism by migrant workers in defence of their economic interests from the 1980s up to the present has resulted in the development of an increasingly acute class consciousness. 'Through their collective actions, workers' class consciousness and strategies towards class organization have steadily advanced in the process of China's integration into the global economy' (Chris Chan 2013: 131). From the analysis of early 1980s small strikes, followed in the 1990s by industrial action that was greater in scale and impact, through to the major strikes (also analysed by Leung and So) of 2010, they see a widening agenda of political as well as economic interests. In this interpretation, the 1980s strikes were about employment conditions and expectations and were largely short, wildcat strikes, not only without union involvement but where the union worked with management to restore industrial order; in the 1990s, strikes were usually concerned with inadequate pay rates, larger in scale, and occasionally attempted to establish independent trade unions; and in the years immediately after China's accession to the WTO (December 2001) there was an increasing labour shortage (Bruni 2011), with strikes being more concerned with employment conditions, including contracts, continuing appointments and severance, leading to partially successful attempts by workers' representatives to establish local unions. The Honda and related strikes of 2010 concerned a substantial pay rise for all workers, but they were also expressing the demand that workers should be able to choose their own democratically elected representatives and trade union leaders, and to establish an independent union, because they saw existing unions as not representing their interests.

The historical dimension of this argument is important. Unlike the workers in the public sector, migrant workers initially had no recent tradition of industrial relations on which to draw. Almost thirty years of migrant-worker experience have inevitably been something of a learning experience, even if there has been turnover in the composition of the migrant-worker labour force. There are now 'second-generation migration workers'. This term refers not to children of migrant workers in the cities who have known no other experience (though there are such children) so much as the second generation in families who have left the countryside to become migrant workers in the cities. It is argued that these second-generation migrant workers have a different attitude to their socio-economic identity, which includes a higher degree of class consciousness and attitude to activism. Moreover, they see themselves as both workers and peasants, and not peasants or peasant workers (Chan and Pun 2010; Pun and Lu 2010b). Indeed, in some cases they even refer to themselves as 'new workers' (Qiu and Wang 2012).

At the same time, historical considerations are also the reason why Anita Chan and Kaxton Siu urge caution in proclaiming the arrival of a new working class (Chan and Siu 2012). Their analysis also works through the (by now) familiar ground of industrial activism in South China during the last three decades. In contrast, however, to Leung, So, Pun (and others), they place their findings in an even longer historical perspective (in China and elsewhere) that highlights the different stages in the emergence of working-class consciousness. Chan and Siu see recent industrial actions as coming from narrow self-interest, with little organization or wider political goals. In their view, industrial action has been neither rights-based (appealing to legal frameworks, such as the various enterprise and labour-contract legislation), nor interest-based (appealing beyond the immediate workplace to include workers elsewhere). Moreover, Chan and Siu argue that striking workers rarely campaign for the election or re-election of workplace trade-union officials, and that even when they do they have still tended to place their trust in official unions and authority generally. In sum, Chan and Siu identify an embryonic trade-union consciousness rather than a new (as yet) working-class consciousness. As they conclude: 'The emergence of a class for itself takes longer than one or two generations. Thus, despite the expectation that this second generation of migrant workers will push through to a new stage of class consciousness, reality militates against this expectation' (Chan and Siu 2012: 99).

In their view, one of those realities is a Party-state concerned that workers' economic demands may indeed become political demands. Another is that 'In a state-controlled society in which the political climate is kept non-ideological . . . migrant workers have little to inspire them to understand their own class position' (Chan and Siu 2012: 99).

PEASANT ACTIVISM

Increased peasant activism is regarded as a potential major challenge to the Party-state not simply because of the latter's control settings, but also because of the origins of the CCP's successful revolution in the pre-1949 countryside and its mobilization of the peasantry. Certainly, peasant activism resulted in a large number of rural protests that started during the 1990s and came to a crescendo in the first decade of the century. Tens and hundreds of thousands of people were involved, violence and death were not uncommon and several hundred million *yuan* RMB of damage was done. On the other hand, these activities have been limited in their political impact. Despite the introduction of some elements of capitalist agriculture (Q. F. Zhang 2008), proletarianization of the rural working population has remained limited because of the household registration system and because of the ways in which decollectivization was implemented and land-usage has developed (Sargeson 1999; Huang, Gao and Peng 2012). The individual's close connection to the village, family and land means that, as a result, peasant collective action has tended to be local and narrowly focused on economic self-interest. Even when governance issues have been an issue for activism, the starting point has been economic self-interest.

Local economic pressures were surely the driver for the transformation of the rural economy during the 1980s, both through increased agricultural production and the development of rural industry in the form of TVEs. Peasant productivity was released by decollectivization and the introduction of the household responsibility system. Across China as a whole the results were dramatic: grain production rose 5 per cent per annum between 1979 and 1984; agricultural output value rose 7.6 per cent per annum (Wright 2010: 139). Commentators later debated the cause. On one side were those who lauded peasant activism (Zhou K. Xiao 1996). The argument was (to quote Lynn White) that during the late 1970s and early 1980s 'the reform syndrome was generally foisted on China's most famous leaders by myriad ex-farmer leaders whose names are not publicly known' (White 1998: 151). The counter-arguments either saw rural reform as a strategic initiative of the new post-Mao leadership, or argued that rural reform was an idea whose time had come. The CCP provided the reform framework that the peasants were able to take advantage of to good effect (Kelliher 1992; Henriot and Shi 1996).

The context for the widespread protests that emerged during the 1990s was a growing economy, administrative reform and, to some extent, Central Government's inattention to rural affairs (Bernstein and Lu 2000). Quite apart from the generally increased cost of managing local economic development for local government, education and health costs were almost totally devolved to townships and villages. Townships have been made responsible for about 80 per cent of revenue in these areas. In addition, villages became responsible for tax collection, family planning and elderly care (Kennedy 2007). Taxes and fees to support these activities were raised but the system was inherently flawed. The fiscal burden was generally way in excess of the 5 per cent that had been announced as a 'reasonable burden'; taxes and fees were levied in an extremely regressive manner so that the poor paid more than the rich and there were no mechanisms of accountability. From the administrative perspective, the decentralized burden presaged crisis (Oi and Zhao 2007). For the peasants it was a recipe for protest, which followed in many places. In their study of rural protest, Bernstein and Lu cite a complainant from 1998:

> It is both reasonable and lawful for the peasants to pay grain (taxes). We peasants are not confused about this. But they just take money from us in a muddled way. We give grain and don't know which 'lord's' (*laoye*) pocket it ends up in. (Bernstein and Lu 2000: 745)

Protest led to demands for independent organizations, detention of local Party committee members, and calls for greater equalization of wealth, sometimes expressed in the language of class. The solutions proposed by the Party-state included the abolition of the Agricultural Tax, restrictions on other fees, and the development of a programme to establish a New Socialist Countryside. A particular feature of this changed rural environment is the introduction of a measure of village accountability with the establishment of village elections and village committees.

The policies of the New Socialist Countryside Programme have certainly not resolved all tensions in the countryside, but they have directed these into more manageable channels, and ones that are acceptable to the Party-state. Whether they are acceptable to the peasants is a different question. There have been complaints that village elections are dominated by the wealthy (Guang and Zheng 2005) and, as Melanie Manion concludes from her study of rural elections, the peasants still 'associate growing inequality with the low moral scruples of those with wealth and power' (Manion 2006: 314).

One area of continuing severe tension, and one where peasant activism is occasionally manifest, is the issue of land development. Although it was only in 2013 that the CCP formalized its policy of encouraging urbanization on a grand scale, it is a process that has been going on for some time. Urbanization has two component parts: the expansion of existing cities and the development of small rural towns into larger cities. In either case, urbanization involves the transformation of farmland into something else, whether it is land for residential real estate, commercial or community use. Particularly after the abolition of the Agricultural Tax, local governments that have been strapped for cash have seen the transformation of farmland as a sure way of raising revenue, by effectively selling land-use rights (there is technically no possibility of a market in land) or by participating in projects as developers or development partners (Tian Li 2008; Hsing 2010: 155ff.). It is estimated that between 1980 and 2003, some 50–66 million peasants lost all or part of their farmland and houses, amounting to about 13 per cent of China's total cultivatable land (Hsing 2010: 182–3).

The processes of land-use purchase, rights assignment and project development are far from transparent. Sometimes land-use is transferred with compensation, sometimes local governments enforce compulsory reassignment, sometimes developers uphold arrangements made with peasants (as well as local authorities) and sometimes peasants find they have subsequent difficulties. A 2011 survey across seventeen provinces found that 43.1 per cent of villages had experienced the transformation of some farmland for non-agricultural purposes since the late 1990s. Some compensation was received in 77.5 per cent of cases, compensation was promised but not delivered in 9.8 per cent of cases and compensation was neither promised nor received in 12.7 per cent of cases. The average compensation paid to peasants was 18,739 *yuan* RMB per *mu*, while authorities received an average of 778,000 *yuan* RMB per *mu* for the land for later development. Moreover, 17.8 per cent of cases of land transfer were the result of forced evictions (Landesa 2012).

Even without forced evictions, a well-known situation is where a peasant agrees to give up their land in return for an urban household registration and housing, but then finds they not only have no community as they did in the past, but also have no livelihood. There is considerable potential for distrust of local officials and for local resistance. It is not surprising that there have been large protests, especially on the fringes of the larger cities. You-tien Hsing quotes the work of Yu Jianrong (of CASS) to the effect that:

> land grabs and forced evictions have become the primary cause of peasants' protests since 2000. Compared to the tax protests of the 1990s, land-related protests tend to be larger and feature more frequent clashes between peasants and police forces. Violence, severe injury, and death are now more common than in the 1990s. (Hsing 2010: 183)

All the same, as You-tien Hsing herself argues, the very processes of land and peasant transformation that lie at the heart of these protests have essentially disempowered the protestors. Relocation destroys trust in the village, and can easily turn the peasant from being a member of a collective into an anomic, and usually very poor, urban resident (Hsing 2010: 191–200).

On the other hand, not all contemporary peasant activism is so desperate. Peasant consciousness has also led to the emergence of urban or peri-urban corporatist villages, sometimes referred to as 'villages in the city'. The peasants in these urban corporatist villages are clearly not dependent on their labour for their livelihood, but the urban corporatist villages do exemplify the argument about peasant actions developing from local and from economic self-interest. They are mainly to be found in Guangdong Province's Pearl River Delta (Hsing 2010: 122ff.; Unger 2012b; Saich and Hu 2012) though something similar also emerged at a fairly early stage of reform in Zhejiang and Jiangsu Provinces (Goodman 1995).

As urban areas started to develop rapidly with reform, local authorities were prepared to strike deals with villages in their jurisdictions that permitted the village to (in practice) retain land for development and residential purposes in return for some surrender of farmland. One result was that the built environment in the village rapidly became indistinguishable from the city surrounding it. Another was that the villagers, who of course stopped engaging in agricultural activities equally rapidly, nonetheless retained their rural household registration. This essentially meant both that the villagers were no longer totally the local urban authority's responsibility for some aspects of their welfare, and that the village to some extent became a self-governing entity. These corporatist villages established shareholding corporations to run their economic activities, and encouraged firms (usually foreign investors) to come and establish factories and production lines on their land, providing housing, jobs, and welfare to their shareholders, and also distributing regular dividends to the shareholding members of the village.

In the corporatist villages, the institutions of the Party-state (village government, Party committee) work together closely with the shareholder corporation and this interaction is usually reinforced by family relationships. In the Pearl River Delta, corporatist villages are almost always based on the local lineage. These family relationships underline the social continuities that extend not just from the early period of the PRC to the reform era, but also from before 1949. In these corporatist villages too, the shareholders are not by any means the labouring workforce. The shareholders are the original inhabitants of the village and their descendants, who hold a local household registration. In Yantian, for example, where the Deng lineage holds sway, there are some 3,000 village resident shareholders in a population that fluctuates with economic activity between 60,000 and 150,000 (Saich and Hu: 2012: 58). In Xiqiao, it is estimated that the Chens, whose village it is, number no more than 2 per cent of the people to be found on the land of the village at any one time. As Jonathan Unger makes clear from his research there over three decades, Chen Village has become a class-based society in which each class is determined by their market position and lifestyle, and certainly knows its own place. He describes the Chens as the local capitalist class, but as he also points out they are by no means the wealthiest people in the village, and they are not held in particularly high esteem by the factory owners, factory managers or the educated, with many of the Chens being distinctly lower-middle class in their lifestyle (Unger 2012b: 29–36).

INEQUALITY AND REGIME LEGITIMACY

Increased inequality and a far higher incidence of public protest have become matters of concern to the leaders of the Party-state, as well as having led some outside the PRC to question whether the regime's legitimacy is under attack (He 2003; Chung, Lai and Xia 2006). For some years (2000–13) the NBS did not publish details of China's Gini coefficent, though admitting when the practice restarted in 2013 that the degree of income inequality had reached a level that gave concern for future social stability (Xinhua 21 January 2013). Public manifestations of dissent of various kinds have indeed risen from 8,700 incidents in 1993 to possibly 230,000 in 2010. While the challenge to the regime from rising inequality should not be minimized, research in China and elsewhere suggests that inequality itself is less the problem than issues of procedural justice and expectation management. Research into revolutions elsewhere in the second half of the last century suggest that while mass unrest is a necessary condition for regime change, it is not a sufficient condition: there is also a need for simultaneously both a state crisis and a divided elite (Goldstone 1991).

Criticism of the rising inequality, and particularly that centred on those 'within the system', is widespread in China's various social media and beyond, especially when position and power are thought to have been abused (Luo Changping 2013). Considerable moral indignation is expressed about both inequality and corruption, with which it is almost inevitably associated, though it is often difficult to know where on the one hand corruption ends, and on the other privilege and inequality begin (Zang 2008). Sun Liping, Professor of Sociology at Tsinghua University in Beijing, has been a powerful voice in this debate, arguing that until the corruption of the political ruling class is brought to heel, it will not be possible to go further in dealing with inequality either. He has called for China to 'build a society which is just and fair', starting with the development of institutions to control corruption (Sun Liping 2006). Most stridently, he has explicitly in his blog linked wealth, government and corruption:

> In the 21st century, China's two most obvious characteristics have been the inflation of power and the failure of power, and these two have become intertwined. The process of the strengthening of the government's capacity to extract resources . . . concentrated more and more money in the hands of the government. And he who has wealth speaks loudest. . . . Vested interests have now become entrenched, the result being tremendous social unfairness. In dealing with this social unfairness, the government has been utterly helpless. It has turned to stability preservation in the hope of ensuring unwelcome things don't happen . . . Recently I raised the issue of the 'license to do evil.' In stability preservation, the overriding concern is that 'nothing happens,' and no one pays any attention to how you achieve that goal. Whatever abuse of power you commit can be justified in the name of stability preservation. (Sun Liping 2013)

An anti-corruption campaign was launched at the end of 2012. In January 2013, President of the PRC and General-Secretary of the CCP Xi Jinping spoke of the corrosive impact of official corruption and the need not only to stop the activities of officials engaged in such illegal practices, but also to ensure that they are held to account. It was a theme he enlarged on further at the National People's Congress (NPC) in March 2013 (Xi 2013). One problem is that some instances and types of corruption exist because without them for structural reasons the system cannot work (Smith 2009). All the same the taking of bribes, the sale of offices and favours, and the abuse of power for excessive personal gain are not only part of the explanation for so much hidden 'grey income' but also regarded by the CCP itself as likely to prove counterproductive to its attempt to retain popular legitimacy.

There are some obvious targets in the public debate. Government and Party officials with extramarital affairs and mistresses are a favoured media item. Indeed, the number of affairs and mistresses is often regarded as an indicator of the level of corruption (Osburg 2013: 175). Consumption and lifestyles have changed dramatically within living memory, especially in the areas of housing, education, travel and personal transport. Typical are the comments (from a researcher at the CASS Institute of Sociology) regarding those 'government officials and entrepreneurs . . . [who] . . . have several sets of condos and buy the best cars . . . their children go abroad at their own expense . . . There is a lot of space and almost a bottomless pit for rent-seeking by those with power' (Yan Ye 2012: 202, 215). China even has a well-established urban myth of the BMW owner who is able to draw the *dibao*.

Inequality more generally is also publicly acknowledged. In February 2013, the State Council issued a detailed thirty-five-point programme for reducing inequality, which included signalling measures to reign in 'hidden income' and requiring SOEs to pay an additional 5 per cent of profits into an expanded social security fund (State Council 2013). A particular target of criticism concerns the children of the wealthy and the powerful, for whom neologisms have been developed: the *fuerdai* (富二代), 'second generation from the rich', and the *guanerdai* (官二代), 'second generation from officials'. While there is some greater tolerance of their parents for having bettered themselves, this does not hold true at all for their children, who often appear in the wider public consciousness to be privileged almost beyond belief (luxury cars, overseas education, exotic holidays, designer clothes) and to do little beyond engaging in ostentatious consumption. Where they are caught behaving badly in public, howls of outrage follow. Where this extends to criminal acts and apparently lenient treatment because of whose children they are, the moral outrage rises exponentially (Oster 2009).

Among social scientists outside China recent research has suggested that neither inequality nor social unrest may be regime threatening. Political change is not the point of the increased number of public manifestations of dissent (Kennedy 2009), nor inequality in itself, but a sense of injustice, largely related to land disputes, environmental issues, labour and ethnic conflicts. In the words of one recent report: 'Social unrest should not be seen as a form of resistance but as a form of participation' (Göbel and Ong 2012: 21). This confirms the results of an earlier large-scale survey that emphasized the greater salience of procedural over distributive justice concerns (Whyte 2010a). This is not to say that there are no class differences in the appreciation of inequality. One study of Beijing revealed:

> most working class respondents mentioned income (wages or pensions) while middle class professionals saw inequality in the uneven distribution of property, life style and status ... The market was widely accepted as an institution for allocating rewards but ordinary people also believed that undue advantages accrued to political elites, and that this seriously compromised the inherent fairness of the market. (Lee 2009: 216)

Moreover, attitudes to inequality are not always associated with occupation and position in society. Resentment of economic inequality is high among urban workers, the urban unemployed and rural migrant workers, but rural residents are considerably more accepting. For their part, the rich and the educated are highly critical of the lack of equal opportunity and extrinsic factors in the creation of inequality even when, as must sometimes be the case, they are also prime beneficiaries (Han and Whyte 2009: 202–5). The comments of a retired cadre are not untypical: 'Under Chairman Mao, workers' pensions and medical care were the same as cadres. Everything was guaranteed. But today, you see, cadres have got everything, cars, a house, and money. What do the laid-offs have today? No wonder they feel left out' (Tang 2013: 66).

Social and economic difference, inequality, feelings of inequality and their role in the formation of class and class identity are the subject of the concluding chapter.

7 Conclusion
Inequality and Class

Explaining social change in China is never easy, not least because of its size, scale and inherent diversity. The socio-economic environment is variable, as might be expected given the size of the population, not just by province, but within provinces. In every province there are distinct subcultures that interact variably with localized economies, social bases of power and political traditions. Moreover, generalizing about social change is also difficult given the speed and intensity of the transformations still under way. In particular, the reform-oriented 3rd Plenum of the 18th Central Committee of the CCP which met in November 2013 signalled changes to the finance and banking systems, the convergence of economic management practices in the public sector and the marketized economy, the development of new solutions to welfare provision, and an almost aggressive programme of urbanization – all of which are likely to impact greatly on structures of class and social stratification.

While the PRC has been transformed since 1978, there remains a need to maintain perspective not only on what has changed, but also on what has not changed or not been achieved. China's GDP grew by a factor of 130 between 1978 and 2011. The growth in the economy has been spectacular, but GDP per capita remains limited (2013) at US$9,300 (PPP). This compares to US$50,700 for the USA or US$37,500 for the United Kingdom. The PRC's 2013 GDP per capita is at roughly the same level the Soviet Union was in 1989 – US$9,211 (CIA *The World Factbook* 1990, 2013).

Despite occasional appearances to the contrary, the period since 1978 has seen the development of a reforming socialist market economy, not the breakdown of Communist rule and the establishment of a capitalist or similar system. Stephen Halper's comment that 'capitalism is now a global phenomenon – with China among its greatest champions' (Halper 2010: 1) is entertaining, but it is not accurate. The PRC now has elements of a redistributive economy as well as elements of a market economy. While the two often coexist uneasily, the Party-state and its redistributive economy are always politically superior to the market economy. The 3rd Plenum of 2013 spelt out its intent in this regard quite specifically. In its formal Decision, it went way beyond the injunction to 'Bear in mind that China is still in the primary stage of socialism' to explain that

> The basic economic system with public ownership playing a dominant role and different economic sectors developing side by side is an important pillar of the socialist system with Chinese characteristics and is the foundation of the socialist market economy. Both the public and non-public sectors are key components of the socialist market economy, and are important bases for the economic and social development of China. We must unswervingly consolidate and develop the public economy, persist in the dominant position of public ownership, give full play to the leading role of the state-owned sector, and continuously increase its vitality, controlling force and influence. We must unwaveringly encourage, support and guide the development of the non-public sector, and stimulate its dynamism and creativity. (CCP Central Committee 2013)

The 3rd Plenum emphasized the need for economic resources to be allocated through the market, though also highlighting the role of the state intervening to correct 'the imperfections of the market'. The balance may change as a result in the future, but the evidence of development to the end of 2013 remains one where the public sector and the Party-state dominate. The Party-state and its cadres still allo-cate economic resources, though no longer through a national Plan, and more usually at the local level (Oi 1995; Schubert and Ahlers 2012). Certainly there is a labour market, but it is maintained in its present form by the state's household registration system which deter-mines the creation of a migrant peasant-worker reserve pool of labour, and which has not been slated for removal. The economic return on being a cadre clearly extends beyond salary, and there is considerable material benefit from being part of a cadre's family. Entrepreneurs, for their part, even those outside the public sector, may take management decisions for political and social rather than economic reasons (Xie and Wu 2008: 560). The state sector of the economy remains domi-nant in many ways despite no longer producing the majority of GDP. The 3rd Plenum of 2013 has adopted a strategy to rectify macro-economic management issues, but to date the banking system has worked to support SOEs overwhelmingly more than other kinds of enterprises, with destabilizing consequences for the entire economy.

In their description of other examples of a 'socialist mixed economy' from Eastern Europe, which emerged during the 1980s as socialist states were experimenting with marketization, Szelényi and Kostello emphasized that the resultant political economy was neither state socialism nor capitalism (a 'capitalist-oriented economy'). In an analysis that could equally apply to the more recent situation in the PRC, they highlighted that in those cases of market socialism the prime benefici-aries of change and the new mixed system were not the capitalists, but rather 'young technocrats and self-interested cadres, the sons and daughters of cadres' (Szelényi and Kostello 1998: 317).

Inequality is a universal social phenomenon. The issue for the analy-sis of any society is not whether there is inequality, but how inequality is conceptualized and managed in society and by the state, as well as the consequences. In particular, if there are relationships between dif-ferent kinds of inequality leading to compound inequalities, and if those compound inequalities are institutionalized over time and have a social base, then there may be a strong basis for identifying classes and a class structure. At the same time, though, this does not imply that the class structure has the same meaning for those living and working in the society as it does for the external analyst: that will depend on the degree of self-awareness and self-identity.

In the case of the PRC, it is clear that there is not only significant economic inequality, but that there are also inequalities of power, social status, culture and lifestyle. It is also clear that these inequalities reinforce one another and are shaped further through the intergenerational transfer of both privilege and disadvantage. There is an apparent emerging class structure that has both been shaped by developments over the period of the PRC, and has its origins in pre-1949 China.

There is a new dominant class of the politically powerful and the wealthy that has begun to emerge both out of the Party-state, and to some extent from the pre-revolutionary local elite. There is a well-established professional and managerial middle class that exists largely under the protection of the Party-state where it is not actually staffing its institutions, and similar close links exist between the Party-state and the entrepreneurial middle class. Last, but by no means least, there are several subordinate classes: among urban residents there are workers in the public sector, laid-off workers, workers in the marketized sector of the economy, and the self-employed; among rural residents there are long-term migrant peasant workers living in urban China, other migrant workers in urban China, migrant peasant workers in rural enterprises, off-farm workers, agricultural labourers, the rural self-employed and peasant farmers.

As of 2013, the weight of evidence suggests that the dominant class is no more than 3 per cent of the population, the middle classes amount to about 12 per cent, and the subordinate classes 85 per cent in total. Understandably, given the PRC's experience before 1978, the public political articulation of class and class conflict is sometimes quite muted, and public expressions of self-awareness and self-identity in class terms seem similarly limited. All the same, the language and ideas of class are never far below the surface, not least because class remains an essential part of the educational curriculum.

INEQUALITY

In the PRC, inequality is often understood only in terms of economic inequality, if only because there are apparent (though often spurious) ready quantifications. Much discussion, for example, has attended the calculation of the Gini coefficient even though, in addition to any problems in statistical analysis, application of the Gini coefficient to the PRC in quite the same way it might be applied to the USA or the economically developed states of Western Europe might not be appropriate. One of the most widely repeated claims related to the Gini coefficient generally is that social stability is threatened when it passes 0.4. This view is widely accepted within the PRC (e.g., Fang and Yu 2012). Yet it is clear that less economically developed countries are also likely to be more unequal as reflected in the Gini coefficient, and that economies with a higher GDP per capita are likely to have lower Gini coefficients (Maddison 2007). A Gini coefficient of 0.48, then, for the PRC when GDP per capita is US$9,300 (PPP) is not quite the same as it might be for other countries with both high GDP per capita and the same level of equality indicated by a Gini coefficient calculation.

At the same time, there clearly is considerable economic inequality in the PRC. Though the precise figure is contested, there is a significant rural–urban economic inequality, most likely of the order of 1:3. The NBS acknowledges that the top 10 per cent of households control about 32 per cent of income, although it also acknowledges that its calculations struggle to incorporate the wealth of the rich (Orlik 2012). Other calculations have different, more unequal, results. The China

Household Finance Survey estimated in 2012 that 10 per cent of households earned 56 per cent of income (Li Gan 2012). In 2013, the China Household Finance Survey estimated that the top 10 per cent of households had 86 per cent of total household assets, and that the top 1 per cent of households had an average disposable income of 559,000 *yuan* RMB a year, while the bottom 25 per cent had an average of 10,800 *yuan* RMB (Li Gan 2013).

Though revealing, the focus on economic inequality in these ways runs the risk of diverting attention from wider interpretations of inequality and its consequences. Whyte's large-scale study, based on research undertaken in 2004, emphasized that objective economic inequality is largely accepted as a part of everyday life. It does not necessarily lead to resentment or action for social and political change (Whyte 2010a). There were, however, greater concerns with procedural justice that showed up in that research, and indeed elsewhere (Ching Kwan Lee 2009). Identification of those concerns suggests that other feelings of inequality may also be important in creating a heightened sense of injustice, and possibly lead to action, beyond perceptions of economic inequality.

There are clear inequalities in the exercise of political power, which can be seen both through the CCP's purposive actions, and where it fails to act (Guo 2013). The Party-state has never suggested that it allocates or manages the reallocation of resources equally. On the contrary, one reason for the CCP's concerns with class in its ideological formulations has been that they identify who is to be the current beneficiary of Party-state policy and action. Thus, peasants and workers were preferred during the 1950s; the workers, peasants and soldiers were privileged during the 1960s and 1970s; and in the reform era, the more 'advanced elements' of wealth creation, political leadership and nationalism came to be recognized in Jiang Zemin's 1990s theory of the 'Three Represents'. The embrace of the middle class since 2002 similarly fits into this schema, though perhaps with less precision. This inequality in the exercise of political power even extends ultimately to the discourse and determination of class, which has an essential role in the symbolic capital controlled by the CCP.

The experience of social change since 1978 provides ample examples of inequalities in social status and culture. Indeed, in China, culture and social status are often equated. Those who have been formally educated are assumed to have gained culture (or at least historically to be socialized in Chinese culture) and subsequently to be of higher social status. The push to identify the middle class, and even to expand its numbers, results in large part from an appreciation of such differences. Migrant peasant workers coming to the cities for work are assumed to have low status and no culture. Lacking in education, they are often regarded as inferior, especially by urban resident workers, all of whom have received some education. Even urban resident workers who have become unemployed tend to look down on migrant workers. There is strict market segmentation in terms of who will take what kind of employment. Unsurprisingly, the migrant workers themselves resent these inequalities, feeling themselves condemned from birth by the accident of a rural household registration and the denial of civil rights and welfare when they work in the cities (Pun and Lu 2010b). These differences between urban workers, migrant workers and the educated were even manifest at the time of the Tiananmen Square protests in May and June 1989. The student demonstrators refused to have anything to do with urban worker demonstrators until it was too late, and neither group worked closely with the migrant-worker demonstrators, who were relegated to an even more minor position in the square (Walder and Gong 1993).

Wanning Sun and Yingjie Guo have detailed the extent to which the PRC is characterized not just by an inequality of culture but also a culture of inequality (Sun and Guo 2013). The language of social interaction is shaped and to some extent limited by reference to education and self-improvement. It is here where the idea of *suzhi* plays a central role in highlighting difference. The emphasis is familiarly elitist in a Chinese context: those who have education are the role models even if the goal is to raise everyone's educational level. While the rhetoric may suggest improvement is possible, practice often delivers other outcomes, as Terry Woronov has also demonstrated through her study of vocational education (Woronov 2012).

Poverty, powerlessness and low social status reinforce one another, but so too do wealth, political power and high social status. The mutual dependence between, and association of, wealth and political power is perhaps most evident in the associational relationship between the Party-state and private entrepreneurs. There is not just a close working relationship between those with political power and those with economic wealth; the two overlap to a high, if precisely indefinable, degree. In addition, a substantial proportion of the entrepreneurs in the private sector, probably about a half, formerly worked in the Party-state, and about a fifth had been serving Party or government cadres.

The CCP has not only encouraged the economic behaviour of the newly emergent private entrepreneurs but, as each has become wealthier, has sought to involve them in the political process. At local levels this may involve the entrepreneur taking on a position of formal leadership in government or even the Party. Entrepreneurs are encouraged to join the CCP – as 'advanced elements' in society – and to serve as delegates to people's congresses and peoples' political consultative conferences at all levels, up to and including the national level (Minglu Chen 2011). Entrepreneurs for their part quickly came to realize the benefits of being involved in local networks of political power and social status. Research based on surveys of small businesses in 2004 and 2006 across thirty-one provinces found that:

> membership in business associations increases the probability of having a loan by 14.8%. . . . hours spent on hospitality and networking positively affect the probability of having loans from commercial banks.

One hour per day spent at social events increases the probability of having a loan by 3.7%. (Talavera et al. 2010)

The relationship between social status through education, on the one hand, and political power or wealth, on the other, is more complex. Formal education remains an important factor in explaining social status and mobility, and is clearly linked to wealth. In other societies, it is clearly the case that education, especially higher education, is the route to social mobility. The elite is formed by graduates from institutions of higher education, and usually from the better reputed of those. This has not been the case in the PRC, where before 1978 there was a distinct dualism in appointments to leadership positions: there were appointments to positions of administrative leadership determined by CCP membership and political performance, and appointments to elite positions in the professions based on educational attainment: 'College education made it more likely that an individual would become a high professional rather than an administrator, while party membership made it more likely that a person would become an administrator rather than a high professional' (Walder et al. 2000: 196). In the post-1978 era, a university education is also required for appointments to positions of administrative leadership. Additionally, appointment to decision-making positions is still determined by political performance and there remains a segmented process of elite appointment, with professional leadership positions resulting from educational success (Walder et al. 2000: 207).

The experience of the reform era has then left the PRC not just socially unequal, but also to a large extent acutely polarized. There is dramatically unequal access to public goods and social mobility between several different pairings of the privileged and the disadvantaged, each of which has permeated this volume. The first and most obvious is that between the rich and the poor (Solinger 2013), the comprehension of which is heightened by the knowledge that the officially recognized income of the richest 10 per cent may be understated by up to 60 per cent. Remarkably, it has been estimated that while the richest quarter of households by income spend 7 per cent of their income on education, the poorest quarter spend 371 per cent (Li Gan 2012: table 4). An equally obvious second pairing is that between those who hold an urban household registration and those who do not, and a (related but not identical) third is that between the urban and the rural areas. A fourth is that between the economically developed coastal areas – particularly those centred on the Pearl River Delta in the South and the Lower Yangtze Delta region of Zhejiang, Jiangsu and Shanghai in the East – and the less developed inland areas (Cartier 2013). A fifth concerns the differences between those 'within the system' of the Party-state, and those who are outside. This includes both those who worked and lived in the work-units of the Party-state at the beginning of the reform era and benefited from the restructuring of economic and social activity at that time, and those who did not (Tomba and Tang 2013), as well as those who continue to work 'within the system' – under the protection and with the support of the Party-state – and those who do not (Zhou Xueguang 2004; Guo 2013). In addition, there remains a clear gender divide in employment, in property ownership and in life chances (Sargeson 2013).

CLASS

Clearly, then, in China as elsewhere, inequalities of different kinds reinforce each other. These inequalities have also been institutionalized to a high degree through the intergenerational transfer of privilege and disadvantage. This was clearly the case in the PRC before 1979 when class labels were operationalized precisely in order to achieve that end. In the countryside, those designated with 'bad' class labels and thereby associated with the former pre-1949 ruling class and its institutions were heavily discriminated against, while those designated as poor and lower-middle peasants (from the old society) received full rural citizenship rights (Unger 1984, 2012b). In the urban areas, there was a similar if more complex pattern of discrimination and preferment, determined by the then accepted history of how class relations had been before 1949 (Whyte 1975; Andreas 2012).

Since 1978, and despite the decline in public and official use of class labels, there has been little evidence of increased social mobility. To some extent this cannot be surprising given the maintenance of the household registration system. Research based on a survey conducted by the Institute of Sociology at CASS at the end of the first decade of reform reported: 'only 33 per cent of men and 30 per cent of women report occupations different from those of their fathers. That is to say, over three-quarters of all working people in China still hold the same occupations as their fathers' (Cheng and Dai 1995: 23). Similar results were found in a 1991–2 enterprise employee survey (Tang, Parish and Feng 1996: 371). Later studies have confirmed that there is a low level of intergenerational social mobility. Research based on household surveys undertaken by the NBS up to 2001 suggests that one consequence of the introduction of the one-child policy has been to reduce the incidence of generational mobility because of 'the increased intensity of investment in child quality'. The study concludes that this is particularly acute for the poor: 'increases in immobility are found to be more prevalent in the lower income quartile, reinforcing notions of "Dynastic Poverty"' (Anderson and Teng 2009: 625–6).

More dramatically still, research based on surveys undertaken in 2004 by Peking University and the NBS notes 'an extremely high level of intergenerational persistence . . . (which) implies that intergenerational mobility is much lower in China than in most developed nations' (Gong, Leigh and Meng 2010: 6). The conclusion from this research is that children's socio-economic position is determined by parents' income, level of education, occupation and CCP membership. As might be expected from these figures, the evidence of this research is that CCP membership, educational experience, occupation and industry of employment are all transmitted from parents to children. In particular, there is a finding of near certainty that a daughter will follow her father's occupation, and a 74 per cent certainty that a son will do the same (Gong, Leigh and Meng 2010: 16).

Still more recent research has highlighted the even longer-term intergenerational transfer of privilege back to before 1949. There is evidence that a significant proportion of the current economic elite consists of direct descendants of the pre-1949 local elites, though more precise quantification is clearly required. Research based on a 1996 recording of life histories has also highlighted the extent to which the late Republican Era local elites and the middle classes contributed to the post-1949 elite. In the first place, the Chinese Communist movement on the eve of 1949 had a substantial number of members from the local elites and the middle classes, and unsurprisingly they transferred in large measure to the post-1949 elite. Moreover, even those from similar backgrounds who had not joined the Chinese Communist movement before 1949 were able to find appointment in a professional capacity, provided they had not actually sided with the previous government or opposed the CCP. The Cultural Revolution disproportionately discriminated against the first of those categories, yet after 1978 individuals and families were rehabilitated and restored to their social and political positions in most cases. In the period since 1978 the second of those categories, members of the former elite and middle class who were not associated with the CCP, have continued their pre-1966 practice of working in the professions, including the rapidly expanding business sector (Walder and Hu 2009).

Both of the findings of that earlier work have been further confirmed and detailed in the work of Hiroshi Sato and Li Shi. Their survey of households in rural China, undertaken in 2002, concluded that 'a class-specific, education-oriented family culture has been shaped as a mixture of, first, family cultural capital inherited from the pre-Maoist era and surfacing again in the post-reform era, and, second, the intergenerational cultural rebound against class-based discrimination' (Sato and Li 2008).

Of course, these appreciations of class are not readily articulated within the political discourse of the PRC. The CCP's legitimacy rests at least in part on the interpretation of the establishment of the PRC in 1949 as having ushered in a new society. Moreover, the politics of class are clearly very ambiguous in contemporary China, for similar reasons. On the one hand, there is an ideological position squarely based in Mao Zedong Thought and Marxism–Leninism that highlights the role of the Worker-Peasant Alliance. On the other hand, there is a political position which seeks to write class conflict out of the script of contemporary politics – not least because of a reaction to the era of the Cultural Revolution – and to replace it with the idea of a growing and preponderant middle class. Paradoxically, both of these positions provide essential elements of legitimacy to the CCP. Reference to the CCP's traditions underwrites its structures, institutions and performance to date; economic growth and a comfortable lifestyle are significant promises for the future, especially for the urban classes.

Despite, or possibly because of, these ambiguities, class and its associated concepts have certainly not dropped out of usage. School and university curricula still include compulsory Marxist–Leninist class education, and in the absence of firmer guidance it has been argued that ordinary people have constructed their own views of class, status and social stratification (Hsu 2007). Certainly, it is now possible to conduct surveys in which interviewees are asked to self-identify their class beyond the categories of worker and peasant, with some reasonable expectation of usable information (Su and Feng 2013).

To some extent, then, as the politics of class have been largely abandoned, the language and practice of class have been socialized. In that process, as might be imagined, grand political narratives have been replaced by lifestyle concerns when people think about class. Amy Hanser's study of the retail sector in Harbin, North-east China, provides examples of this and goes a little further. She worked in three separate retail environments – a state-owned department store catering to the urban working class; a 'high-end private department store' targeted at the new rich; and an underground bazaar full of stallholders selling cheap goods. The cultural distinctions that were on display in each location, in material terms as well as in the performance of both customers and sales staff, not only explained class to those involved but also legitimated inequality (Hanser 2008).

As with shopping sites, housing preferences provide another example that also reinforces class identity. Housing developments are almost always class-based, even when, as has sometimes occurred for political reasons, mixed-class occupation has been forced on the developers (Tang and Tomba 2008). Housing projects target specific classes and market accordingly.

On the other hand, the socialization of class is not just about class identity rehearsed through consumption. A somewhat different example that is less immediately focused on economic inequality comes from personal experience. In March 2012, I was riding in a taxi past a Provincial Party School. Talking to the taxi driver about his work, on a whim I asked if he were a member of the CCP. He laughed good-naturedly. 'No,' he said. 'We're just simple members of the working class. The Party is not for people like us.'

Bibliography

Abercrombie, Nicholas and John Urry (1983) *Capital, Labour and the Middle Classes*. London: George Allen and Unwin.

Ahlers, Anna Lisa and Gunter Schubert (2013) 'Strategic Modelling: "Building a New Socialist Countryside" in Three Chinese Counties' in *The China Quarterly* 216: 831–49.

Alpermann, Bjorn (2006) '"Wrapped up in cotton wool": the political integration of private entrepreneurs in rural china' in *The China Journal* 56: 33–61.

Anagnost, Ann (2004) 'The corporeal politics of quality (*suzhi*)' in *Public Culture* 16: 189–208.

Anagnost, Ann (2008) 'From "class" to "social strata": grasping the social totality in reform-era China' in *Third World Quarterly* 29: 497–519.

Anderlini, Jamil (2013) 'Chinese National People's Congress has 83 billionaires' in the *Financial Times*, 7 March.

Anderson, Gordon and Wah Leo Teng (2009) 'Child poverty, investment in children and generational mobility: the short and long term wellbeing of children in urban China after the one child policy' in *Review of Income and Wealth* 55/1: 607–29.

Andreas, Joel (2012) 'Industrial restructuring and class transformation in China' in Beatriz Carrillo and David S. G. Goodman (eds), *China's Peasants and Workers: Changing Class Identities*. Cheltenham: Edward Elgar, pp. 102–23.

Appleton, Simon, John Knight, Linda Song and Qingjie Xia (2006a) 'Labour retrenchment in China: determinants and consequences' in Li Shi and Hiroshi Sato (eds), *Unemployment, Inequality and Poverty in Urban China*. Abingdon: Routledge, pp. 19–42.

Appleton, Simon, John Knight, Linda Song and Qingjie Xia (2006b) 'Contrasting paradigms – segmentation and competiveness in the formation of the Chinese labour market' in Li Shi and Hiroshi Sato (eds), *Unemployment, Inequality and Poverty in Urban China*. Abingdon: Routledge, pp. 212–35.

Bai, Limin (2006) 'Graduate unemployment: dilemmas and challenges in China's move to mass higher education' in *The China Quarterly* 185: 128–44.

Baoru (2010) 'Shanghai's seven social classes' in *Jiefang Ribao* [*Liberation Daily*], 15 September.

Barboza, David (2012) 'Billions in hidden riches for family of a Chinese leader' in *New York Times*, 25 October.

Barboza, David and Keith Bradsher (2012) 'Foxconn factory in China is closed after worker riot' in *New York Times*, 23 September.

Barton, Dominic, Yougang Chen and Amy Jin (2013) 'Mapping China's middle class' in *McKinsey Quarterly* 3, June. At: <http://www.mckinsey.com/insights/consumer_and_retail/mapping_chinas_middle_class>.

Becker, Jeffrey and Manfred Elfstrom (2010) *The Impact of China's Labor Contract Law on Workers*. Washington, DC: International Labor Rights Forum.

Bernstein, Thomas P. (1977) *Up to the Mountains and Down to the Villages: The Transfer of Youth from Urban to Rural China*. New Haven, CT: Yale University Press.

Bernstein, Thomas and Xiaobo Lu (2000) 'Taxation without representation: peasants, the central and local states in reform China' in *The China Quarterly* 163: 742–63.

Bian, Yanjie (2002) 'Chinese social stratification and social mobility' in *Annual Review of Sociology* 28: 91–116.

Bian, Yanjie and J. R. Logan (1996) 'Market transition and the persistence of power: The changing stratification system in urban China' in *American Sociological Review* 61: 739–58.

Bian, Yanjie and Lu Hanlong (1996) 'Reform and socioeconomic inequality: status perception in Shanghai' in Jixuan Hu, Zhaohui Hong and E. Stavrou (eds), *In Search of a Chinese Road Towards Modernization*. New York: Mellen University Press, pp. 109–42.

Bian, Yanjie and Zhang Zhanxin (2004) 'Urban elites and income differential in China: 1988–1995' in *Japanese Journal of Political Science* 5: 51–68.

Blecher, Marc J. (2002) 'Hegemony and workers' politics in China' in *The China Quarterly* 170: 283–303.

Blecher, Marc and Vivienne Shue (1996) *Tethered Deer: Government and Economy in a Chinese County*. Redwood City: Stanford University Press.

Boehler, Patrick (2013) 'The Chinese Dream in Surveys: A Happy Middle Class' in the *South China Morning Post*, 18 December.

Bosker, Bianca (2013) *Original Copies*. Honolulu: University of Hawaii Press.

Bourdieu, Pierre (1998) *Practical Reason: On the Theory of Action* [1994]. Redwood City: Stanford University Press.

Bramall, Chris (2001) 'The quality of China's Household Income Surveys' in *The China Quarterly* 167: 689–705.

Brandt, Loren, Jijun Huang, Guo Li and Scott Rozelle (2002) 'Land rights in rural China' in *The China Journal* 47: 67–97.

Bray, David (2005) *Social Space and Governance in Urban China: The Danwei System from Origins to Urban Reform*. Redwood City: Stanford University Press.

Brodsgaard, Kjeld Erik (2006) '*Bianzhi* and cadre management in China: the case of Yangpu' in Kjeld-Erik Brodsgaard and Yongnian Zheng (eds), *The Chinese Communist Party in Reform*. New York: Routledge.

Bruni, Michele (2011) 'China's new demographic challenge: from unlimited supply of labour to structural lack of labour supply. Labour market and demographic scenarios: 2008–2048'. Center for the Analysis of Public Policies discussion paper, University of Modena and Reggio.

Buckley, Christopher (1999) 'How a revolution becomes a dinner party: stratification, mobility, and the new rich in urban China' in Michael Pinches (ed.), *Culture and Privilege in Capitalist Asia*. London: Routledge.

Burns, John P. (1989) *The Chinese Communist Party's Nomenklatura System*. New York: M. E. Sharpe.

Burns, John P. (1994) 'Strengthening central CCP control of leadership selection: the 1990 *Nomenklatura*' in *The China Quarterly* 138: 474–80.

Burns, John P. (2003) 'Downsizing the Chinese State: government retrenchment in the 1990s' in *The China Quarterly* 175: 775–802.

Burns, John P. (2006) 'The Chinese Communist Party's nomenklatura system as a leadership selection mechanism: an evaluation' in Kjeld Erik Brodsgaard and Zheng Yongnian (eds), *The Chinese Communist Party in Reform*. Abingdon: Routledge.

Cai, Yongshun (2002) 'The resistance of Chinese laid-off workers in the reform period' in *The China Quarterly* 170: 327–44.

Cai, Yongshun (2005) 'China's moderate middle class: the case of homeowners resistance' in *Asian Survey* 45: 777–99.

Cai, Zhenfeng (2004) 'China's middle class has not taken form yet' in *Global Times*, 28 January.

Carrillo, Beatriz (2011) *Small Town China: Rural Labour and Social Inclusion*. London: Routledge.

Cartier, Carolyn (2008) 'The Shanghai-Hong Kong connection: fine jewelry consumption and the demand for diamonds' in David S. G. Goodman (ed.), *The New Rich in China*. London: Routledge, pp. 187–200.

Cartier, Carolyn (2013) 'Uneven development and the time/space economy' in Wanning Sun and Yingjie Guo (eds), *Unequal China*. Abingdon: Routledge, pp. 77–90.

Castells, Manuel and Alejandro Portes (1989) 'World underneath: the origins, dynamics, and effects of the informal economy' in Alejandro Portes, Manuel

Castells and Lauren Benton (eds), *The Informal Economy: Studies in Advanced and Less Developed Countries*. Baltimore: Johns Hopkins University Press.

CCP Central Committee (2013) *Decision of the Central Committee of the Communist Party of China on Some Major Issues Concerning Comprehensively Deepening the Reform 12 November 2013* China.org.cn, 16 January 2014. At: <http://www.china.org.cn/china/third_plenary_session/2014-01/16/content_31212602.htm>.

CCP Organization Department (2002) *Zuzhi he renyuan tongxin* [*Organization and Personnel Communications*]. Beijing: Dangjian wenxian chubanshe.

Chan, Anita (1995) 'The emerging patterns of industrial relations in China and the rise of two new labour movements' in *China Information* 9/4: 36–59.

Chan, Anita (2005) 'Recent trends in Chinese labour issues' in *China Perspectives* 57: 23–31.

Chan, Anita and Kaxton Siu (2012) 'Chinese migrant workers: factors constraining the emergence of class consciousness' in Beatriz Carrillo and David S. G. Goodman (eds) (2012), *China's Peasants and Workers: Changing Class Identities*. Cheltenham: Edward Elgar, pp. 79–101.

Chan, Anita, Richard Madsen and Jonathan Unger (2009) *Chen Village: Revolution to Globalization*. Berkeley: University of California Press.

Chan, Chris King-Chi (2012) 'Class or citizenship? Debating workplace conflict in China' in *Journal of Contemporary Asia* 42: 308–27.

Chan, Chris King-Chi (2013) 'Contesting class organization: migrant workers' strikes in China's Pearl River Delta, 1978–2010' in *International Labor and Working-Class History* 83: 112–36.

Chan, Chris King-Chi and Pun Ngai (2009) 'The making of a new working class? A study of collective actions of migrant workers in South China' in *The China Quarterly* 198: 287–303.

Chan, Jenny and Pun Ngai (2010) 'Suicide as protest for the new generation of Chinese migrant workers: Foxconn, global capital, and the state' in *The Asia-Pacific Journal: Japan Focus* 37: 23–37.

Chan, Kam Wing (2009) 'The Chinese Hukou System at 50' in *Economic Geography and Economics* 50: 197–221.

Chan, Kam Wing (2012) 'Migration and development in China: trends, geography and current issues' in *Migration and Development* 1: 187–205.

Chan, Kam Wing and Will Buckingham (2008) 'Is China abolishing the *hukou* system?' in *The China Quarterly* 195: 582–606.

Chen, Danqing (2013) 'Zhiyou shangji shehui meiyou shangliu shehui' ['There's only a ruling class; there's no upper class'] in *Nanfang Zhoumou* [*Southern Weekend*], 7 February.

Chen, Feng (2003) 'Industrial restructuring and workers' resistance in China' in *Modern China* 29: 237–62.

Chen, Feng (2006) 'Privatization and its discontents in Chinese factories' in *The China Quarterly* 185: 42–60.

Chen Guangjin (2013) 'Bujin you "xiangdui boduo" haiyou "shengcun jiaolu" – Zhongguo zhuguan renting jieceng fenbu shinian bianqian de shizheng fenxi (2001–2011)' ['Survival anxiety as well as relative deprivation: An empirical analysis of subjective class identification and changes in China, 2001–2011'] in *Heilongjiang Shehui Kexue [Heilongjiang Social Sciences]* 5.

Chen, Guangjin, Jun Li and Harry Matlay (2006) 'Who are the Chinese private entrepreneurs? A study of entrepreneurial attributes and business governance' in *Journal of Small Business and Enterprise Development* 13: 148–60.

Chen, Jerome (1973) 'The development and Logic of Mao Tse-tung's Thought, 1928–1949' in Chalmers Johnson (ed.), *Ideology and Politics in Contemporary China.* Seattle: University of Washington Press.

Chen, Jiandong, Dai Dai, Ming Pu, Wenxuan Hou, Qiaobin Feng (2010) 'The Trend of the Gini Coefficient of China'. Brooks World Poverty Institute Working Paper 109.

Chen, Jie (2013) *A Middle Class Without Democracy: Economic Growth and the Prospects for Democratization in China.* New York: Oxford University Press.

Chen, Jie and Bruce J. Dickson (2010) *Allies of the State: China's Private Entrepreneurs and Democratic Change.* Cambridge, MA: Harvard University Press.

Chen, Minglu (2011) *Tiger Girls: Women and Enterprise in the People's Republic of China.* Abingdon: Routledge.

Chen, Minglu (2012) 'Being Elite, 1931–2011: Three generations of social change' in *Journal of Contemporary China* 21: 741–56.

Chen, Peng (2009) 'Cong "chanquan" zouxiang "gongminquan". Dangqian zhongguo chengshi yezhu weiquan yanjiu' ['From property rights to citizens' rights. A study on homeowners' rights defence in contemporary urban China'] in *Kaifang Shidai [Open Times]* 4: 126–39.

Chen, Yiping (2005) *Fenhua yu zuhe: Zhongguo zhongchan jieceng yanjiu* [Separation and coherence: Research on China's Middle Class]. Guangzhou: Guangdong renmin chubanshe.

Cheng, Tiejun and Mark Selden (1994) 'The origins and social consequences of China's hukou system' in *The China Quarterly* 139: 644–68.

Cheng, Yuan and Dai Jianzhong (1995) 'Intergenerational Mobility in Modern China' in *European Sociological Review* 11: 17–35.

Cheng, Yuk-shing and Tsang Shu-kai (1996) 'Agricultural land reform in a mixed system' in *China Information* 10/3–4: 1–29.

China Briefing (2013) 'China revises labor conract law' in *China Briefing*, 18 March, pp. 1–3

China Labour Bulletin (2013) 'China's migrants seek answers closer to home' in *China Labour Bulletins*, 2 July: 1–8

Chung, Jae Ho, Hongyi Lai and Ming Xia (2006) 'Mounting challenges to governance in China: surveying collective protestors, religious sects, and criminal organizations' in *The China Journal* 56: 1–31.

Chung, Jae Ho, Hongyi Lai and Jang-Hwan Joo (2009) 'Assessing the "revive the northeast" (*zhenxing dongbei*) programme: origins, policies and implementation' in *The China Quarterly* 197: 108–25.

CIA (nd) *The World Factbook*. At: <https://www.cia.gov/library/publications/the-world-factbook/>.

Cohen, Philip N. and Wang Feng (2009) 'Market and gender pay equity: have Chinese reforms narrowed the gap?' in Deborah Davis and Wang Feng (eds), *Creating Wealth and Poverty in Postsocialist China*. Redwood City: Stanford University Press, pp. 37–53.

Crompton, Rosemary (2006) 'Class and Family' in *The Sociological Review* 54: 658–77.

Davis, Deborah S. (1985) 'Intergenerational inequalities and the Chinese revolution' in *Modern China* 11: 177–201.

Davis, Deborah S. (1992) 'Skidding: downward mobility among children of the Maoist middle class' in *Modern China* 18: 410–37.

Davis, Deborah S. (2003) 'From welfare benefit to capitalized asset' in R. Forrest and J. Lee (eds), *Chinese Urban Housing Reform*. London: Routledge, pp. 183–96.

Davis, Deborah S. (2005) 'Urban consumer culture' in *The China Quarterly* 183: 677–94.

Deng, Xiaoping (1956) 'Report on the work of the secretariat' in *Eighth National Congress of the Communist Party of China*, vol. 2. Peking: Foreign Languages Press, pp. 198–232.

Dickson, Bruce J. (2007) 'Integrating wealth and power in China: The Communist Party's embrace of the private sector' in *The China Quarterly* 192: 827–54.

Dickson, Bruce J. (2008) *Wealth into Power: The Communist Party's Embrace of China's Private Sector*. Cambridge: Cambridge University Press.

Dickson, Bruce J. (2010) 'China's cooperative capitalists: the business end of the middle class' in Cheng Li (ed.), *China's Emerging Middle Class*. Washington: Brookings Institution Press, pp. 291–306.

Ding, X. L. (2000) 'The illicit asset stripping of Chinese state firms' in *The China Journal* 43: 1–28.

Economist (2013) 'Gini out of the bottle', 26 January.

Edgell, Stephen (1993) *Class*. London: Routledge.

Esherick, Joseph (1981) 'Numbers games: a note on land distribution in prerevolutionary China' in *Modern China* 7: 387–411.

Fan, Ping (2012) '2011 nian nongmin fazhan baogao' ['Report on peasant development in 2011'] *2012 Shehui lanpishu [2012 Blue Book of China's Society]*. Beijing: Shehui kexue wenxian chubanshe, pp. 284–97.

Fang, Xuyan and Lea Yu (2012) 'Government refuses to release Gini Coefficient' in *Caixin [Financial News]*, 18 January, p. 1.

Fang, Yu (2001) 'Weishenme shuo zai xinde lishi shiqi Zhongguo gongren jiejide xianjinxing bujin jixu baochi erqie zai buduan fazhan? – Xuexi Jiang Zemin tongzhi "Qiyi" zhongyao jianghua xilietan' ['Why China's working class is not only advanced but is also expanding in the new historical era – Study Comrade Jiang Zemin's important speech from Party Day'] in *Renmin Ribao [The People's Daily]*, 5 September, p. 1.

Frazier, Mark (2004) 'China's pension reform and its discontents' in *The China Journal* 51: 97–114.

Freeman, Carla (2012) 'From "Blood Transfusion" to "Harmonious Development": the political economy of fiscal allocations to China's ethnic regions' in *Journal of Current Chinese Affairs* 41: 11–44.

Friedman, Eli and Ching Kwan Lee (2010) 'Remaking the world of Chinese labour: a 30-year retrospective' in *British Journal of Industrial Relations* 48: 507–33.

Gao, Qin and Carl Riskin (2009) 'Market versus social benefits: explaining China's changing income inequality' in Deborah Davis and Wang Feng (eds), *Creating Wealth and Poverty in Postsocialist China*. Redwood City: Stanford University Press, pp. 20–36.

Gao, Yong (2013) 'Diwei cengji renting weihe xiayi: jian lun diwei cengji renting jichu de zhuanbian' ['Downward status identification: Changes on the basis of the status hierarchy'] in *Shehui [Society]* 4: 17–31.

Garnaut, John (2012) *The Rise and Fall of the House of Bo: How a Murder Exposed the Cracks in China's Leadership*. Harmondsworth: Penguin.

Garnaut, Ross, Ligang Song and Yang Yao (2006) 'Impact and significance of state-owned enterprise restructuring in China' in *The China Journal* 55: 35–63.

Gerth, Karl (2003) *China Made: Consumer Culture and the Creation of the Nation*. Cambridge, MA: Harvard University Press.

Giddens, A. (1973) *The Class Structure of Advanced Societies*. London: Hutchinson.

Glassman, Ronald M. (1991) *China in Transition: Communism, Capitalism and Democracy*. New York: Praeger.

Global Times (2013) 'New study shows children of officials earn more in first professional job', 7 May, p. 3.

Global Times (2013) 'Lover sold out NDRC official to journalist', 13 May, p. 2.

Göbel, Christian and Lynette H. Ong (2012) *Social Unrest in China*. London: ECRAN Steinbeis.

Gold, Thomas (1989) 'Guerrilla interviewing among the *getihu*' in Perry Link, Richard Madsen and Paul G. Pickowicz (eds), *Unofficial China: Popular Culture and Thought in the People's Republic*. Boulder: Westview Press, pp. 175–92.

Gold, Thomas (1990) 'Urban private business and social change' in Deborah Davis and Ezra F. Vogel (eds), *Chinese Society on the Eve of Tiananmen*. Cambridge, MA: Harvard University Press, pp. 157–78.

Goldstone, Jack A. (1991) 'An analytical framework' in Jack A. Goldstone, Ted Robert Gurr and Farrokh Moshiri (eds), *Revolutions of the Late Twentieth Century*. Boulder: Westview Press, pp. 37–51.

Goldthorpe, John H. (1980) *Social Mobility and Class Structure in Modern Britain*. Oxford: Clarendon Press.

Gong, Cathy Honge, Andrew Leigh and Xin Meng (2010) 'Intergenerational income mobility in urban China'. IZA DP No. 4811.

Goodman, David S. G. (1985) 'The Chinese political order after Mao: "Socialist Democracy" and the exercise of state power' in *Political Studies* 33: 218–35.

Goodman, David S. G. (1995) 'Collectives and connectives, capitalism and corporatism: structural change in China' in *The Journal of Communist Studies and Transition Politics* 11/1: 12–32.

Goodman, David S. G. (1999) 'The new middle class' in M. Goldman and R. MacFarquhar (eds), *The Paradox of China's Post-Mao Reforms*. Cambridge, MA: Harvard University Press, pp. 241–61.

Goodman, David S. G. (2000) 'The localism of local leadership: cadres in reform Shanxi' in *Journal of Contemporary China* 9: 159–83.

Goodman, David S. G. (2001) 'The interdependence of state and society: the political sociology of local leadership' in Chien-min Chao and Bruce J. Dickson (eds), *Remaking the Chinese State: Strategies, Society and Security*. London: Routledge, pp. 132–56.

Goodman, David S. G. (2004a) 'Localism and entrepreneurship: history, identity and solidarity as factors of production' in Barbara Krug (ed.), *China's Rational Entrepreneurs: The Development of the New Private Business Sector*. Routledge, London, pp. 139–65.

Goodman, David S. G. (2004b) 'The campaign to "Open up the West": national, provincial-level, and local perspectives' in *The China Quarterly* 178: 317–34.

Goodman, David S. G. (2007) 'Narratives of change: culture and local economic development' in Barbara Krug and Hans Hendrsichke (eds), *The Chinese*

Economy in the 21st Century: Enterprise and Business Behaviour. Cheltenham: Edward Elgar, pp. 175–201.

Goodman, David S. G. (2014) 'New Economic Elites: Family histories and social change' in Sujian Guo (ed.), *State Society Relations and Governance in China*. Lexington: Rowman and Littlefield, pp. 35–53.

Gu, Qiang and Zongbao Luo (2004) 'Lun qiye de gufen hezuozhi gaizao' ['Reforming the enterprise shareholder cooperative system'] in *Jishu jingji yu guanli yanjiu [Journal of Technological Economy and Management Research]* 5: 117–18.

Guan, Xiaofeng (2007) 'Most people free to have more children' in *China Daily*, 11 July, p. 1.

Guang, Lei (2005) 'Guerilla workfare: migrant renovators, state power, and informal work in urban China' in *Politics and Society* 33: 481–506.

Guang, Lei and Fanmin Kong (2010) 'Rural prejudice and gender discrimination in China's urban market' in Martin K. Whyte (ed.), *One Country, Two Societies: Rural–Urban Inequality in Contemporary China*. Cambridge, MA: Harvard University Press, pp. 241–64.

Guang, Lei and Lu Zheng (2005) 'Migration as the second best option: local power and off-farm employment' in *The China Quarterly* 181: 22–45.

Guo, Yingjie (2008) 'Class, stratum and group: the politics of description and prescription' in David S. G. Goodman (ed.), *The New Rich in China*. Abingdon: Routledge, pp. 38–52.

Guo, Yingjie (2009) 'Farewell to class, except the middle class: the politics of class analysis in contemporary China' in *The Asia-Pacific Journal* 26: 189–205.

Guo, Yingjie (2012) 'Class without class consciousness and class consciousness without classes: the meaning of class in the People's Republic of China' in *Journal of Contemporary China* 21: 723–39.

Guo, Yingjie (2013) 'Political power and social inequality' in Wanning Sun and Yingie Guo (eds), *Unequal China*. Abingdon: Routledge, pp. 12–26.

Gustafsson, Bjorn and Ding Sai (2010) 'New light on China's rural elites'. UNU-WIDER WP No. 2010/108.

Gustafsson, Bjorn, Li Shi and Terry Sicular (eds) (2008) *Inequality and Public Policy in China*. Cambridge: Cambridge University Press.

Halper, Stefan (2010) *The Beijing Consensus: How China's Authoritarian Model Will Dominate the Twenty-first Century*. New York: Basic Books.

Han, Chunping and Martin King Whyte (2009) 'The social contours of distributive injustice feelings in contemporary China' in Deborah Davis and Wang Feng (eds), *Creating Wealth and Poverty in Postsocialist China*. Redwood City: Stanford University Press, pp. 193–212.

Hannum, Emily and Jennifer Adams (2009) 'Beyond cost: rural perspectives on barriers to education' in Deborah Davis and Wang Feng (eds), *Creating Wealth and Poverty in Postsocialist China*. Redwood City: Stanford University Press, pp. 156–71.

Hanser, Amy (2008) *Service Encounters: Class, Gender, and the Market for Social Distinction in Urban China*. Redwood City: Stanford University Press.

Harvey, David (2007) *A Brief History of Neoliberalism*. New York: Oxford University Press.

He, Qinglian (1998) *Xiandaihua de xianjing: Dangdai Zhongguo de jingji shehui wenti* [*Pitfalls of Modernization: Economic and Social Problems in Contemporary China*]. Beijing: Jinri Zhongguo chubanshe.

He, Qinglian (2000) 'Dangqian Zhongguo shehui jiegou yanbian de zongtixing fenxi' ['A comprehensive analysis of the evolution of China's social formation'] in *Shuwu* [*Book Room*] 3: 1–31.

He, Qinglian (2003) 'A Volcanic stability' in *Journal of Democracy* 14: 66–72.

Heberer, Thomas (2007) *Doing Business in Rural China: Liangshan's New Ethnic Entrepreneurs*. Washington, DC: University of Washington Press.

Hendrischke, Hans (2013) 'Institutional determinants of the political consciousness of private entrepreneurs' in Minglu Chen and David S. G. Goodman (eds), *Middle Class China: Identity and Behaviour*. Cheltenham: Edward Elgar, pp. 135–48.

Henriot, Christian and Lu Shi (1996) *La Réforme des Enterpises en China*. Paris: L'Harmattan.

Hsiao, Hsin-huang M. (1993) (ed.) *Discovery of the Middle Classes in East Asia*. Taipei: Institute of Ethnology, Academia Sinica.

Hsing, You-tien (2010) *The Great Urban Transformation: Politics of Land and Property in China*. Oxford: Oxford University Press.

Hsu, Carolyn L. (2007) *Creating Market Socialism: How Ordinary People are Shaping Class and Status in China*. Durham, NC: Duke University Press.

Hu, Jianguo, Li Chunling and Li Wei (2012) 'Social class structure' in Lu Xueyi (ed.), *Social Structure of Contemporary China*. Singapore: World Scientific Publishing, pp. 397–436.

Hu, Xiuhong and David H. Kaplan (2001) 'The emergence of affluence in Beijing: residential social stratification in China's capital city' in *Urban Geography* 22: 54–77.

Huang, Philip C. (1995) 'Rural class struggle in the Chinese revolution' in *Modern China* 21: 105–43.

Huang, Philip C. (2009) 'China's neglected informal economy: reality and theory' in *Modern China* 35: 405–38.

Huang, Philip C. (2011a) 'The theoretical and practical implications of China's development experience: The role of informal economic practices' in *Modern China* 37: 3–43.

Huang, Philip C. (2011b) 'The modern Chinese family: in light of economic and legal history' in *Modern China* 37: 450–97.

Huang, Philip C. (2012) 'Profit-making state firms and China's development experience: "State Capitalism" or "Socialist Market Economy"?' in *Modern China* 38: 591–629.

Huang, Philip C. (2013) 'Misleading Chinese legal and statistical categories: labour, individual entities, and private enterprises' in *Modern China* 39: 347–79.

Huang, Philip C., Yuan Gao and Yusheng Peng (2012) 'Capitalization without proletarianization in Chinese agriculture' in *Modern China* 38: 139–73.

Huang, Yasheng (2008) *Capitalism with Chinese Characteristics: Entrepreneurship and the State.* Cambridge: Cambridge University Press.

Huang, Youqin (2005) 'From work-unit compounds to gated communities: housing inequality and residential segregation in transitional Beijing' in L. J. C. Ma and F. Wu (eds), *Restructuring the Chinese City: Changing Society, Economy and Space.* New York: Routledge, pp. 192–221.

Huntington, Samuel P. (1991) *The Third Wave: Democratization in the Late Twentieth Century.* Oklahoma: University of Oklahoma Press.

Hurst, William (2009) *The Chinese Worker After Socialism.* Cambridge: Cambridge University Press.

Hurst, William and Kevin O'Brien (2002) 'China's contentious pensioners' in *The China Quarterly* 170: 345–60.

Hurun (2012) Group M Knowledge and Hurun Wealth Report, *The Chinese Millionaire Wealth Report 2012.*

Jiang, Zemin (2001) 'Zai qingzhu Zhongguo gongchandang chengli bashi zhouniandahu shang de jianghua' ['Speech at the Celebration of the Eightieth Anniversary of the Founding of the Chinese Communist Party'] in Jiang Zemin *Lun Sange Daibiao* [*On the Three Represents*]. Beijing: Zhongyang wenxian chubanshe, p. 169.

Jiang, Zemin (2002) '*Quanmin* jianshe xiaokang shehui, kaichuang Zhongguo tese shehui zhuyi shiye xin jumian – zai Zhongguo gongchandang di shiliu ci quanguo daibiao dahui shang de baogao' ['Build a Comprehensive *Xiaokang* Society and Create a New Order of Socialism with Chinese Characteristics: Report to the 16th Congress of the CCP'] in *Renmin Ribao* [*The People's Daily*], 18 November, p.1.

Jones, David M. (1995) 'Democratization and the myth of the liberalizing middle class' in Daniel Bell et al. (eds), *Towards Illiberal Democracy in Pacific Asia*. Basingstoke: Palgrave Macmillan, pp. 78–106.

Kelliher, D. (1992) *Peasant Power in China: The Era of Rural Reform, 1979–1989*. New Haven, CT: Yale University Press.

Kelly, David (2013) 'Between social justice and social order: The framing of inequality' in Sun Wanning and Yingjie Guo (eds), *Unequal China: The Political Economy and Cultural Politics of Inequality*. Abingdon, Routledge, pp. 43–58.

Kennedy, John James (2007) 'The implementation of village elections and tax-for-fee reform in rural Northwest China' in Elizabeth J. Perry and Merle Goldman (eds), *Grassroots Political Reform in Contemporary China*. Cambridge, MA: Harvard University Press, pp. 48–74.

Kennedy, John James (2009) 'Maintaining political support for the Chinese Communist Party: the influence of education and the state-controlled media' in *Political Studies* 57: 517–36.

Khan, Azizur Rahman (2005) 'An evaluation of World Bank assistance to China for poverty reduction in the 1990s'. World Bank OED Paper no.32904.

Khan, Azizur and Carl Riskin (2005) 'China's household income distribution, 1995 and 2002' in *The China Quarterly* 182: 356–84.

Kharas, H. and G. Geertz (2010) 'The new global middle class: a cross-over from West to East' in Cheng Li (ed.), *China's Emerging Middle Class: Beyond Economic Transformation* Washington, DC: Brookings Institution Press, pp. 32–51.

Kipnis, Andrew (2006) 'Suzhi: A keyword approach' in *The China Quarterly* 186: 295–313.

Kong, Tao Sherry and Jonathan Unger (2013) 'Egalitarian redistributions of agricultural land in China through community concensus: Findings from two surveys' in *The China Journal* 69: 1–19.

Korzec, M. and M. K. Whyte (1981) 'The Chinese wage system' in *The China Quarterly* 86: 248–73.

Kou, Chien-Wen and Xiaowei Zang (2013) *Choosing China's Leaders*. Abingdon: Routledge.

Kraus, Richard Curt (1981) *Class Conflict in Chinese Socialism*. Columbia: Columbia University Press.

Landesa (2012) Rural Development Institute *Summary of 2011 17-Province Survey's Findings*. Seattle.

Landry, Pierre F. (2008) *Decentralized Authoritarianism in China: The Communist Party's Control of Local Elites in the Post-Mao Era*. Cambridge: Cambridge University Press.

Lau, W. K. (1999) 'The 15th Congress of the Chinese Communist Party: milestone in China's privatization' in Capital and Class 68: 50–87.

Lee, Ching Kwan (1998) Gender and the South China Miracle: Two Worlds of Factory Women. California: University of California Press.

Lee, Ching Kwan (2005) 'Livelihood struggles and market reform: (un)marking Chinese abour after state socialism'. United Nations Research Institute for Social Development Paper.

Lee, Ching Kwan (2007) Against the Law: Labor Protests in China's Rustbelt and Sunbelt. California: University of California Press.

Lee, Ching Kwan (2009) 'From inequality to inequity: popular conceptions of social (in)justice in Beijing' in Deborah Davis and Wang Feng (eds), Creating Wealth and Poverty in Postsocialist China. Redwood City: Stanford University Press, pp. 213–31.

Lee, Ching Kwan (2010) 'Pathways of labour activism' in Perry, Elizabeth J. and Mark Selden (eds), Chinese Society: Change, Conflict and Resistance. New York: Routledge, pp. 57–79.

Leung, Pak Nang and Pun Ngai (2009) 'Radicalization of the new Chinese working class' in Third World Quarterly 30: 551–65.

Leung, Parry and Alvin Y. So (2012) 'The making and re-making of the working class in South China' in Beatriz Carrillo and David S. G. Goodman (eds), China's Peasants and Workers: Changing Class Identities. Cheltenham, Edward Elgar, pp. 62–78.

Lewis, John W. and Xue Litai (2003) 'Social change and political reform in China: meeting the challenge of success' in The China Quarterly 176: 926–42.

Li, Bingin and Mark Duda (2011) 'Life considerations and the housing of rural to urban migrants: the case of Taiyuan' in Beatriz Carrillo and Jane Duckett (eds), China's Changing Welfare Mix: Local perspectives. Abingdon: Routledge, pp. 151–70.

Li, Cheng (2001) China's Leaders: The New Generation. Lanham, MD: Rowman and Littlefield.

Li, Cheng (2010) 'Chinese scholarship on the middle class: from social stratification to political potential' in Cheng Li (ed.), China's Emerging Middle Class. Washington: Brookings Institution Press, pp. 55–83.

Li, Cheng (2012) 'The end of the CCP's resilient authoritarianism? A tripartite assessment of shifting power in China' in The China Quarterly 211: 595–623.

Li, Chunling (2003) 'Zhongguo dangdai zhongchan jieceng de goucheng ji bili' ['The composition and proportion of the present Chinese middle class'] in Zhongguo renkou kexue [Chinese Population Science] 6: 25–32.

Li, Chunling (2005) *Duanlie yu suipian: dangdai Zhongguo shehui jieceng fenhua shizheng fenxi* [*Cleavage and Fragmentation: An Empirical Analysis of Social Stratification in Contemporary China*]. Beijing: Shehui kexue wenxian chubanshe.

Li, Chunling (2010) 'Characterizing China's middle class: heterogeneous composition and multiple identities' in Cheng Li (ed.), *China's Emerging Middle Class*. Washington: Brookings Institution Press, pp. 135–56.

Li, Chunling (2013) 'Sociopolitical attitude of the middle class and the implications for political transition' in Minglu Chen and David S. G. Goodman (eds), *Middle Class China: Identity and Behaviour*. Cheltenham: Edward Elgar, pp. 12–33.

Li, Gan (2012) 'China Household Finance Survey 2012', Texas A&M University and Southwestern University of Finance and Economics.

Li, Gan (2013) 'Findings from China Household Finance Survey', Texas A&M University and Southwestern University of Finance and Economics, China Household Finance Survey.

Li, He (2003) 'Middle class: friends or foes of Beijing's new leadership' in *Journal of Chinese Political Science* 8: 87–100.

Li, Hongbin and Scott Rozelle (2003) 'Privatizing rural China: insider privatization, innovative contracts and the performance of township enterprises' in *The China Quarterly* 176: 981–1005.

Li, Jian and Xiaohan Niu (2003) 'The new middle class(es) in Peking: a case study' in *China Perspectives* 45: 4–20.

Li, Linda Chelan (2006) 'Path creation? Processes and networks: how the Chinese rural tax reform began' in *Policy and Society* 25: 61–84.

Li, Lulu (2003) *Zai shengchan de yanxu – zhidu zhuanxing yu chengshi shuhui fencing jiegou* [*The Continuation of Reproduction – Systemic Transformation and Patterns of Social Stratification in Chinese Cities*]. Beijing: Zhongguo renmin daxue chubanshe.

Li, Peilin (1995) *Zhongguo xin shiqi jieji jieceng baogao* [*Social Stratification during China's Market Transition in China*]. Shenyang: Liaoning renmin chubanshe.

Li, Peilin (2004) 'Zhongguo jingji shehui fazhande wenti he qushi' ['Issues and trends in China's economic and social development'] in Xin Ru, Lu Xueyi and Li Peilin (eds), *2004 nian: Zhongguo shehui xingshi fenxi yu yuce* [*2004: Analysis and forecast of China's society*]. Beiing: Shehui kexue wenxian chubanshe.

Li, Peilin and Zhang Yi (2009) 'Zhongguo zhongchan jiejide guimo, rentong, he shehui taidu' ['The scale, identification and attitudes of China's middle class'] in Tang Jin (ed.), *Daguoce tongxiang Zhongguo zhilude Zhongguo minzhu* [*A Chinese Democratic Great Power Strategy for China*]. Beijing: Renmin chubanshe, pp. 188–98.

Li, Qiang (2001) 'Guanyu zhongchan jieji he zhongjian jieceng' ['On the middle class and the middle stratum'] in *Renmin daxue xuebao* [*Journal of People's University*] 2: 17–20.

Li, Qiang (2002) *Zhuanxing shiqi de Zhongguo shehui fenceng jiegou* [*Patterns of Social Stratification during China's Transition*]. Harbin: Heilongjiang jiaoyu chubanshe.

Li, Shenming (2002) *Dangdai woguo de shehui jieji jieceng jiegou* [*The Class and Stratum Structure of Contemporary China*]. Beijing: Shehui kexue wenxian chubanshe.

Li, Shi, Luo Chuliang and Terry Sicular (2012) 'Overview: income inequality and poverty in China, 2002–2007. Working Paper 2011–10, University of Western Ontario, Department of Economics, CIBC Working Paper Series.

Li, Shi, Hiroshi Sato and Terry Sicular (eds) (2013) *Rising Inequality in China: Challenges to a Harmonious Society*. Cambridge: Cambridge University Press.

Liang, Xiaosheng (1997) *Zhongguo shehui ge jieceng fenxi* [*The Analysis of China's Social Classes*]. Beijing: Jingji ribao chubanshe.

Lin, Boye and Shen Zhe (1981) 'Ping suowei fandui guanliao zhuyi zhe jieji' ['Commenting on the so-called opposition to the class of bureaucrats'] in *Hongqi* [*Red Flag*] (5 March): 12–8.

Lin, Jing and Xiaoyan Sun (2010) 'Higher education expansion and China's middle class' in Cheng Li (ed.), *China's Emerging Middle Class*. Washington: Brookings Institution Press, pp. 217–42.

Lin, Min with Maria Galikowski (1999) 'Liang Xiaosheng's moral critique of China's modernization process' in Lin, Min and Maria Galikowski (eds), *The Search for Modernity: Chinese Intellectuals and Cultural Discourse in the Post-Mao Era*. New York: St Martin's Press, pp. 123–42.

Lin, Nan and Chih-Jou Jay Chen (1999) 'Local elites as officials and owners: shareholding and property rights in Daqiuzhuang' in Jean Oi and Andrew Walder (eds), *Property Rights and Economic Reform in China*. Redwood City: Stanford University Press, pp. 145–70.

Lin, Yimin and Zhanxin Zhang (1999) 'Backyard profit centers: the private assets of public agencies' in Jean Oi and Andrew Walder (eds), *Property Rights and Economic Reform in China*. Redwood City: Stanford University Press, pp. 203–25.

Liu, Changjiang (2006) '"Zhongchan jieji" yanjiu: yiwen yu tanyuan' ['Studies of the middle class: questions and origins'] in *Shehui* [*Society*] 4: 43–56.

Liu, Jieyu (2007) *Gender and Work in Urban China: Women Workers of the Unlucky Generation*. London: Routledge.

Liu, Jieyu (2011) 'Life goes on: redundant woman workers in Nanjing' in Carrillo, Beatriz and Jane Duckett, *China's Changing Welfare Mix: Local Perspectives*. Abingdon: Routledge, pp. 82–103

Liu, Jun (2005) 'The Chinese middle class will account for 40 per cent of the whole population of employment within 20 years' in *China Daily*, 21 October, p. 1.

Liu, Xin (2009) 'Institutional basis of social stratification in transitional China' in Deborah Davis and Wang Feng (eds), *Creating Wealth and Poverty in Postsocialist China*. Redwood City: Stanford University Press, pp. 85–96.

Liu, Yia-ling (1992) 'Reform from below: the private economy and local politics in the rural industrialization of Wenzhou' in *The China Quarterly* 130: 1132–49.

Loyalka, Michelle Dammon (2012) *Eating Bitterness: Scenes from the Front Lines of China's Great Urban Migration*. California: University of California Press.

Lu, Hanlong (2010) 'The Chinese middle class and *Xiaokang* society' in Cheng Li (ed.), *China's Emerging Middle Class*. Washington: Brookings Institution Press, pp. 104–31.

Lu, Peng (2013) 'Xin gudian shehui xue zhong de "a'er jizhi mi": Zhongguo di yi dai zui fuyou siying qiye jia de shehui qiyuan' ['The Horatio Alger myth in neo-classical sociology: origins of the first generation of visibly rich Chinese private entrepreneurs'] in *Xuehai* 3: 46–61.

Lu, Xueyi (2002) (ed.) *Dangdai Zhongguo shehui jieceng yanjiu baogao* [*Report on Research into Social Stratification in Contemporary China*]. Beijing: Shehui kexue wenxian chubanshe.

Lu, Xueyi (2004) *Dangdai Zhongguo Shehui Liudong* [*Social Mobility in Contemporary China*]. Beijing: Shehui kexue wenxian chubanshe.

Lu, Xueyi (2005) *Social Mobility in Contemporary China*. Montreal: American Quantum Media.

Lu, Xueyi (2012) (ed.) *Social Structure of Contemporary China*. Singapore: World Scientific Publishing.

Luo, Changping (2013) *Gaoguan fanfu lu* [Record of anti-corruption amongst officials]. Guangdong: Nanfang ribao chubanshe.

Maddison, Angus (2007) *Chinese Economic Performance in the Long Run 960–2030 AD*. Paris: OECD Publishing, Development Centre Studies.

Man, Joyce Yanyun (2010) 'China's housing reform and emerging middle class' in Cheng Li (ed.), *China's Emerging Middle Class*. Washington: Brookings Institution Press, pp. 179–92.

Manion, Melanie (2006) 'Democracy, community, and trust: The impact of elections in rural China' in *Comparative Political Studies* 39: 301–24.

Mao, Zedong (1949) 'On the people's democratic dictatorship' in *Selected Works of Mao Tse-tung Vol.4*. Beijing, Foreign Languages Press [1961], pp. 411–24.

Mao, Zedong (1957a) 'On the correct handling of contradictions among the people' in *Selected Works of Mao Tse-tung Vol.5*. Beijing: Foreign Languages Press [1977], pp. 384–421.

Mao, Zedong (1957b) 'Things are beginning to change' in *Selected Works of Mao Tse-tung Vol.5*. Beijing: Foreign Languages Press [1977], pp. 440–46.

Michelson, Ethan (2007) 'Lawyers, political embeddedness, and institutional continuity in China's transition from socialism' in *American Journal of Sociology* 113: 352–414.

Michelson, Ethan and Sida Liu (2010) 'What do Chinese lawyers want? Political values and legal practice' in Cheng Li (ed.), *China's Emerging Middle Class*. Washington: Brookings Institution Press, pp. 310–33.

Mok, Ka-ho and Cai He (1999) 'Beyond organized dependence: A study of workers' actual and perceived living standards in Guangzhou' in *Work, Employment, and Society* 13: 67–82.

Moore, Barrington (1967) *Social origins of Dictatorship and Democracy: Lord and Peasant in the Making of the Modern World*. Boston: Beacon Press.

Murphy, Rachel (2002) *How Migrant Labour is Changing Rural China*. Cambridge: Cambridge University Press.

Naughton, Barry (1995) *Growing Out of the Plan: Chinese Economic Reform, 1978–1993*. Cambridge: Cambridge University Press.

Naughton, Barry (2007) *The Chinese Economy: Transitions and Growth*. Cambridge: Cambridge University Press.

Naughton, Barry (2010) 'China's distinctive system: can it be a model for others?' in *Journal of Contemporary China* 19: 437–60.

NBS (2005) National Bureau of Statistics *China Statistical Yearbook 2005*. Beijing: China Statistics Press.

NBS (2012) National Bureau of Statistics *China Statistical Yearbook 2012*. Beijing: China Statistics Press.

NBS (2013) 'Statistical Communiqué of the People's Republic of China on the 2012 National Economic and Social Development', 22 February.

Nee, Victor (1989) 'A theory of market transition: from redistribution to markets in state socialism' in *American Sociological Review* 54: 663–81.

Nee, Victor (1991) 'Social inequalities in reforming state socialism: between redistribution and markets in China' in *American Sociological Review* 56: 267–82.

Nee, Victor (1992) 'Organizational dynamics of market transition: hybrid forms, property rights, and mixed economy in China' in *Administrative Science Quarterly* 37: 1–27.

Nee, Victor (1996) 'The emergence of a market society: changing mechanisms of stratification in China' in *American Journal of Sociology* 101: 908–49.

Nee, Victor and Cao Yang (1999) 'Path dependent societal transformation: stratification in hybrid mixed economy' in *Theory and Society* 28: 799–834.

Nee, Victor and Cao Yang (2002) 'Postsocialist inequality: the causes of continuity and discontinuity' in *The Future of Market Transition* 19: 3–39.

Nee, Victor and P. Lian (1994) 'Sleeping with the enemy: a dynamic model of declining political commitment in state socialism' in *Theory and Society* 23: 253–96.

Nee, Victor and R. Matthews (1996) 'Market transition and societal transformation in reforming state socialism' in *Annual Review of Sociology* 22: 401–35.

Nee, Victor and Sonja Opper (2012) *Capitalism from Below: Markets and Institutional Change in China*. Cambridge, MA: Harvard University Press.

Nee, Victor and S. Su (1998) 'Institutional foundations of robust economic performance: public sector industrial growth in China' in J. Henderson (ed.), *Industrial Transformation in Eastern Europe in the Light of East Asian Experience*. New York: St Martin's Press, pp. 167–87.

O'Brien, Kevin and Lianjiang Li (2006) *Rightful Resistance in Rural China*. Cambridge: Cambridge University Press.

Oi, Jean C. (1995) 'The role of the local state in China's transitional economy' in *The China Quarterly* 144: 1132–49.

Oi, Jean C. (1999) *Rural China Takes Off: Institutional Foundations of Economic Reform*. Cambridge: University of California Press.

Oi, Jean C. and Han Chaohua (2011) 'China's Corporate Restructuring: a multistep process' in Jean Oi (ed.), *Going Private in China: The Politics of Corporate Restructuring and System Reform*. Redwood City: Stanford University Press. pp. 20–37.

Oi, Jean C. and Andrew Walder (1999) 'Property rights in the Chinese economy: contours of process of change' in Jean C. Oi and Andrew Walder (eds), *Property Rights and Economic Reform in China*. Redwood City: Stanford University Press, pp. 1–26.

Oi, Jean and Shukai Zhao (2007) 'Fiscal crisis in China's townships' in Elizabeth J. Perry and Merle Goldman (eds), *Grassroots Political Reform in China*. Cambridge, MA: Harvard University Press, pp. 75–96.

Oksenberg, Michael (1974) 'Political changes and their causes in China, 1949–1972' in *The Political Quarterly* 45: 45–72.

Orlik, Tom (2012) 'China's inequality gini out of the bottle' in *Wall Street Journal*, 17 September.

Osburg, John (2013) *Anxious Wealth: Money and Morality among China's New Rich*. Redwood City: Stanford University Press.

Oster, Shai (2009) 'China's rich youth spark bitter divide' in *The Wall Street Journal*, 23 September, p. A16.

Otis, Eileen M. (2009) 'The labour of luxury: gender and generational inequality in a Beijing hotel' in Deborah Davis and Wang Feng (eds), *Creating Wealth and Poverty in Postsocialist China*. Redwood City: Stanford University Press, pp. 54–68.

Parish, William (1984) 'Destratification in China' in James L. Watson (ed.), *Class and Social Stratification in Post-Revolution China*. Cambridge: Cambridge University Press, pp. 84–120.

Parish, W. L. and E. Michelson (1996) 'Politics and markets: dual transformations' in *American Journal of Sociology* 101: 1042–59.

Parish, W. L. and M. K. Whyte (1978) *Village and Family in Contemporary China*. Chicago: University of Chicago Press.

Parish, William, X. Zhen and F. Li (1995) 'Nonfarm work and marketization of the Chinese countryside' in *The China Quarterly* 143: 697–730.

Parker, Richard (1972) *The Myth of the Middle Class: Notes on Affluence and Inequality*. New York: Harper and Row.

Parris, Kristen (1993) 'Local initiative and national reform: The Wenzhou model of development' in *The China Quarterly* 134: 242–63.

Pearson, Margaret M. (1994) 'The Janus face of business associations in China: socialist corporatism in foreign enterprises' in *Australian Journal of Chinese Affairs* 31: 25–46.

Pearson, Margaret M. (1997) *China's New Business Elite: The Political Consequences of Economic Reform*. California: University of California Press.

Perlin, Ross (2013) 'Chinese workers Foxconned' in *Dissent* (spring): 1–8.

Pieke, Frank N. (1995) 'Bureaucracy, friends, and money: the growth of capital socialism in China' in *Comparative Studies in Society and History* 37: 494–518.

Pieke, Frank N. (2009) *The Good Communist: Elite Training and State Building in Today's China*. Cambridge: Cambridge University Press.

Pow, Choon-Piew (2009) *Gated Communities in China: Class, Privilege and the Moral Politics of the Good Life*. Abingdon: Routledge.

Pun, Ngai (1999) 'Becoming Dagongmei: The politics of identity and difference in reform China' in *The China Journal* 42: 1–19.

Pun, Ngai and Lu, Huilin (2010a) 'A culture of violence: The labour subcontracting system and collective action by construction workers in post-socialist China' in *The China Journal* 64: 143–58.

Pun, Ngai and Lu, Huilin (2010b) 'Unfinished proletarianization: self, anger, and class action among the second generation of peasant-workers in present-day China' in *Modern China* 36: 493–519.

Qiao, Jian (2004) '2003 nian: Xin yilun jiegou tiaozheng xiade laogong guanxi' ['2003: Labour relations under a new round of structural adjustment'] in Xin Ru, Lu Xueyi and Li Peilin (eds), 2004 nian: Zhongguo shehui xingshi fenxi yu yuce [2004: Analysis and Forecast of China's Society]. Beiing: Shehui kexue wenxian chubanshe.

Qiu, Jack Linchuan and Hongzhe Wang (2012) 'Working-class cultural spaces: comparing the old and the new' in Beatriz Carrillo and David S. G. Goodman (eds), China's Peasants and Workers: Changing Class Identities. Cheltenham: Edward Elgar, pp. 124–46.

Ravaillon, Martin (2009) 'The developing world's bulging (but vulnerable) "middle class"'. Policy Research Working Paper 4816, World Bank Development Research Group.

Ravaillon, Martin and Shaohua Chen (2007) 'China's (uneven) progress against poverty' in Journal of Development Economics 82: 1–42.

RMRB (2011) 'China higher education students exceed 30 million' in People's Daily Online (in English), 11 March. At: <http://english.peopledaily.com .cn/90001/98649/7315789.html>.

RMRB (2012) '"Geng gongping" yiweizhe shenme' ['The significance of greater equity'] in Renmin Ribao [The People's Daily], 12 November, A2.

Robison, Richard and David S. G. Goodman (1992) 'The new rich in Asia: affluence, mobility and power' in The Pacific Review 5: 321–27.

Rocca, Jean-Louis (2003) 'Old working class, new working class' in Fisac Badell and Leila Fernandez-Stembridge (eds), China Today: Economic Reforms, Social Cohesion and Collective Identities. London: Routledge, pp. 77–104.

Rocca, Jean-Louis (2008) 'Power of knowledge: the imaginary formation of the Chinese middle class stratum in an era of growth and stability' in Christophe Jaffrelot and Peter van der Veer (eds), Patterns of Middle Class Consumption. Beverly Hills: Sage, pp. 127–39.

Rocca, Jean-Louis (2010) Une sociologie de la Chine. Paris: Editions La Découverte.

Rocca, Jean-Louis (2013) 'Homeowners' movements: narratives on the political behaviours of the middle class' in Minglu Chen and David S. G. Goodman (eds), Middle Class China: Identity and Behaviour. Cheltenham: Edward Elgar, pp. 110–34.

Saich, Tony and Biliang Hu (2012) Chinese Village, Global Market: New Collectives and Rural Development. New York: Palgrave Macmillan.

Sargeson, Sally (1999) Reworking China's Proletariat. New York: St Martin's Press.

Sargeson, Sally (2013) 'Gender as a categorical source of property inequality in urbanizing poverty' in Wanning Sun and Yingjie Guo (eds), Unequal China. Abingdon: Routledge, pp. 168–83.

Sato, Hiroshi and Shi Li (2008) 'Class origin, family culture, and intergenerational correlation of education in rural China'. Hi-Stat Discussion Paper 007, Hitotsubashi University.

Savage, Mike (1995) 'Class analysis and social research' in Tim Butler and Mike Savage (eds), *Social Change and the Middle Classes*. London: UCL Press, pp. 15–25.

Savage, Mike (2000) *Class Analysis and Social Transformation*. Buckingham: Open University Press.

Schram, Stuart R. (1981) 'To utopia and back: a cycle in the history of the Chinese Communist Party' in *The China Quarterly* 87: 407–39.

Schram, Stuart R. (1983) *Mao Zedong: A Preliminary Reassessment*. Hong Kong: Chinese University Press.

Schram, Stuart R. (1984) 'Classes, old and new, in Mao Zedong's thought, 1949–1976' in James L. Watson (ed.), *Class and Social Stratification in Post-Revolution China*. Cambridge: Cambridge University Press, pp. 29–55.

Schubert, Gunter and Anna L. Ahlers (2012) 'County and township cadres as a strategic group' in *The China Journal* 67: 67–86.

Selden, Mark (1988) *The Political Economy of Chinese Socialism*. New York: M. E. Sharpe.

Shen, Hui (2005) 'Zhongchan jiecengde rentong jiqi goujian' ['Middle class identity and structure'] in Zhou Xiaohong (ed.), *Zhongguo zhongchan jieceng diaocha* [*Survey of the Chinese Middle Class*]. Beijing: Shehui kexue chubanshe, pp. 20–61.

Shi, Xiuyin (2012) 'Employment structure' in Lu Xueyi (ed.), *Social Structure of Contemporary China*. Singapore: World Scientific Publishing, pp. 133–83.

Shih, Victor, Wei Shan and Mingxing Liu (2010) 'The Central Committee past and present' in Allen Carlson, Mary E. Gallagher, Kenneth Lieberthal and Melanie Manion (eds), *Contemporary Chinese Politics*. Cambridge: Cambridge University Press, pp. 51–68.

Shih, Victor, Christopher Adolph and Liu Minxing (2012) 'Getting ahead in the Communist Party' in *American Political Science Review* 106: 166–87.

Shirk, Susan L. (1984) 'The decline of virtuocracy in China' in James L. Watson (ed.), *Class and Social Stratification in Post-Revolution China*. Cambridge: Cambridge University Press, pp. 56–83.

Silverstein, Michael J., Abheek Singhi, Carol Liao and David Michael (2012) *The $10 Trillion Prize: Captivating the Newly Affluent in China and India*. Cambridge, MA: Harvard Business Review Press.

Smith, Graeme (2009) 'Political machinations in a rural county' in *The China Journal* 62: 29–59.

So, Alvin Y. (2003a) 'The changing pattern of classes and class conflict in China,' in *Journal of Contemporary Asia* 33: 363–76.

So, Alvin Y. (2003b) 'The making of the cadre-capitalist class in China' in Joseph Cheng (ed.), *China's Challenges in the Twenty-First Century*. Hong Kong: City University of Hong Kong Press, pp. 73–87.

So, Alvin Y. (2012) 'Global capitalist crisis and the rise of China to the world scene' in Berch Berberoglu (ed.), *Beyond the Global Capitalist Crisis: The World Economy in Transition*. Aldershot: Ashgate, pp. 123–44.

So, Alvin Y. (2013) *Class and Class Conflict in Post-Socialist China*. Singapore: World Scientific Publishing.

Solinger, Dorothy (1981) 'Economic reform via reformulation in China: where do rightist ideas come from?' in *Asian Survey* 9: 947–60.

Solinger, Dorothy (1997) 'The impact of the floating population on the *danwei*: shifts in the pattern of labor mobility control and entitlement provision' in Xiaobo Lu and Elizabeth Perry (eds), *Danwei: The Changing Chinese Workplace in Historical and Comparative Perspective*. New York: M. E. Sharpe, pp. 195–224.

Solinger, Dorothy (1999a) *Contesting Citizenship in Urban China: Peasant Migrants, the State, and the Logic of the Market*. California: University of California Press.

Solinger, Dorothy (1999b) 'China's floating population' in Merle Goldman and Roderick MacFarquhar (eds), *The Paradox of China's Post-Mao Reforms*. Cambridge, MA: Harvard University Press, pp. 220–40.

Solinger, Dorothy (2001a) 'Clashes between reform and opening: Labour market formation in three cities' in Bruce Dickson and Chao Chien-min (eds), *Remaking the Chinese State: Strategies, Society, and Security*. London: Routledge, pp. 103–31.

Solinger, Dorothy (2001b) 'Why we cannot count the "unemployed"' in *The China Quarterly* 167: 671–88.

Solinger, Dorothy (2002) 'Labour market reform and the plight of the laid-off proletariat' in *The China Quarterly* 170: 304–26.

Solinger, Dorothy (2004) 'The new crowd of the dispossessed' in Peter Gries and Stanley Rosen (eds), *State and Society in 21st Century China*. New York: Routledge, pp. 50–66.

Solinger, Dorothy (2006) 'The creation of a new underclass in China and its implications' in *Environment and Urbanization* 18: 177–93.

Solinger, Dorothy (2011) '*Dibaohu* in distress: the meagre minimum livelihood guarantee system in Wuhan' in Beatriz Carrilloand and Jane Duckett (eds), *China's Changing Welfare Mix: Local Perspectives*. Abingdon: Routledge, pp. 36–63.

Solinger, Dorothy (2012) 'The new urban underclass and its consciousness: is it a class?' in *Journal of Contemporary China* 21: 1011–29.

Solinger, Dorothy (2013) 'Temporality as trope in delineating inequality: progress for the prosperous, time warp for the poor' in Wanning Sun and Yingjie Guo (eds), *Unequal China*. Abingdon: Routledge, pp. 59–76.

Song, Shengxia (2013) 'GDP per capita record masks economic woes, didn't transform lives: experts' in *Global Times*, 23 February, p. 1.

State Council (2013) PRC State Council *Guofa* [State Council Circular] No.6 'Guanyu shenhua shouru fenpei zhidu gaigede ruogan yijian' ['Some opinions on deepening income distribution system reform'], 3 February.

Stockman, Norman (2000) *Understanding Chinese Society*. Cambridge: Polity.

Su, Yang and Shizheng Feng (2013) 'Adapt or voice: class, *Guanxi*, and protest propensity in China' in *The Journal of Asian Studies* 72: 45–67.

Sun, Laixiang (2005) 'Ownership reform in China's township and village enterprises' in Stephen Green and Guy S. Liu (eds), *Exit the Dragon? Privatization and State Control in China*. Oxford: Blackwell, pp. 90–110.

Sun, Liping (2002) 'Jiushi niandai zhongqi yilai Zhongguo shehui jieguo yanbian de xinqushi' ['New Trends in China's Social Structural Evolution since the Mid-1990s'] in *Dangdai Zhongguo yanjiu* [*Research on Contemporary China*] 3: 1–20.

Sun, Liping (2006) 'Duanlie: ershi shiji jiushiniandai yilai Zhongguo shehui jieguo' ['Fracture: China's social structure since the 1990s'] in Y. Li, L. Sun and Y. Shen (eds), *Dangdai Zhongguo shehui fenceng: lilun yu shizheng* [*Social Stratification in Contemporary China: Theory and Evidence*]. Beijing: Shehui kexue wenxian chubanshe, pp. 1–35.

Sun, Liping (2013) 'Quanli kuibai de di san jieduan' ['The third stage in the failure of power'], 11 March.

Sun, Wanning and Yingjie Guo (2013) (eds) *Unequal China: The Political Economy and Cultural Politics of Inequality*. Abingdon: Routledge.

Szelényi, Ivan (1978) 'Social inequalities in state socialist redistributive economies' in *International Journal of Comparative Sociology* 19: 63–87.

Szelényi, Ivan (1988) *Socialist Entrepreneurs: Embourgeoisement in Rural Hungary*. Madison: University of Wisconsin Press.

Szelényi, Ivan (2008) 'A theory of transitions' in *Modern China* 34: 165–75.

Szelényi, Ivan and Eric Kostello (1998) 'Outline of an institutional theory of inequality: The case of socialist and postcommunist Eastern Europe' in Mary C. Brinton and Victor Nee (eds), *The New Institutionalism in Sociology*. Redwood City: Stanford University Press, pp. 305–26.

Talavera, Oleksandr, Lin Xiong and Xiong Xiong (2010) 'Social capital and access to bank financing: the case of Chinese entrepreneurs'. University of East

Anglia Applied and Financial Economics Working Paper Series 019, Norwich: School of Economics, University of East Anglia.

Tang, Beibei (2013) 'Urban housing status groups: consumption, lifestyles, and identity' in Minglu Chen and David S. G. Goodman (eds), *Middle Class China: Identity and Behaviour*. Cheltenham: Edward Elgar, pp. 54–74.

Tang, Beibei and Luigi Tomba (2008) 'The forest city: homeownership and new wealth in Shenyang' in David S. G. Goodman (ed.), *The New Rich in China*. Abingdon: Routledge, pp. 171–86.

Tang, Beibei and Jonathan Unger (2013) 'The socio-economic status, co-optation and political conservatism of the educational middle class: a case study of university teachers' in Minglu Chen and David S. G. Goodman (eds), *Middle Class China: Identity and Behaviour*. Cheltenham: Edward Elgar, pp. 90–109.

Tang, Min, Dwayne Woods and Zhao Jujun (2009) 'The attitudes of the Chinese middle class towards democracy' in *Journal of Chinese Political Science* 14: 81–95.

Tang, Wenfang, William Parish and Tongqing Feng (1996) 'Chinese labor relations in a changing work environment' in *Journal of Contemporary China* 5: 367–89.

Taylor, Bill and Qi Li (2010) 'China's creative approach to "union" organizing' in *Labor History* 51: 411–28.

Thireau, Isabelle and Hua Linshan (2003) 'The moral universe of aggrieved Chinese workers' in *The China Journal* 50: 83–103.

Tian, Li (2008) 'The Chengzhongcun land market in China: boon or bane? A perspective on property rights' in *International Journal of Urban and Regional Research* 32: 282–304.

Tomba, Luigi (2002) *The Paradoxes of Labour Reform: Chinese Labour Theory and Practice from Socialism to Market*. Honolulu: University of Hawaii Press.

Tomba, Luigi (2004) 'Creating an urban middle class: social engineering in Beijing' in *The China Journal* 51: 1–26.

Tomba, Luigi (2011) 'Who's afraid of China's middle class' in *East Asia Forum*, 25 August 2011, At: <http://www.eastasiaforum.org/2011/08/25/whos-afraid-of-chinas-middle-class/>.

Tomba, Luigi (2012) 'Awakening the God of Earth: land, place and class in urbanizing Guangdong' in Beatriz Carrillo and David S. G. Goodman (eds), *China's Peasants and Workers: Changing Class Identities*. Cheltenham: Edward Elgar, pp. 40–61.

Tomba, Luigi and Beibei Tang (2013) 'The great divide: institutionalized inequality in market socialism' in Wanning Sun and Yingjie Guo (eds), *Unequal China*. Abingdon: Routledge, pp. 91–110.

Tsai, Kellee S. (2005) 'Capitalists without a class: political diversity among private entrepreneurs in China' in *Comparative Political Studies* 38: 1130–58.

Tsai, Kellee S. (2007) *Capitalism without Democracy: The Private Sector in Contemporary China*. Ithaca, NY: Cornell University Press.

Tsai, Kellee S. (2011) 'Comparing China's capitalists: neither democratic nor exceptional' in Scott Kennedy (ed.), *Beyond the Middle Kingdom*. Redwood City: Stanford University Press, pp. 136–58.

Unger, Jonathan (1984) 'The class system in rural China: a case study' in James Watson (ed.), *Class and Social Stratification in Post-revolution China*. Cambridge: Cambridge University Press, pp. 121–41.

Unger, Jonathan (2002) *The Transformation of Rural China*. New York: M. E. Sharpe.

Unger, Jonathan (2012a) 'Continuity and change in rural China's organization' in Ane Bislev and Stig Thøgersen (eds), *Organizing Rural China – Rural China Organizing*. Lanham: Lexington, pp. 15–33.

Unger, Jonathan (2012b) 'Status groups and classes in a Chinese village: from the Mao era through post-Mao industrialization' in Beatriz Carrillo and David S. G. Goodman (eds), *China's Peasants and Workers: Changing Class Identities*. Cheltenham: Edward Elgar, pp. 15–39.

Walder, Andrew (1984) 'The remaking of the Chinese working class, 1949–1981' in *Modern China* 10: 3–48.

Walder, Andrew (1986) *Communist Neo-traditionalism: Work and Authority in Chinese Industry*. California: University of California Press.

Walder, Andrew (1992) 'Property rights and stratification in socialist redistributive economies' in *American Sociology Review* 57: 524–39.

Walder, Andrew (1996) 'Markets and inequality in transitional economies: towards testable theories' in *American Journal of Sociology* 101: 1060–173.

Walder, Andrew (2002) 'Markets and income inequality in rural China: political advantage in an expanding economy' in *American Sociological Review* 67: 231–53.

Walder, Andrew (2003) 'Elite opportunity in transitional economies' in *American Sociological Review* 68: 899–917.

Walder, Andrew (2006a) 'China's private sector: a global perspective' in A. S. Tsui, Y. J. Bian and L. Cheng (eds), *China's Domestic Private Firms: Multidisciplinary Perspectives on Management and Performance*. New York: M. E. Sharpe, pp. 311–26.

Walder, Andrew (2006b) 'The party elite and China's trajectory of change' in Kjeld-Erik Brodsgaard and Yongnian Zheng (eds), *The Chinese Communist Party in Reform*. New York: Routledge.

Walder, Andrew and Xiaoxia Gong (1993) 'Workers in the Tiananmen protests' in *The Australian Journal of Chinese Affairs* 29: 1–29.

Walder, Andrew G. and Songhua Hu (2009) 'Revolution, reform, and status inheritance: urban China, 1949–1996' in *American Journal of Sociology* 114: 1395–427.

Walder, Andrew J., Li Bobai and Donald J. Treiman (2000) 'Politics and life chances in a socialist regime: dual career paths into the urban Chinese elite, 1949–1996' in *American Sociological Review* 65: 191–209.

Wang, An (2012) 'Zhongguo shuifu he guanminbi' ['China's tax burden and the ratio of officials'] in *Qiushi* [*Seeking Truth*] (September): 48–52.

Wang, Chunguang (2012) 'Urban–rural structure' in Lu Xueyi (ed.), *Social Structure of Contemporary China*. Singapore: World Scientific Publishing, pp. 265–300.

Wang, Haiyan, Richard P. Appelbaum, Francesca Deguili and Nelson Lichtenstein (2009) 'China's new Labour Contract Law: is China moving towards increased power for workers?' in *Third World Quarterly* 30: 485–501.

Wang, Jianying and Deborah Davis (2010) 'China's new upper middle classes: the importance of occupational disaggregation' in Cheng Li (ed.), *China's Emerging Middle Class*. Washington, DC: Brookings Institution Press, pp. 157–76.

Wang, Renzhong (1982) 'Unify thinking, conscientiously rectify party work style' in Hongqi [*Red Flag*] (1 March): 2–13, translated in FBIS-CHI-82-055-K3.

Wang, Shaoguang (2006) 'Regulating death at coalmines: changing mode of governance in China' in *Journal of Contemporary China* 46: 1–30.

Wang, Xiaobing, Chengfang Liu, Linxiu Zhang, Yaojiang Shi and Scott Rozelle (2013) 'College is rich, Han, urban, male club' in *The China Quarterly* 214: 456–70.

Wang, Xiangwei (2013) 'Key questions on shamed rail chief left unanswered' in *South China Morning Post*, 24 June, p. 1.

Wang, Xiaolu and Wing Thye Woo (2010) 'The size and distribution of hidden household income in China'. At: <http://scholar.google.com.au/scholar _url?hl=en&q=http://old.econ.ucdavis.edu/faculty/woo/9.Wang-Woo.Hid den%2520Income%2520in%2520China.2010-12-25.pdf&sa=X&scisig=AA GBfm2xWakayE5It-AV8SzRV-vMdl4Xag&oi=scholarr&ei=cqQaU4G2N 8SHrgfgn4HYCg&ved=0CCgQgAMoADAA>.

Wang, Yi (2003) 'How many middle class people are there in China?' in *East Day*, cited in Zhou Xiaohong 'Chinese middle class: reality and illusion?' in Christophe Jaffrelot and Peter van der Veer (eds), *Patterns of Middle Class Consumption*. London: Sage [2008], p. 14.

Wang, Zhuoqiong (2013) 'China's billionaires on rise' in *China Daily*, 1 March, p. 1.

White, Gordon (1976) *The Politics of Class and Class Origin: The Case of the Cultural Revolution*. Canberra: ANU, Contemporary China Paper no.9.

White, Lynn T. III (1998) *Unstately Power: Local Causes of China's Economic Reforms*. New York: M. E. Sharpe.

Whiting, Susan H. (2001) *Power and Wealth in Rural China: The Political Economy of Institutional Change*. Cambridge: Cambridge University Press.

Whyte, Martin King (1975) 'Inequality and social stratification in China' in *The China Quarterly* 64: 684–711.

Whyte, Martin King (2010a) *Myth of the Social Volcano: Perceptions of Inequality and Distributive Injustice in Contemporary China*. Redwood City: Stanford University Press.

Whyte, Martin King (2010b) (ed.) *One Country, Two Societies: Rural–Urban Inequality in Contemporary China*. Cambridge, MA: Harvard University Press.

Wolf, Margaret (1985) *Revolution Postponed: Women in Contemporary China*. Redwood City: Stanford University Press.

World Bank with Development Research Center of the State Council, PRC (2012) *China 2030: Building a Modern Harmonious, and Creative Society*. Washington: International Bank for Reconstruction and Development.

Woronov, T. E. (2012) 'Class consciousness, service work: Youth and class in Nanjing vocational secondary schools' in *Journal of Contemporary China* 21: 779–91.

Wright, Erik Olin (1997) *Class Counts: Comparative Studies in Class Analysis*. Cambridge: Cambridge University Press.

Wright, Teresa (2010) *Accepting Authoritarianism: State-Society Relations in China's Reform Era*. Redwood City: Stanford University Press.

Wu, Jiao (2007) '50% of people will be middle class by 2020' in *China Daily*, 27 December, p. 1.

Wu, Xiaogang (2006) 'Communist cadres and market opportunities' in *Social Forces* 85: 389–411.

Xi, Jinping (2013) 'Zhongguo meng, renminde meng' ['The China dream, the people's dream']. Closing Speech at Plenary Session of 12th National People's Congress, 17 March, in *Renmin Ribao* [*The People's Daily*], 18 March.

Xie, Yu and Emily Hannum (1996) 'Regional variation in earnings inequality in Reform Era urban China' in *American Journal of Sociology* 101: 950–92.

Xie, Yu and Xiaogang Wu (2008) 'Danwei profitability and earnings inequality in urban China' in *The China Quarterly* 195: 558–81.

Xinhua [New China News Agency] (2005) 'Middle class to reach 40 per cent of workforce', 15 September. At: <http://www.china.org.cn/english/China/142303.htm>.

Xinhua [New China News Agency] (2007) 'CPC amends constitution to foster private sector', 21 October. At: <http://www.china.org.cn/english/congress/229123.htm>.

Xinhua [New China News Agency] (2013) 'Urban Chinese per capita income grows in 2012', 18 January. At: <http://news.xinhuanet.com/english/china/2013-01/18/c_132111609.htm>.

Xinhua [New China News Agency] (2013) 'Gini coefficient release highlights China's resolve to bridge wealth gap', 21 January. At: <http://news.xinhuanet.com/english/china/2013-01/21/c_132116852.htm>.

Xinhua [New China News Agency] (2013) 'China has 10m private enterprises', 2 February. At: <http://news.xinhuanet.com/english/indepth/2013-02/2/c_133148233.htm>.

Xinhua [New China News Agency] (2013) 'Tough job market for Chinese college graduates', 25 June. At: <http://news.xinhuanet.com/english/china/2013-06/25/c_132484919.htm>.

Xinhua [New China News Agency] (2013) 'China advances diverse forms of ownership', 12 November. At: <http://english.cntv.cn/20131112/104993.shtml>.

Yan, Hairong (2008) *New Masters, New Servants: Migration, Development and Women Workers in China.* Duke University Press.

Yan, Ye (2012) 'Income distribution structure' in Lu Xueyi (ed.), *Social Structure of Contemporary China.* Singapore: World Scientific Publishing, pp. 185–224.

Yan, Zhimin (2002) *Zhongguo xian jieduan jieji jieceng yanjiu* [Research on Class and Stratum in Contemporary China]. Beijing: Zhonggong zhongyang dangxiao chubanshe.

Yang, Jing (2013) 'Understanding entrepreneurs' in Minglu Chen and David S. G. Goodman (ed.), *Middle Class China: Identity and Behaviour.* Cheltenham: Edward Elgar, pp. 149–68.

Yang, Jisheng (2000) *Zhongguo shehui ge jieceng fenxi baogao* [Analysis of the Social Strata in China]. Wulumuqi: Xinjiang renmin chubanshe.

Yao, Wen-yuan (1975) *On the Social Basis of the Lin Piao Anti-Party Clique.* Beijing: Foreign Languages Press.

Ye, Jianying (1979) *Speech at the Meeting in Celebration of the Founding of the 30th Anniversary of the People's Republic of China* (29 September). Beijing: Foreign Languages Press.

Yeh, Emily T., Kevin O'Brien, and Jingzhong Ye (2013) 'Rural politics in contemporary China' in *Journal of Peasant Studies* 40/6: 915–928.

Ying Yiyuan (2013) 'Private sector contributes over 60% to GDP' in CCTV English, 6 February.

Yip, Winnie (2010) 'Disparities in health care and health status: the rural–urban gap and beyond' in Martin K. Whyte (ed.), *One Country, Two Societies: Rural–Urban Inequality in Contemporary China*. Harvard University Press, pp. 147–65.

Zang, Xiaowei (2001) 'Educational credentials, elite dualism, and elite stratification in China' in *Sociological Perspectives* 44: 189–205.

Zang, Xiaowei (2004) *Elite Dualism and Leadership Selection in China*. London: Routledge.

Zang, Xiaowei (2008) 'Market transition, wealth and status claims' in David S. G. Goodman (ed.), *The New Rich in China*. Abingdon: Routledge, pp. 53–70.

Zang, Xiaowei (2012) 'Scaling the socioeconomic ladder: Uyghur perceptions of class status' in *Journal of Contemporary China* 21: 1029–43.

Zeng, Jin and Kellee S. Tsai (2011) 'The local politics of restructuring state-owned enterprises in China' in Jean Oi (ed.), *Going Private in China: The Politics of Corporate Restructuring and System Reform*. Redwood City: Stanford University Press, pp. 40–69.

Zhang, Chunqiao [Chang Ch'un-chiao] (1958) 'Pochu zichan jiejide faquan sixiang' ['Eradicate the ideology of bourgeois right'] in *Renmin Ribao* [*The People's Daily*], 13 October.

Zhang, Chunqiao [Chang Ch'un-chiao] (1975) *On Exercising all-Round Dictatorship over the Bourgeoisie*. Beijing: Foreign Languages Press.

Zhang, Houyi (2004) 'Jinru xinshiqide Zhongguo saying qiyezhu jiceng' ['Private entrepreneurs in China enter a new era'] in *2004 nian: Zhongguo shehui xingshi fenxi yu yuce* [*Blue Book of China's Society 2004: Analysis and Forecast of China's Social Development*]. Beijing: Shehui kexue wenxian chubanshe.

Zhang, Houyi (2012) 'Zhongguo siying qiyezhu jieceng 20 nian' ['Twenty Years Development of China's Entrepreneurs in Private Sector'] in *2012 Shehui lanpishu* [*2012 Blue Book of China's Society*]. Beijing: Shehui kexue wenxian chubanshe, pp. 273–83.

Zhang, Houyi and Ming Zhili (1999) (eds) *Zhongguo saying qiye fazhan baogao 1978–1998* [*Report on the Development of Private Enterprises in China 1978–1998*]. Beijing: Shehui kexue wenxuan chubanshe.

Zhang, Jianjun (2007) 'Marketization, Class structure, and democracy in China: contrasting regional experiences' in *Democratization* 14: 159–84.

Zhang, Jing (2009) 'Resolution mechanisms for land rights disputes' in Deborah Davis and Wang Feng (eds), *Creating Wealth and Poverty in Postsocialist China*. Redwood City: Stanford University Press, pp. 126–39.

Zhang, Li (2010) *In Search of Paradise: Middle-class Living in a Chinese Metropolis.* Ithaca, NY: Cornell University Press.

Zhang, Qi and Mingxing Liu (2010) 'Local political elite, partial reform symptoms, and the business and market environment in rural China' in *Business and Politics* 12: Article 5.

Zhang, Qian Forrest (2008) 'Retreat from Equality or Advance towards Efficiency? Land Markets and Inequality in Rural Zhejiang' in *The China Quarterly* 195: 535–57.

Zhao, Suisheng (2010) 'The China model: can it replace the Western model of modernization?' in *Journal of Contemporary China* 19: 419–36.

Zheng, Yongnian (2006) 'The party, class, and democracy in China' in Kjeld-Erik Brodsgaard and Yongnian Zheng (eds), *The Chinese Communist Party in Reform.* New York: Routledge, pp. 231–60.

Zhou, Feizhou (2009) 'Creating wealth: land seizure, local government, and farmers' in Deborah Davis and Wang Feng (eds), *Creating Wealth and Poverty in Postsocialist China.* Redwood City: Stanford University Press, pp. 112–25.

Zhou, K. Xiao (1996) *How the Farmers Changed China: Power of the People.* Boulder: Westview Press.

Zhou, Wubiao (2009) 'Bank financing in China's private sector: the payoffs of political capital' in *World Development* 37: 787–99.

Zhou, Xiaohong (2005) *Zhongguo zhongchanjieceng diaocha* [*Survey of the Chinese Middle Classes*]. Beijing: Shehui kexue wenxian chubanshe.

Zhou, Xiaohong (2008) 'Chinese middle class: reality or illusion?' in Christophe Jaffrelot and Peter van der Veer (eds), *Patterns of Middle Class Consumption.* London: Sage, pp. 110–26.

Zhou, Xiaohong and Qin Chen (2010) 'Globalization, social transformation, and the construction of China's middle class' in Cheng Li (ed.), *China's Emerging Middle Class.* Washington: Brookings Institution Press, pp. 84–103.

Zhou, Xueguang (2004) *The State and Life Chances in Urban China.* Cambridge: Cambridge University Press.

Zhu, Guanglei (1998) *Dangdai Zhongguo shehui ge jieceng fenxi* [*Analysis of the Social Strata in Contemporary China*]. Tianjin: Tianjin remin chubanshe.

Index

Giddens, Anthony, 28, 58
Gini coefficient, 2–3, 45–6, 172, 181
Göbel, Christian, 175
Goldthorpe, John, 28, 56
Great Leap Forward, 19, 21
'grey income', 45, 63
gross domestic product (GDP)
  gender inequality, 51
  increase in, 104, 177
  inequality, 40, 48, 181
  private sector, 154, 155
  public sector, 74–5, 155
Guang, Lei, 143
Guangdong
  corporatist villages, 170
  economic elite, 83
  entrepreneurs, 89
  income inequality, 48, 49
  migrant workers, 141, 142
  peasants, 144
  town and village enterprises, 78
Guangxi, 87
Guangzhou, 101, 103, 106
Guizhou, 48, 141
Guo, Yingjie, 183

Halper, Stephen, 178
Hangzhou, 106
Hannum, Emily, 47
Hanser, Amy, 190
He Qinglian, 54–5, 66
health
  housing and access to, 53
  migrant workers, 44
  public-sector benefits, 35, 52, 129
  rural–urban divide, 42
Hebei, 84, 87
Henan, 141

higher education
  admissions based on political merit, 22
  expansion of, 38–9, 110, 111–13, 120–1
  middle classes, 95, 107, 111–14, 118, 119
  political elite, 70, 71
  social mobility, 185
  university teachers, 157
  see also education
homeownership, 94, 96, 99, 115, 156, 158, 186
Hoogewerf, Rupert, 75
household registration system, 13, 30, 35–6, 39, 107, 186
  discrimination, 41
  lack of social mobility, 187
  migrant workers, 37, 43, 44, 123, 142, 179
  peasants, 145, 166, 171
household responsibility system, 37, 41, 145, 167
housing
  class identity, 190
  inequality, 47–8, 52–3
  middle classes, 96, 114–16, 158
  migrant workers, 44
  price disparities, 104
  public-sector benefits, 35, 52, 129
  reforms, 38
  see also homeownership
Hsiao, Michael, 56
Hsing, You-tien, 170
Hu, Biliang, 144
Hu, Jianguo, 113
Hu Jintao, 40
Huang, Philip, 122, 123, 136
Huawei Technologies, 137